THE CASE FOR GOLD

THE CASE FOR GOLD

Edited by
William Rees-Mogg

Volume 2

LONDON
PICKERING & CHATTO
2002

Published by Pickering & Chatto (Publishers) Limited
21 Bloomsbury Way, London, WC1A 2TH

2252 Ridge Road, Brookfield, Vermont 05036, USA

www.pickeringchatto.com

BRITISH LIBRARY CATALOGUING IN PUBLICATION DATA
The Case for Gold
1. Gold Standard 2. Gold Standard – Early Works to 1800
I. Rees-Mogg, Sir William
332.4'222

ISBN 1851967575

LIBRARY OF CONGRESS CATALOGING-IN-PUBLICATION DATA
A catalogue record for this title is available from the Library of Congress

∞
This publication is printed on acid-free paper that conforms to
the American National Standard for Permanence of Paper in Printed Library Materials.

Typeset by
P&C

Printed and bound in Great Britain by
Cromwell Press, Trowbridge

CONTENTS

Francis Horner (1778–1817)

Report, together with Minutes of Evidence, and Accounts, from the Select Committee on the High Price of Gold Bullion (1810)

I.

It will be found by the Evidence, (*Minutes of Evidence*, pp. 41 – 45. 135, 136. 178, 179.) that the high price of Gold is ascribed, by most of the Witnesses, entirely to an alleged scarcity of that article, arising out of an unusual demand for it upon the Continent of Europe. This unusual demand for Gold upon the Continent is described by some of them as being chiefly for the use of the French Armies, though increased also by that state of alarm, and failure of confidence, which leads to the practice of hoarding.

Your Committee are of opinion, that, in the sound and natural state of the British currency, the foundation of which is Gold, no increased demand for Gold from other parts of the world, however great, or from whatever causes arising, can have the effect of producing here, for a considerable period of time, a material rise in the market price of Gold. But before they proceed to explain the grounds of that general opinion, they wish to state some other reasons which alone would have led them to doubt whether, in point of fact, such a demand for Gold, as is alleged, has operated in the manner supposed.

If there were an unusual demand for Gold upon the Continent, such as could influence its market price in this country, it would of course influence also, and indeed in the first instance, its price in the Continental markets; and it was to be expected that those who ascribed the high price here to a great demand abroad, would have been prepared to state that there was a corresponding high price abroad. Your Committee did not find that they grounded their inference upon any such information; and so far as Your Committee have been enabled to ascertain, it does not appear that during the period when the price of Gold Bullion was rising here, as valued in our paper, there was any corresponding rise in the price of Gold Bullion in the market of the Continent, as valued in their respective currencies. Mr. *Whitmore*, indeed, the late Governor of the Bank, stated, (*Min.* p. 178, 179.) that in his opinion it was the high price abroad which had carried our Gold coin out of this Country; but he did not offer to Your Committee any proof of this high price. Mr. *Greffulhe*, a Continental Merchant, (*Min.* p. 70.) who appeared to be remarkably well informed in the details of trade, being asked by the Committee, If he could state whether any change had taken place in the price of Gold in any of the foreign

3

markets within the last year? answered, 'No very material change that I am aware of.' Upon a subsequent day, (*Min.* p. 131, 132.) having had time to refer to the actual prices, he again stated to the Committee, 'I beg leave to observe, that there has been no alteration of late in the Mint price of Gold in foreign places, nor have the market prices experienced an advance at all relative to the rise that has taken place in England; one of the papers I have delivered shews the foreign prices reduced into sterling money at the present low rates of Exchange, and the excess above our market price may be considered as about equal to the charges of conveyance.' The paper he refers to will be found in the Appendix; (*Appendix of Accounts:* No 56, 57, 58.) and this statement made by Mr. Greffulhe throws great light upon this part of the subject; as it shews, that the actual prices of Gold in the foreign markets are just so much lower than its market price here, as the difference of Exchange amounts to. Mr. Greffulhe's paper is confirmed by another, (*Acc.* No 59, *Min.* p. 116.) which has been laid before Your Committee, that, during that part of last year when the market price of Gold here rose so high, its price at Hamburgh did not fluctuate more than from 3 to 4 per cent.

Here Your Committee must observe, that both at Hamburgh and Amsterdam, where the measure of value is not Gold as in this Country, but Silver, an unusual demand for Gold would affect its money price, that is, its price in Silver; and that as it does not appear that there has been any considerable rise in the price of Gold, as valued in Silver, at those places in the last year, the inference is, that there was not any considerable increase in the demand for Gold. That permanent rise in the market price of Gold above its Mint price, which appears by Mr. Greffulhe's paper to have taken place for several years both at Hamburgh and Amsterdam, may in some degree be ascribed, as Your Committee conceive, to an alteration which has taken place in the relative value of the two precious metals all over the world; concerning which, much curious and satisfactory Evidence will be found in the Appendix, particularly in the documents laid before Your Committee by Mr. Allen. (*Acc.* No 21. to 33.) From the same cause, a fall in the relative price of Silver appears to have taken place in this Country for some time before the increase of our paper currency began to operate. Silver having fallen in its relative value to Gold throughout the world, Gold has appeared to rise in price in those markets where Silver is the fixed measure, and Silver has appeared to fall in those where Gold is the fixed measure.

With respect to the alleged demand for Gold upon the Continent for the supply of the French Armies, Your Committee must further observe, that, if the wants of the military chest have been latterly much increased, the general supply of Europe with Gold has been augmented by all that quantity which this great commercial Country has spared in consequence of the substitution of another medium of circulation. And Your Committee cannot omit remarking, that though the circumstances which might occasion such an increased demand may recently have existed in greater force than at former periods, yet in the former wars and convulsions of the Continent, they must have existed in such a degree as to produce some effect. *Sir Francis Baring* has very justly referred (*Min.* p. 199.) to the seven years war and to the American war, and remarks, that no want of Bullion was then felt in this Country. And upon referring for a course of years to the tables which are published for the use of the Merchants, such as Lloyd's Lists and Wettenhall's Course of Exchange, Your Committee have found that from the middle of the year 1773, when the reformation of the Gold coin took place, till about the middle of the year 1799, two years after the suspension of the cash payments of the Bank, the market price of standard Gold in bars remained steadily uniform at the price of £. 3. 17. 6. [being, with the small allowance for loss by detention at the Mint, equal to the Mint price of £. 3. 17. 10½.] with the exception of one year, from May 1783 to May 1784, when it was occasionally £. 3. 18. During the same period it is to be noticed, the price of Portugal Gold coin was occasionally as high as £. 4. 2. 0.; and Your Committee also observe, that it was stated to the Lords' Committee in 1797 by Mr. Abraham Newland, (*Report Comm. of Secresy*, p. 66.) that the Bank had been frequently obliged to buy Gold higher than the Mint price, and upon one particular occasion gave as much for a small quantity, which their agent procured from Portugal, as £. 4. 8. But Your Committee find, that the price of standard Gold in bars was never for any length of time materially above the Mint price, during the whole period of 24 years which elapsed from the reformation of the Gold coin to the suspension of the cash payments of the Bank. The two most remarkable periods prior to the present, when the market price of Gold in this country has exceeded our Mint price, were in the reign of King William, when the Silver coin was very much worn below its standard, and in the early part of His present Majesty's reign, when the Gold coin was very much worn below its standard. In both those periods, the excess of the market price of Gold above its Mint price was found to be owing to the bad state of the currency; and in both instances, the reformation of the currency effectually lowered the market price of Gold to the level of the Mint price. During the whole of the years 1796 and 1797, in which there was such a scarcity of Gold, occasioned by the great demands of the country Bankers in order to increase their deposits, the market price of Gold never rose above the Mint price.

Your Committee have still further to remark upon this point, that the Evidence laid before them has led them to entertain much doubt of the alleged fact, that a scarcity of Gold Bullion has been recently experienced in this country. That Guineas have disappeared from the circulation, there can be no question; but that does not prove a scarcity of Bullion, any more than the high price proves that scarcity. If Gold is rendered dear by any other cause than scarcity, those who cannot purchase it without paying the high price, will be very apt to conclude that it is scarce. A very extensive home dealer who was examined, and who spoke very much of the scarcity of Gold, acknowledged, (*Min.* p. 35.) that he found no difficulty in getting any quantity he wanted, if he was willing to pay the price for it. And it appears to Your Committee, that, though in the course of the last year there have been large exportations of Gold to the Continent, there have been also very considerable importations of it into this Country from South America, chiefly through the West Indies. The changes which have affected Spain and Portugal, combined with our maritime and commercial advantages, would seem to have rendered this country a channel through which the produce of the mines of New Spain and the Brazils passes to the rest of the world. In such a situation, the imports of Bullion and Coin give us the opportunity of first supplying ourselves; and must render this the last of the great markets in which a scarcity of that article will be felt. This is remarkably illustrated by the fact, that Portugal Gold coin is now sent regularly from this Country to the Cotton Settlements in the Brazils, Pernambuco, and Maranham, while Dollars are remitted in considerable quantities to this country from Rio Janiero.

It is important also to observe, that the rise in the market price of Silver in this country, which has nearly corresponded to that of the market price of Gold, cannot in any degree be ascribed to a scarcity of Silver. The importations of Silver have of late years been unusually large, while the usual drain for India and China has been stopped. (*Acc.* Nos. 9. & 10.)

For all these reasons, Your Committee would be inclined to think, that those who ascribe the high price of Gold to an unusual demand for that article, and a consequent scarcity, assume facts as certain of which there is no evidence. But even if these assumptions were proved, – to ascribe the high price of Gold in this Country to its scarcity, seems to your Committee to involve a misconception, which they think it important to explain.

In this Country, Gold is itself the measure of all exchangeable value, the scale to which all money prices are referred. It is so, not only by the usage and commercial habits of the country, but likewise by operation of law, ever since the Act of the 14th of His present Majesty [finally rendered perpetual by an Act of the 39th year of the reign] disallowed a legal tender in Silver coin beyond the sum of £. 25. Gold being thus our measure of prices, a commodity is said to be dear or cheap according as more or less Gold is given in exchange for a given quantity of that commodity; but a given quantity of Gold itself will never be exchanged for a greater or a less quantity of Gold of the same standard fineness. At particular times it may be convenient, in exchange for Gold in a particular coin, to give more than an equal quantity of other Gold; but this difference can never exceed a certain small limit: and thus it has happened that the Bank, while liable to pay its notes in specie, has under particular emergencies been put to the necessity of purchasing Gold at a loss, in order to keep up or to repair its stock. But, generally speaking, the price of Gold, being itself measured and expressed in Gold, cannot be raised or lowered by an increased or diminished demand for it. An ounce of Gold will exchange for neither more nor less than an ounce of Gold of the same fineness, except so far as an allowance is to be made, if the one ounce is coined or otherwise manufactured and the other is not, for the expense of that coinage or manufacture. An ounce of standard Gold Bullion will not fetch more in our market than £. 3. 17. 10.½, unless £. 3. 17. 10½, in our actual currency is equivalent to less than an ounce of Gold. An increase or diminution in the demand for Gold, or, what comes to the same thing, a diminution or increase in the general supply of Gold, will, no doubt, have a material effect upon the money prices of all other articles. An increased demand for Gold, and a consequent scarcity of that article, will make it more valuable in proportion to all other articles; the same quantity of Gold will purchase a greater quantity of any other article than it did before: in other words, the real price of Gold, or the quantity of commodities given in exchange for it, will rise, and the money prices of all commodities will fall; the money price of Gold itself will remain unaltered, but the prices of all other commodities will fall. That this is not the present state of things is abundantly manifest; the prices of all commodities have risen, and Gold appears to have risen in its price only in common with them. If this common effect is to be ascribed to one and the same cause, that cause can only be found in the state of the currency of this Country.

Your Committee think it proper to state still more specifically, what appear to them to be the principles which govern the relative prices of Gold in Bullion and Gold in Coin, as well as of Paper circulating in its place and exchangeable for it. They cannot introduce this subject more properly, than by adverting to those simple principles and regulations, on which a coinage issuing from the King's Mint is founded.

The object is, to secure to the people a standard of a determinate value, by affixing a stamp, under the Royal authority, to pieces of Gold, which are thus certified to be of a given weight and fineness. Gold in Bullion is the standard to which the Legislature has intended that the coin should be conformed, and with which it should be identified as much as possible. And if that intention of the Legislature were completely fulfilled, the coined Gold would bear precisely the same price in exchange for all other commodities, as it would have borne had it continued in the shape of Bullion; but it is subject to some small fluctuations.

7

First, there is some expense incurred in converting Bullion into coin. They who send Bullion to be coined, and it is allowed to any one to send it, though they are charged with no seignorage, incur a loss of interest by the detention of their Gold in the Mint. This loss may hitherto have amounted to about £. 1. per cent., but it is to be presumed that the improvements of the system of the new Mint will cause the detention and consequent loss to be much smaller. This £. 1. per cent. has formed the limit, or nearly the limit, to the possible rise of the value of coin above that of Bullion; for to suppose that coin could, through any cause, advance much above this limit, would be to assume that there was a high profit on a transaction, in which there is no risk, and every one has an opportunity of engaging.

The two following circumstances conjoined, account for the depression of the Coin below the price of Bullion, and will show what must have been the limit to its extent before 1797, the period of the suspension of the Cash payments of the Bank of England. First, the Coin, after it had become current, was gradually diminished in weight by use, and therefore if melted would produce a less quantity of Bullion. The average diminution of weight of the present current Gold Coin below that of the same Coin when fresh from the Mint, appears by the Evidence (*Acc.* No 20.) to be nearly £1. per cent. This evil, in more ancient times, was occasionally very great. It was particularly felt in an early period of His present Majesty's reign, and led to the reformation of the Gold Coin in 1773. But it is now carefully guarded against, not only by the legal punishment of every wilful deterioration of the Gold Coin, but also by the regulation of the Statute, that Guineas, of which the full weight when fresh from the Mint is 5 dwts. 9 $\frac{39}{89}$ grains, shall not be a legal tender if worn below 5 dwts. 8 grs.; the depreciation thus allowed being at the utmost 1.11 per cent. A still more material cause of depression is the difficulty under which the holders of Coin have been placed when they wished to convert it into Bullion. The Law of this Country forbids any other Gold Coin than that which has become light to be put into the melting-pot, and, with a very questionable policy prohibits the exportation of our Gold Coin, and of any Gold, unless an oath is taken that it has not been produced from the Coin of this realm. It appears by the Evidence, that the difference between the value of Gold Bullion which may be sworn off for exportation, and that of the Gold produced or supposed to be produced from our own Coin, which by Law is convertible only to domestic purposes, amounts at present to between 3s. and 4s. per ounce.

The two circumstances which have now been mentioned have unquestionably constituted, in the judgement of Your Committee, the whole cause of that depression of the value of the Gold Coin of this Country in exchange for commodities, below the value of Bullion in exchange for commodities, which has occasionally arisen or could arise at those times when the Bank paid in specie, and Gold was consequently obtainable in the quantity that was desired; and the limit fixed, by those two circumstances conjoined, to this excess of the market price of Gold above the Mint price, was therefore a limit of about 5½ per cent. The chief part of this depression is to be ascribed to that ancient but doubtful policy of this Country, which, by attempting to confine the Coin within the Kingdom, has served, in the same manner as permanent restrictions on the export of other articles, to place it under a disadvantage, and to give to it a less value in the market than the same article would have if subject to no such prohibition.

The truth of these observations on the causes and limits of the ordinary difference between the market and Mint price of Gold, may be illustrated by a reference to the mode, explained in the Evidence, of securing a fixed standard of value for the great commercial payments of Hamburgh. The payments in the ordinary transactions of life are made in a currency composed of the coins of the several surrounding States; but Silver is the standard there resorted to in the great commercial payments, as Gold is in England. No difference analogous to that which occurs in this Country, between the Mint and market price of Gold, can ever arise at Hamburgh with regard to Silver, because provision is made that none of the three causes above specified, [the expense of coinage, the depreciation by wear, or the obstruction to exportation] shall have any operation. The large payments of Hamburgh are effected in Bank money, which consists of actual Silver of a given fineness, lodged in the Hamburgh Bank by the merchants of the place, who thereupon have a proportionate credit in the Bank books, which they transfer according to their occasions. The Silver being assayed and weighed with scarcely any loss of time, the first-mentioned cause of fluctuation in the relative value of the current medium compared with Bullion is avoided. Certain masses of it being then certified (without any stamp being affixed on the metal) to be of a given quantity and fineness, the value is transferred from individual to individual by the medium merely of the Bank books, and thus the wearing of the Coin being prevented, one cause of depreciation is removed. A free right is also given to withdraw, melt, and export it; and thus the other and principal source of the occasional fall of the value of the current medium of payment, below that of the Bullion which it is intended to represent, is also effectually precluded.

In this manner, at Hamburgh, Silver is not only the measure of all exchangeable value, but it is rendered an invariable measure, except in so far as the relative value of Silver itself varies with the varying supply of that precious metal from the mines. In the same manner the usage, and at last the law, which made Gold Coin the usual and at last the only legal tender in large payments here, rendered that metal our measure of value: and from the period of the reformation of the Gold Coin down to the suspension of the Bank

9

payments in specie in 1797, Gold Coin was not a very variable measure of value; being subject only to that variation in the relative value of Gold Bullion which depends upon its supply from the mines, together with that limited variation which, as above described, might take place between the market and the Mint price of Gold Coin.

The highest amount of the depression of the Coin which can take place when the Bank pays in Gold, has just been stated to be about 5½ per cent.; and accordingly it will be found, that in all the periods preceding 1797, the difference between what is called the Mint price and market price of Gold never exceeded that limit.

Since the suspension of Cash payments in 1797, however, it is certain, that, even if Gold is still our measure of value and standard of prices, it has been exposed to a new cause of variation, from the possible excess of that paper which is not convertible into Gold at will; and the limit of this new variation is as indefinite as the excess to which that paper may be issued. It may indeed be doubted, whether, since the new system of Bank of England payments has been fully established, Gold has in truth continued to be our measure of value; and whether we have any other standard of prices than that circulating medium, issued primarily by the Bank of England and in a secondary manner by the country Banks, the variations of which in relative value may be as indefinite as the possible excess of that circulating medium. But whether our present measure of value, and standard of prices, be this paper currency thus variable in its relative value, or continues still to be Gold, but Gold rendered more variable than it was before in consequence of being interchangeable for a paper currency which is not at will convertible into Gold, it is, in either case, most desirable for the public that our circulating medium should again be conformed, as speedily as circumstances will permit, to its real and legal standard, Gold Bullion.

If the Gold Coin of the Country were at any time to become very much worn and lessened in weight, or if it should suffer a debasement of its standard, it is evident that there would be a proportionable rise of the market price of Gold Bullion above its Mint price: for the Mint price is the sum in coin, which is equivalent in intrinsic value to a given quantity, an ounce for example, of the metal in Bullion; and if the intrinsic value of that sum of Coin be lessened, it is equivalent to a less quantity of Bullion than before. The same rise of the market price of Gold above its Mint price will take place, if the local currency of this particular Country, being no longer convertible into Gold, should at any time be issued to excess. That excess cannot be exported to other countries, and, not being convertible into specie, it is not necessarily returned upon those who issued it; it remains in the channel of circulation, and is gradually absorbed by increasing the prices of all commodities. An increase in the quantity of the local currency of a particular country, will raise prices in that country exactly in the same manner as an increase in the general supply of precious metals raises prices all over the world. By means of the increase of quantity, the value of a given portion of that circulating medium, in exchange for other commodities, is lowered; in other words, the money prices of all other commodities are raised, and that of Bullion with the rest. In this manner, an excess of the local currency of a particular country will occasion a rise of the market price of Gold above its Mint price. It is no less evident, that, in the event of the prices of commodities being raised in one country by an augmentation of its circulating medium, while no similar augmentation in the circulating medium of a neighbouring country has led to a similar rise of prices, the currencies of those two countries will no longer continue to bear the same relative value to each other as before. The intrinsic value of a given portion of the one currency being lessened, while that of the other remains unaltered, the Exchange will be computed between those two countries to the disadvantage of the former.

In this manner, a general rise of all prices, a rise in the market price of Gold, and a fall of the Foreign Exchanges, will be the effect of an excessive quantity of circulating medium in a country which has adopted a currency not exportable to other countries, or not convertible at will into a Coin which is exportable.

II.

Your Committee are thus led to the next head of their inquiry; the present state of the Exchanges between this Country and the Continent. And here, as under the former head, Your Committee will first state the opinions which they have received from practical men, respecting the causes of the present state of the Exchange.

Mr. *Greffulhe*, a general merchant, trading chiefly to the Continent, ascribed the fall of Exchange between London and Hamburgh, near 18 per cent. below par, in the year 1809, (*Min.* p. 68.) 'altogether to the commercial situation of this Country with the Continent; to the circumstance of the imports, and payments of Subsidies, &c. having very much exceeded the exports.' He stated, however, that he formed his judgment of the balance of trade in a great measure from the state of the Exchange itself, though it was corroborated by what fell under his observation. He insisted particularly on the large imports from the Baltic, and the wines and brandies brought from France, in return for which no merchandize had been exported from this Country. He observed on the other hand, that the export of Colonial produce to the Continent had increased in the last year compared with former years; and that during the last year there was an excess, to a considerable amount, of the exports of colonial produce and British manufactures to Holland above the imports from thence, but not nearly equal, he thought, to the excess of imports from other parts of the world, judging from the state of the Exchange as well as from what fell generally under his observation. He afterwards explained, (*Min.* p. 74.) that it was not strictly the balance of trade, but the balance of payments, being unfavourable to this Country, which he assigned as the principal cause of the rate of Exchange; observing also, that the balance of payments for the year may be against us, while the general exports exceed the imports. He gave it as his opinion, (*Min.* p. 72.) that the cause of the present state of Exchange was entirely commercial, with the addition of the foreign expenditure of Government; and that an excess of imports above exports would account for the rates of Exchange continuing so high as 16 per cent. against this country, for a permanent period of time.

It will be found in the Evidence, that several other Witnesses agree in substance with *Mr. Greffulhe*, in this explanation of the unfavourable state of the Exchange; particularly *Mr. Chambers* and *Mr. Coningham*.

Sir Francis Baring stated to the Committee, (*Min.* p. 198.) that he considered the two great circumstances which affect the Exchange in its present unfavourable state, to be the restrictions upon trade with the Continent, and the increased circulation of this Country in paper as productive of the scarcity of Bullion. And he instanced, as examples of a contrary state of things, the seven years war, and the American war, in which there were the same remittances to make to the Continent for naval and military expenditure, yet no want of Bullion was ever felt.

The Committee likewise examined a very eminent Continental Merchant, whose evidence will be found to contain a variety of valuable information. That Gentleman states, (*Min.* pp. 78. 82. 96. 102.) that the Exchange cannot fall in any country in Europe at the present time, if computed in coin of a definitive value, or in something convertible into such coin, lower than the extent of the charge of transporting it, together with an adequate profit in proportion to the risk attending such transmission. He conceives (*Min.* p. 84.) that such fall of our Exchange as has exceeded that extent in the last 15 months, must certainly be referred to the circumstance of our paper currency not being convertible into specie; and that if that paper had been so convertible, and Guineas had been in general circulation, an unfavourable balance of trade could hardly have caused so great a fall in the Exchange as to the extent of 5 or 6 per cent. He explains his opinion upon the subject more specifically in the following Answers, which are extracted from different parts of his Evidence.

'To what causes do you ascribe the present unfavourable course of Exchange? – The first great depreciation took place when the French got possession of the North of Germany, and passed severe penal decrees against a communication with this Country; at the same time that a sequestration was laid upon all English goods and property, whilst the payments for English account were still to be made, and the reimbursements to be taken on this Country; many more bills were in consequence to be sold than could be taken by persons requiring to make payments in England. The communication by letters being also very difficult and uncertain, middle men were not to be found, as in usual times, to purchase and send such bills to England for returns; whilst no suit at law could be instituted in the Courts of Justice there against any person who chose to resist payment of a returned bill, or to dispute the charges of re-exchange. Whilst those causes depressed the Exchange, payments due to England only came round at distant periods; the Exchange once lowered by those circumstances, and Bullion being withheld in England to make up those occasional differences, the operations between this Country and the Continent have continued at a low rate, as it is only matter of opinion what rate a pound sterling is there to be valued at, not being able to obtain what it is meant to represent.' (*Min.* p. 88.)

'The Exchange against England fluctuating from 15 to 20 per cent. how much of that loss may be ascribed to the effect of the measures taken by the enemy in the North of Germany, and the interruption of intercourse which has been the result, and how much to the effect of the Bank of England paper not being convertible into cash, to which you have ascribed a part of that depreciation? – I ascribe the whole of the depreciation to have taken place originally in consequence of the measures of the enemy; and its not having recovered, to the circumstance of the paper of England not being exchangeable for cash.' (*Min.* p. 90.)

'Since the conduct of the enemy which you have described, what other causes have continued to operate on the Continent to lower the course of Exchange? – Very considerable shipments from the Baltic, which were drawn for and the bills negotiated immediately on the shipments taking place, without consulting the interest of the Proprietors in this country much, by deferring such a negotiation till a demand should take place for such bills: The continued difficulty and uncertainly in carrying on the correspondence between this Country and the Continent: The curtailed number of houses to be found on the Continent willing to undertake such operations, either by accepting bills for English account drawn from the various parts where shipments take place, or by accepting bills drawn from this Country, either against property shipped, or on a speculative idea that the Exchange either ought or is likely to rise: The length of time that is required before goods can be converted into cash, from the circuitous routes they are obliged to take: The very large sums of money paid to foreign Ship Owners, which in some instances, such as on the article of Hemp, has amounted to nearly its prime cost in Russia: The want of middle men who as formerly used to employ great capitals in Exchange operations, who, from the increased difficulties and dangers to which such operations are now subject, are at present rarely to be met with, to make combined exchange operations, which tend to anticipate probable ultimate results.' (*Min.* p. 96.)

The preceding Answers, and the rest of this Gentleman's Evidence, all involve this principle, expressed more or less distinctly, that Bullion is the true regulator both of the value of a local currency and of the rate of Foreign Exchanges; and that the free convertibility of paper currency into the precious metals, and the free exportation of those metals, place a limit to the fall of Exchange, and not only check the Exchanges from falling below that limit, but recover them by restoring the balance.

14

Your Committee need not particularly point out in what respects these opinions, received from persons of practical detail, are vague and unsatisfactory, and in what respects they are contradictory of one another; considerable assistance however may be derived from the information which the evidence of these persons affords, in explaining the true causes of the present state of the Exchanges.

Your Committee conceive that there is no point of trade, considered politically, which is better settled, than the subject of Foreign Exchanges. The PAR of Exchange between two Countries is that sum of the currency of either of the two, which, in point of intrinsic value, is precisely equal to a given sum of the currency of the other; that is, contains precisely an equal weight of Gold or Silver of the same fineness. If 25 livres of France contained precisely an equal quantity of pure Silver with twenty shillings sterling, 25 would be said to be the Par of Exchange between London and Paris. If one country uses Gold for its principal measure of value, and another uses Silver, the par between those countries cannot be estimated for any particular period, without taking into account the relative value of Gold and Silver at that particular period; and as the relative value of the two precious metals is subject to fluctuation, the Par of Exchange between two such countries is not strictly a fixed point, but fluctuates within certain limits. An illustration of this will be found in the Evidence, (*Min.* p. 78, 79.) in the calculation of the Par between London and Hamburgh, which is estimated to be 34/3½ Flemish shillings for a pound sterling. That *rate* of exchange, which is produced at any particular period by a balance of trade or payments between the two countries, and by a consequent disproportion between the supply and the demand of bills drawn by the one upon the other, is a departure on one side or the other from the real and fixed Par. But this real Par will be altered if any change takes place in the currency of one of the two countries, whether that change consists in the wear or debasement of a metallic currency below its standard, or in the discredit of a forced paper currency, or in the excess of a paper currency not convertible into specie; a fall having taken place in the intrinsic value of a given portion of one currency, that portion will no longer be equal to the same portion, as before, of the other currency. But though the real Par of the currencies is thus altered, the dealers, having little or no occasion to refer to the par, continue to reckon their course of Exchanges from the former denomination of the par; and in this state of things a distinction is necessary to be made between the *real* and *computed* course of Exchange. The computed course of Exchange, as expressed in the tables used by the Merchants, will then include, not only the real difference of exchange arising from the state of trade, but likewise the difference between the original par and the new par. Those two sums may happen to be added together in the calculation, or they may happen to be set against each

15

other. If the country, whose currency has been depreciated in comparison with the other, has the balance of trade also against it, the computed rate of exchange will appear to be still more unfavourable than the real difference of exchange will be found to be; and so if that same country has the balance of trade in its favour, the computed rate of exchange will appear to be much less favourable than the real difference of exchange will be found to be. Before the new coinage of our silver in King William's time, the Exchange between England and Holland, computed in the usual manner according to the standard of their respective mints, was 25 per cent against England; but the value of the current coin of England was more than 25 per cent. below the standard value; so that if that of Holland was at its full standard, the real exchange was in fact in favour of England. It may happen in the same manner, that the two parts of the calculation may be both opposite and equal, the real exchange in favour of the country by trade being equal to the nominal exchange against it by the state of its currency: in that case, the computed exchange will be at par, while the real exchange is in fact in favour of that country. Again, the currencies of both the countries which trade together may have undergone an alteration, and that either in an equal degree, or unequally: in such a case, the question of the real state of the exchange between them becomes a little more complicated, but it is to be resolved exactly upon the same principle. Without going out of the bounds of the present inquiry, this may be well illustrated by the present state of the Exchange of London with Portugal, as quoted in the tables for the 18th of May last. The exchange of London on Lisbon appears to be 67½; 67½ d. sterling for a mill ree is the old established par of exchange between the two countries; and 67½ accordingly is still said to be the par. But by the evidence of Mr. *Lyne*, it appears, (*Min.* p. 50.) that, in Portugal, all payments are now by law made one-half in hard money, and one-half in Government paper; and that this paper is depreciated at a discount of 27 per cent. Upon all payments made in Portugal, therefore, there is a discount or loss of 13½ per cent.; and the exchange at 67½, though nominally at par, is in truth 13½ per cent. against this Country. If the exchange were really at par, it would be quoted at 56 $^{65}/_{100}$, or apparently 13½ per cent. in favour of London, as compared with the old par which was fixed before the depreciation of the Portuguese medium of payments. Whether this 13½ per cent. which stands against this Country by the present Exchange on Lisbon, is a real difference of Exchange, occasioned by the course of trade and by the remittances to Portugal on account of Government, or a nominal and apparent Exchange occasioned by something in the state of our own currency, or is partly real and partly nominal, may perhaps be determined by what Your Committee have yet to state.

It appears to Your Committee to have been long settled and understood as a principle, that the difference of Exchange resulting from the state of trade and payments between two countries is limited by the expence of conveying and insuring the precious metals from one country to the other; at least, that it cannot for any considerable length of time exceed that limit. The real difference of Exchange, resulting from the state of trade and payments, never can fall lower than the amount of such expence of carriage, including the Insurance. The truth of this position is so plain, and it is so uniformly agreed to by all the practical authorities, both commercial and political, that Your Committee will assume it as indisputable.

It occurred however to Your Committee, that the amount of that charge and premium of insurance might be increased above what it has been in ordinary periods even of war, by the peculiar circumstances which at present obstruct the commercial intercourse between this Country and the Continent of Europe; and that as such an increase would place so much lower than usual the limit to which our Exchanges might fall, an explanation might thereby be furnished of their present unusual fall. Your Committee accordingly directed their enquiries to this point.

It was stated to Your Committee, by the Merchant who has been already mentioned as being intimately acquainted with the trade between this Country and the Continent, (*Min.* p. 83, 84.) that the present expence of transporting Gold from London to Hamburgh, independent of the premium of Insurance, is from 1½ to 2 per cent.; that the risk is very variable from day to day, so that there is no fixed premium, but he conceived the average risk, for the fifteen months preceding the time when he spoke, to have been about 4 per cent.: making the whole cost of sending Gold from London to Hamburgh for those fifteen months, at such average of the risk, from 5½ to 6 per cent. – Mr. *Abraham Goldsmid* stated, that in the last five or six months of the year 1809, the expence of sending Gold to Holland varied exceedingly, from 4 to 7 per cent. for all charges, covering the risk as well as the costs of transportation. By the Evidence which was taken before the Committees upon the Bank affairs in 1797, it appears that the cost of sending specie from London to Hamburgh in that time of war, including all charges as well as an average insurance, was estimated at a little more than 3½ per cent. It is clear, therefore, that in consequence of the peculiar circumstances of the present state of the war, and the increased difficulties of intercourse with the Continent, the cost of transporting the precious metals thither from this Country has not only been rendered more fluctuating than it used to be, but, upon the whole, is very considerably increased. It would appear, however, that upon an average of the risk for that period when it seems to have been highest, the last half of the last year, the cost and insurance of transporting Gold to Hamburgh or to Holland

17

did not exceed 7 per cent. It was of course greater at particular times, when the risk was above that average. It is evident also that the risk, and consequently the whole cost of transporting it to an inland market, to Paris for example, would, upon an average, be higher than that of carrying it to Amsterdam or Hamburgh. It follows, that the limit to which the Exchanges, as resulting from the state of trade, might fall and continue unfavourable for a considerable length of time, has, during the period in question, been a good deal lower than in former times of war; but it appears also, that the expence of remitting specie has not been increased so much, and that the limit, by which the depression of the Exchanges is bounded, has not been lowered so much, as to afford an adequate explanation of a fall of the Exchanges so great as from 16 to 20 per cent. below par. The increased cost of such remittance would explain, at those moments when the risk was greatest, a fall of something more than 7 per cent. in the Exchange with Hamburgh or Holland, and a fall still greater perhaps in the Exchange with Paris; but the rest of the fall, which has actually taken place, remains to be explained in some other manner.

Your Committee are disposed to think, from the result of the whole evidence, contradictory as it is, that the circumstances of the trade of this Country, in the course of the last year, were such as to occasion a real fall of our Exchanges with the Continent to a certain extent, and perhaps at one period almost as low as the limit fixed by the expence of remitting Gold from hence to the respective markets. And Your Committee is inclined to this opinion, both by what is stated regarding the excess of imports from the Continent above the exports, though that is the part of the subject which is left most in doubt; and also by what is stated respecting the mode in which the payments in our trade have been latterly effected, an advance being paid upon the imports from the Continent of Europe, and a long credit being given upon the exports to other parts of the world.

Your Committee, observing how entirely the present depression of our Exchange with Europe is referred by many persons to a great excess of our imports above our exports, have called for an account of the actual value of those for the last five years; and Mr. Irving, the Inspector General of Customs, has accordingly furnished the most accurate Estimate of both that he has been enabled to form. He has also endeavoured to forward the object of the Committee, by calculating how much should be deducted from the value of goods imported, on account of articles in return for which nothing is exported. These deductions consist of the produce of Fisheries, and of imports from the East and West Indies, which are of the nature of rents, profits, and

capital remitted to Proprietors in this Country. The balance of trade in favour
of this Country, upon the face of the Account thus made up, was

In	1805	about	£. 6,616,000
	1806		£. 10,437,000
	1807		£. 5,866,000.
	1808		£. 12,481,000.
	1809		£14,834,000.

So far therefore, as any inference is to be drawn from the balance thus exhibited, the Exchanges during the present year, in which many payments to this
Country on account of the very advantageous balances of the two former years
may be expected to take place, ought to be peculiarly favourable.

Your Committee, however, place little confidence in deductions made even
from the improved document which the industry and intelligence of the
Inspector General has enabled him to furnish. It is defective, as Mr. Irving has
himself stated, inasmuch as it supplies no account of the sum drawn by Foreigners (which is at the present period peculiarly large) on account of freight
due to them for the employment of their shipping, nor, on the other hand, of
the sum receivable from them (and forming an addition to the value of our
exported articles) on account of freight arising from the employment of British
shipping. It leaves out of consideration all interest on capital in England possessed by Foreigners, and on capital abroad belonging to Inhabitants of Great
Britain, as well as the pecuniary transactions between the Governments
of England and Ireland. It takes no cognizance of contraband trade, and of
exported and imported Bullion, of which no account is rendered at the Cus-
tomhouse. It likewise omits a most important article, the variations of which, if
correctly stated, would probably be found to correspond in a great degree with
the fluctuations of the apparently favourable balance; namely, the bills drawn
on Government for our naval, military, and other expences in Foreign parts.
Your Committee had hoped to receive an account of these from the table of
the House; but there has been some difficulty and consequent delay in execut-
ing a material part of the Order made for them. It appears from 'an Account,
as far as it could be made out, of sums paid for Expences Abroad in 1793, 4, 5,
and 6,' inserted in the Appendix of the Lords' Report on the occasion of the
Bank Restriction Bill, that the sums so paid were,

In 1793	—	£ 2,785,252.
4	—	£ 8,335,591.
5	—	£ 11,040,236.
6	—	£ 10,649,916.

19

The following is an account of the official value of our Imports and Exports with the Continent of Europe alone, in each of the last five years:

	IMPORTS.	EXPORTS.	Balance in favour of Great Britain, reckoned in Official Value.
	£	£	£
1805	10,008,649	15,465,430	5,456,781
1806	8,197,256	13,216,386	5,019,130
1807	7,973,510	12,689,590	4,716,080
1808	4,210,671	11,280,490	7,069,819
1809	9,551,857	23,722,615	14,170,758

The balances with Europe alone in favour of Great Britain, as exhibited in this imperfect statement, are not far from corresponding with the general and more accurate balances before given. The favourable balance of 1809 with Europe alone, if computed according to the actual value, would be much more considerable than the value of the same year, in the former general statement.

A favourable balance of trade on the face of the Account of Exports and Imports, presented annually to Parliament, is a very probable consequence of large drafts on Government for foreign expenditure; an augmentation of exports, and a diminution of imports, being promoted and even enforced by the means of such drafts. For if the supply of bills drawn abroad, either by the Agents of Government, or by individuals, is disproportionate to the demand, the price of them in foreign money falls, until it is so low as to invite purchasers; and the purchasers, who are generally Foreigners, not wishing to transfer their property permanently to England, have a reference to the terms on which the bills on England will purchase those British commodities which are in demand, either in their own country, or in intermediate places, with which the account may be adjusted. Thus, the price of the bills being regulated in some degree by that of British commodities, and continuing to fall till it becomes so low as to be likely to afford a profit on the purchase and exportation of these commodities, an actual exportation nearly proportionate to the amount of the bills drawn can scarcely fail to take place. It follows, that there cannot be, for any long period, either a highly favourable or unfavourable balance of trade; for the balance no sooner affects the price of bills, than the price of bills, by its re-action on the state of trade, promotes an equalization of commercial exports and imports, Your Committee have here considered Cash and

Bullion as forming a part of the general mass of exported or imported articles, and as transferred according to the state both of the supply and the demand; forming however, under certain circumstances, and especially in the case of great fluctuations in the general commerce, a peculiarly commodious remittance.

Your Committee have enlarged on the documents supplied by Mr. Irving, for the sake of throwing further light on the general question of the balance of trade and the Exchanges, and of dissipating some very prevalent errors which have a great practical influence on the subject now under consideration.

That the real Exchange against this Country with the Continent cannot at any time have materially exceeded the limit fixed by the cost at that time of transporting specie, Your Committee are convinced upon the principles which have been already stated. That in point of fact, those Exchanges have not exceeded that limit, seems to receive a very satisfactory illustration from one part of the evidence of Mr. Greffulhe, who, of all the Merchants examined, seemed most wedded to the opinion, that the state of the balance of payments alone was sufficient to account for any depression of the Exchanges, however great. From what the Committee have already stated with respect to the par of Exchange, it is manifest that the Exchange between two countries is *at its real par*, when a given quantity of Gold or Silver in the one country is convertible at the market price into such an amount of the currency of that country, as will purchase a bill of Exchange on the other country for such an amount of the currency of that other country, as will there be convertible at the market price into an *equal* quantity of Gold or Silver of the same fineness. In the same manner the real Exchange is *in favour* of a country having money transactions with another, when a given quantity of Gold or Silver in the former is convertible for such an amount in the currency of that latter country, as will there be convertible into a *greater* quantity of Gold or Silver of the same fineness.

Upon these principles, Your Committee desired Mr. Greffulhe to make certain calculations, which appear in his Answers to the following Questions; viz.

'Supposing you had a pound weight troy of Gold of the English standard at Paris, and that you wished by means of that to procure a Bill of Exchange upon London, what would be the amount of the Bill of Exchange which you would procure in the present circumstances? – I find that a pound of Gold of the British standard at the present market price of 105 francs, and the exchange at 20 livres, would purchase a Bill of Exchange of £. 59. 8s.

'At the present market price of Gold in London, how much standard Gold can you purchase for £. 59. 8s.? – At the price of £. 4. 12s. I find it will purchase 12 ounces of Gold, within a very small fraction.

21

'Then what is the difference per cent. in the quantity of Standard Gold which is equivalent to £. 59. 8s. of our currency as at Paris and in London? – About 8½ per cent.

'Suppose you have a pound weight troy of our standard Gold at Hamburgh, and that you wished to part with it for a Bill of Exchange upon London, what would be the amount of the Bill of Exchange, which, in the present circumstances, you would procure? – At the Hamburgh price of 101, and the Exchange at 29, the amount of the Bill purchased on London would be £. 58. 4s.

'What quantity of our standard Gold, at the present price of £. 4. 12s. do you purchase for £. 58. 4s.? – About 12 ounces and 3 dwts.

'Then what is the difference per cent. between the quantity of standard Gold at Hamburgh and in London, which is equivalent to £. 58. 4s. sterling? – About 5½ per cent.

'Suppose you had a pound weight troy of our standard Gold at Amsterdam, and wished to part with it for a Bill of Exchange upon London, what would be the amount sterling of the Bill of Exchange which you would procure? – At the Amsterdam price of 14½, Exchange 31. 6. and Bank agio 1 per cent. the amount of the Bill on London would be £. 58. 18s.

'At the present price of £. 4. 12s. what quantity of our standard Gold do you purchase in London for £. 58. 18s. sterling? – 12 oz. 16 dwts.

'How much is that per cent.? – 7 per cent.' (*Min.* p. 133.)

Similar calculations, but made upon different assumed data, will be found in the evidence of Mr. Abraham Goldsmid. (*Min.* pp. 115, 116.) From these answers of Mr. Greffulhe, it appears, that when the computed Exchange with Hamburgh was 29, that is, from 16 to 17 per cent. below par, the real difference of Exchange, resulting from the state of trade and balance of payments was no more than 5½ per cent. against this Country; that when the computed Exchange with Amsterdam was 31. 6. that is about 15 per cent. below par, the real Exchange was no more than 7 per cent. against this Country; that, when the computed Exchange with Paris was 20, that is 20 per cent. below par, the real Exchange was no more than 8½ per cent. against this Country. (*Min.* p. 133.) After making these allowances, therefore, for the effect of the balance of trade and payments upon our Exchanges with those places, there will still remain a fall of 11 per cent. in the Exchange with Hamburgh, of above 8 per cent. in the Exchange with Holland, and of 11½ per cent. in the Exchange with Paris, to be explained in some other manner.

If the same mode of calculation be applied to the more recent statements of the Exchange with the Continent, it will perhaps appear, that though the computed Exchange is at present against this Country, the real Exchange is in its favour.

From the foregoing reasonings relative to the state of the Exchanges, if they are considered apart, Your Committee find it difficult to resist an inference, that a portion at least of the great fall which the Exchanges lately suffered must have resulted not from the state of trade, but from a change in the relative value of our domestic currency. But when this deduction is joined with that which Your Committee have stated, respecting the change in the market price of Gold, that inference appears to be demonstrated.

Thomas Robert Malthus (1766–1834)

'Depreciation of Paper Currency', *The Edinburgh Review* 17
(February 1811)

THE two first of these pamphlets deserve particular commendation, for having given a beginning to the interesting discussion which is still going on, with regard to the present extraordinary depreciation of our paper currency. The attention which was drawn to the same important question a few years ago, by the very clear and masterly view of the subject given by Lord King, and the uncommon combination of extensive knowledge of detail with just principles, exhibited in the work of Mr H. Thornton, seems to have had the effect of checking the progress of the evil, though not of entirely removing it. The great subsequent prosperity of our commerce, owing to our peculiarly fortunate situation compared with the rest of Europe, having improved our foreign exchanges, the depreciation of our currency, which still existed in a certain degree, was no longer thought of; and the subject, as might be expected, was allowed to drop.

Within the last two years, however, the progress of depreciation has been so rapid, as to force itself on the attention of all who were in any degree acquainted with its symptoms; and as it is not the practice of the public to resort to advice called forth on temporary occasions when similar occasions recur, Mr Mushet and Mr Ricardo seem to have been fully justified in their endeavours to excite fresh attention to so important a subject by new publications.

Nor are their *endeavours* alone entitled to our commendation: the manner in which they have executed their tasks, deserves a very considerable degree of praise. Mr Mushet has the great merit of stating some very important truths in so clear and simple a manner, as admirably to fit them for admission into the minds of those who are not very familiar with such investigations; while his errors are so inconsiderable, that the reader is in no danger of being led far from the right course. His suggestions respecting a recoinage of silver, and the mode of preserving it from degradation, well deserve the attention of the government. It should also be observed, that the judicious selection of tables subjoined to this publication, give it a very great additional interest, which has not been superseded even by the valuable Appendix to the Report of the Bullion Committee.

Mr Ricardo's pamphlet contains an excellent view of the general principles of circulation, and of the various results which are occasioned in different countries by the variations in their respective currencies. He is, in our opinion, particularly entitled to praise for the manner in which he has laid down two most important docrines, – long known, indeed, and acknowledged by those who have maturely considered these subjects, but not unfrequently overlooked by others.

The first is the grand doctrine, which may be said to be the main hinge on which the principles of circulation, whether consisting of a paper currency, or of the precious metals, must necessarily turn; – the doctrine, that every kind of circulating medium, as well as every other kind of commodity, is necessarily depreciated by excess, and raised in value by deficiency, compared with the demand, without reference either to confidence or intrinsic use. This doctrine follows immediately from the general principles of supply and demand, which are unquestionably the foundation on which the whole superstructure of political economy is built. And if we deny the application of these principles to the currencies of different countries, it will be quite impossible to explain the reason why the wants of some countries do not absolutely exhaust them of the precious metals, and the desireable products of others overload them with bullion; – and why, instead of such a state of things, the precious metals are, on the whole, maintained in such proportions in the different countries of the commercial world, as, in reference to the commodities which form the subjects of their mutual intercourse, to be nearly of the same value in each.

The other doctrine, to which we have alluded, nearly compacted with the former, and, from its being less generally known, even more important on the present occasion, is the doctrine; that excess and deficiency of currency are only *relative* terms; that the circulation of a country can never be superabundant; except in relation to other countries; that, as, after the discovery of the American mines, the different countries of Europe absorbed into their circulation three or four times the quantity of gold and silver which they before possessed, so, if the paper currency of one country would pass in another, or if proportional issues were made in all the different countries of the commercial world at the same time, there is no limit to the quantity which might be absorbed, without any such redundancy as would overfill the circulation, and occasion the efflux of the precious metals, though it might be continually occasioning the melting of coin into bullion.

A clear understanding of this doctrine is absolutely necessary, in order to explain what is meant by *excessive* issues of paper; and to enable us fully to comprehend the grand distinction, between the wants of the circulation, in order to maintain it on a level with bullion or the currencies of surrounding countries, – and the wants of private merchants, and of the government for the purposes of business, and national expenditure.

These two important doctrines are, in the course of Mr Ricardo's discussion, explained with great clearness and precision; and both he and Mr Mushet appear to us to have completely succeeded in proving the actual depretiation of our currency, and in tracing it to its true cause. They have both also the satisfaction of having seen their main views of the subject, and the remedy which they recommend, sanctioned by a Report, drawn up with great care and ability by a committee of the House of Commons, consisting of some of the best informed men of their time; and founded upon a body of curious evidence, and a set of instructive documents, which would have been utterly beyond the reach of private individuals.

The great fault of Mr Ricardo's performance, is the partial view which he takes of the causes which operate upon the course of Exchange.

Independently of the wearing or the adulteration of the coin, the effects of which are readily intelligible, there are, we conceive, two causes, perfectly distinct in their origin, though nearly similar in their effects, by which the exchange is affected. The first, and the most ordinary, is the varying demand for different sorts of produce arising from the varying desires and necessities of the nations connected with each other by commerce: The second is a comparative redundancy or deficiency of currency, in whatever way it may be occasioned.

If, for instance, in consequence of the sudden adoption of some foreign commodity into general use, or the sudden deficiency of some commodity of home growth, which must be supplied from abroad, the imports of a particular country should exceed its exports, the exchange might be turned greatly against it; and it might be obliged to make some of its payments in bullion, although, previous to the extraordinary imports occasioned by these new desires or new wants, both its bullion and its currency might have been precisely of the same value as those of the country into which they were now flowing.

In this case, it is quite clear, that the exportation of bullion was the *effect of a balance of trade*, originating in causes which may exist without any relation whatever to redundancy or deficiency of currency.

In other cases, a redundancy or deficiency of currency is the exciting *cause of the balance of trade* and payments, and of the exportation or the importation of bullion.

An efflux or influx of the precious metals, for instance, originating in the first cause, could exist but a very short time, before it would produce a comparative deficiency in one country, and redundancy in the other; and, by the convertibility of bullion into coin, and coin into bullion, a proportional change in the bullion value of their respective currencies.

But the country, with a diminishing quantity of bullion, would evidently soon be limited in its powers of paying with the precious metals, while, at the same time, it would be encouraged to sell by the low bullion prices of its goods, and the foreign demand for them, occasioned by the fall in its bills. On the other hand, the country, with an increasing quantity of bullion, would have its power of purchasing with the precious metals increased, and its encouragement to sell diminished, by the advanced bullion prices of its goods, and the diminished foreign demand for them occasioned by the premium upon its bills. This state of things could not fail to have a speedy effect in changing the direction of the balance of payments, and in restoring that equilibrium of the precious metals, which had been for a time disturbed by the naturally unequal wants and necessities of the countries which trade with each other.

A similar effect would be produced upon the imports and exports, by the discovery of a new mine, or the increased issues of paper, as long as such issues continued to throw coin out of circulation. In these cases, the redundancy or deficiency of currency is the *cause* of an unfavourable or favourable balance of trade, an unfavourable or favourable course of the real exchanges, and the consequent exportation or importation of bullion.

It is of the utmost importance to keep these two distinct causes, which affect the course of exchange, constantly in view; because they sometimes act in conjunction, and sometimes in opposition to each other; and the results produced by their sum, or their difference, cannot of course be accounted for by either the one or the other taken separately. Mr Ricardo, however, instead of directing his attention to both these causes, confines it to only one of them. He attributes a favourable or unfavourable exchange *exclusively* to a redundant or deficient currency, and overlooks the varying desires and wants of different societies, as an original cause of a temporary excess of imports above exports, or exports above imports.

To point out more explicitly the effects of these partial views on the reasoning of Mr Ricardo, we will quote his criticism on a passage in Mr Thornton's work on *Paper credit*, in which the error of his principles appears in a very striking light.

Mr Thornton had stated in substance, that a very unfavourable balance of trade might be occasioned in this country by a bad harvest; that there might be at the same time an unwillingness in the country to which we were indebted, to receive our goods in payment; and that, under these circumstances, the balance due must be paid in part by bullion. On this statement Mr Ricardo observes, that 'Mr Thornton has not explained to us, why any unwillingness should exist in the foreign country to receive our goods in exchange for their corn; and it would be necessary for him to show, that if such an unwillingness were to exist, we should agree to indulge it so far, as to part with 'our coin. If we consent to give coin in exchange for goods, it must be from choice, not necessity. We should not import more goods than we export, unless we had a redundancy of currency which it therefore suits us to make a part of our exports. The exportation of coin is caused by its cheapness; and is not the effect, but the cause, of an unfavourable balance. We should not export it, if we did not send it to a better market; or if we had any commodity which we could export more profitably. It is a salutary remedy for a redundant currency; and as I have endeavoured to prove that redundancy or excess is only a relative term, it follows, that the demand for it abroad arises only from the comparative deficiency of the currency of the importing country which there causes its superior value.' This reasoning, Mr Ricardo applies equally to the stronger case of the payment of a subsidy to a foreign power.

Now, we would ask, what necessary connexion there is between the wants of a nation for unusual importations of corn, occasioned by a bad harvest, or its desire to transmit a large subsidy to a foreign power occasioned by a treaty to that effect, – and the question of redundant or deficient currencies? Surely, such wants or desires might occur in one of two countries, where, immediately previous to their existence, the precious metals circulated as nearly as possible on a level. And the unwillingness of the country to which the debt is owing, to receive in payment a great quantity of goods, beyond what it is in the habit of giving orders for, and consuming, stands much less in need of explanation, than that a bad harvest, or the necessity of paying a subsidy in one country, should be immediately and invariably accompanied by an unusual demand for muslins, hardware, and colonial produce in some other. We know indeed, that such a demand will to a certain degree exist, owing to the fall in the bills upon the debtor country, and the consequent opportunity of purchasing its commodities at a cheaper rate than usual. But if the debt for the corn or the subsidy be considerable, and require prompt payment, the bills on the debtor country will fall below the price of the transport of the precious metals. A part of the debt will be paid in these metals; and a part by the increased exports of commodities. But, as far as it is paid by the transmission of bullion, this transmission does not merely originate in redundancy of currency. It is not occasioned by its cheapness. It is not, as Mr Ricardo endeavours to persuade us, the cause of the unfavourable balance, instead of the effect. It is not merely a salutary remedy for a redundant currency: But it is owing precisely to the cause mentioned by Mr Thornton – the unwillingness of the creditor nation to receive a great additional quantity of goods not wanted for immediate consumption, without being bribed to it by excessive cheapness; and its willingness to receive bullion – the currency of the commercial world – without any such bribe. It is unquestionably true, as stated by Mr Ricardo, that no nation will pay a debt in the precious metals, if it can do it cheaper by commodities; but the prices of commodities are liable to great depressions from a glut in the market; – whereas the precious metals, on account of their having been constituted, by the universal consent of society, the general medium of exchange, and instrument of commerce, will pay a debt of the largest amount at its nominal estimation, according to the quantity of bullion contained in the respective currencies of the countries in question. And, whatever variations between the quantity of currency and commodities, may be stated to take place subsequent to the commencement of these transactions, it cannot be for a moment doubted, that the cause of them is to be found in the wants and desires of one of the two nations, and not in any original redundancy or defi-ciency of currency in either of them.

The same kind of error which we have here noticed, pervades other parts of Mr Ricardo's pamphlet, particularly the opening of his subject. He seems to think, that when once the precious metals have been divided among the dif-ferent countries of the earth, according to their relative wealth and commerce, that each having an equal necessity for the quantity actually in use, no temp-tation would be offered for their importation or exportation, till either a new mine, or a new bank was opened; or till some marked change had taken place in their relative prosperity.

That the discovery of a new mine, or the opening of a new bank, on which Mr Ricardo lays his principal stress, are most powerful causes of the efflux and influx of bullion, we are most ready to acknowledge; but they certainly are not the sole causes. The wants of different nations with different climates, and dif-ferent degrees of fertility, cannot, with any degree of probability, be supposed, in the first instance, *exactly* to balance each other. They are only forced to this kind of level by the absolute impossibility, if they have no mines, of continuing to purchase more than they sell; and the rapid effect which the exportation of even a very moderate quantity of the precious metals has in raising the cur-rency of the exporting, and lowering that of the importing country. But, while this level is, on the whole, maintained, we cannot doubt that the varying wants of these nations frequently subject them to unfavourable or favourable balances of payment, beyond what can be easily settled by bills: and that to settle these, and to carry on the various roundabout foreign trades of con-sumption, there ever has been, and always will be, a quantity of the precious metals in use destined to perform the same part with regard to the different nations connected with each other by commerce, which the currency of a par-ticular country performs with regard to its distant provinces.

To the pamphlet of Mr Ricardo succeeded, we believe, the able and original observations of Mr Blake, on the principles which regulate the course of exchange; and the public is certainly indebted to him for a very valuable addi-tion to their stock of information on the important subject which now occupies so much of their attention. We wish that we had room to point out to the reader many of the clear and masterly statements contained in this publi-cation; but when we consider the quantity of matter still before us, we are compelled to confine ourselves chiefly to the more invidious task of pointing out what we conceive to be its errors. Mr Blake observes, in his introduction, that 'the computed exchange varies from two causes totally distinct from each other. The first, arising from the abundance or scarcity of bills in the market, is the foundation of what may be called the *real* exchange; which depends upon the payments which a country has to make, compared with those it has to receive, and has no reference to the state of the currency. The second, arising from alterations in the value of the currency, is the foundation of what may be called the *nominal* exchange; which has no reference whatever to the state of debt and credit of the country.' He then proceeds, in three distinct sections, to comment, first, upon the real exchange; secondly, upon the nominal exchange; and, thirdly, upon the computed exchange, or the combined results of both, as they appear in the printed accounts.

In discussing the first branch of his subject, he has entirely avoided the error of Mr Ricardo, and has traced the causes of the real exchange to the varying desires and necessities of different nations, which naturally make them sometimes debtors, and sometimes creditors, to the countries with which they deal, although their respective currencies may be in a state of the most perfect equality of value. The great fault which appears in this part of Mr Blake's work, is, that though he has explained certain causes of the real exchange, and their various effects on mercantile transactions, in the clearest and most satisfactory manner, yet, he has omitted to notice one of the principal causes; and, so far, has left his section on the real exchange incomplete.

In proceeding to the discussion of the nominal exchange, he assumes as a postulatum, for the sake of clearness, that the real exchange remains unaltered: he, at the same time, considers an alteration in the total amount of the currency of a country, without a corresponding alteration of the commodities to be circulated by it, as the main cause which, in the present times, affects the nominal exchange; and the cause, therefore, to which he intends to direct his chief attention. He is thus at once led into the grave error of implying, what indeed he distinctly maintains afterwards, that an alteration in the amount of the currency of a country, without a corresponding alteration in its commodities, has no tendency to affect the real exchange, and to cause an exportation or importation of bullion.

We are quite ready to agree with Mr Blake, that the *nominal* exchange, as far as it is *merely nominal*, has no tendency of this kind; but, we are firmly persuaded, with Mr Ricardo, that, as long as there is any quantity of coin to be displaced, and converted into bullion by increased issues of paper, so long will such increased issues continue to raise the bullion, as well as the nominal prices of commodities; that if the bullion prices of commodities be raised, what Mr Blake calls the real prices current will be raised; and the raising of the real prices current cannot fail to discourage the sale of home produce, and encourage the purchase of foreign produce, occasion a discount upon home bills, and a premium on foreign bills, affect unfavourably the real exchange, and terminate in the exportation of bullion.

Connected with this important error, of supposing that the real exchange is not affected by a redundancy or deficiency of currency, is another, which supposes that the bullion trade may be carried on between two countries while their real exchanges are at par. Now, we would ask, in the first place, whether it is readily conceivable that such a difference should exist between the real prices of bullion in two countries connected with each other, as to cover the expenses of transport, and offer a fair profit to the bullion merchant, without affecting the real prices of commodities in such countries. By the real prices of commodities, in the present discussion, Mr Blake explains himself to mean (p. 48) 'the prices at which those commodities would be bought and sold, if no depreciation of currency existed, which, from the convertibility of coin into bullion, and bullion into coin, can be no other than what we should call the bullion prices. But if the bullion prices, or real prices current, were lowered in one of two countries, so as more than to cover the expense of transport, the exports would undoubtedly exceed the imports, and the exchange could no longer remain at par.

Secondly, We would ask, in what manner the bullion merchant pays for the bullion which he imports? It can only be by the purchase and remittance of a foreign bill, or by ordering a bill to be drawn upon him. In either case, funds in goods must have gone out, or must go out, to provide for the payment of these bills; and if a balance of goods had not gone out before, that is, if the exchange had not before been favourable, the additional quantity which must go out to pay for the bullion would at once make the exports exceed the imports, and prevent the exchange from being at par. It appears, therefore, from the very terms of the proposition, that bullion cannot be purchased for importation without an excess of exports, and a consequent favourable exchange. We are aware, indeed, that on the supposition of the exports and imports of the produce of two countries being exactly balanced, and the exchange at par, the fresh competition of a bullion merchant for a bill to pay for the bullion which he wished to import, would rather tend to raise the price of foreign bills, and render the exchange unfavourable; but this only shows that such a competition at such a time could never occur. It is indeed impossible to suppose, with Mr Blake, that the bullion dealer would be the most engaged at the time that the real exchange was at its least deviation from par, (p. 35.), when, in the purchase of a commodity for which there is rarely any very urgent and sudden demand, by waiting till the exchange was decidedly favourable, he could import any quantity that he might want, with so much greater profit. Mr Blake seems to be quite unconscious of the grand difference between bullion and other commodities. The bullion prices of particular commodities may easily vary in such a manner, from plenty or scarcity, as to make it answer to import them when the exchange is at par, or even decidedly unfavourable. But how can the bullion prices of *bullion* experience such variations? The prices of that commodity, which is the general medium of exchange, can properly be said to vary only in reference to the sum of all other commodities; but a variation in the sum of all other commodities compared with bullion, cannot take place in any country which has a ready communication with others, without affecting the exchange. To us, therefore, it appears quite clear, that there are really no other variations in the prices at which bullion can be bought and sold for import or export, than those which appear in the exchange.

In our commerce with all those countries which are nearly connected with the mines, and where, in consequence, bullion is comparatively cheap, the real exchange has been almost invariably in our favour; and we believe it may be laid down as a rule that admits of no exception, that, whenever the real exchange with any country is either at par, or unfavourable, it is cheaper to purchase bullion in the home markets than to import it from such country.

To the same error of Mr Blake is to be ascribed his criticism upon Lord King (p. 35.), who has stated, if we recollect, in substance, that the bullion sent to India has a tendency to render our exchanges with Europe favourable. Now, if, from what we have just said, it appears that bullion cannot flow into a country except in consequence of a favourable real exchange; and if any unusual demand for bullion in a particular country must tend to render bullion scarcer and dearer, and, by lowering the real prices of commodities, to encourage an excess of exports above imports, and to render the real exchange favourable, we conceive that Lord King must be right, and Mr Blake's correction unfounded.

We are fearful that the subject of exchanges will not admit of that distinctness and simplicity of division with which Mr Blake has treated it; because it is unquestionable, that one of the most powerful causes of the nominal exchange – a redundancy or deficiency of currency – invariably influences the real exchange, as long as there is any coin that can be converted with advantage into bullion, or any bullion to be converted into coin. All that can be done, as it appears to us, is, to rank among the causes of the real exchange, not only the varying desires and necessities of different nations, but every such alteration in their currencies as tends to affect the bullion prices of commodities. The causes of the nominal exchange will then be all that part of every alteration in the currencies of different countries, which does not affect the bullion prices of commodities; and the computed exchange will of course be the result of both Notwithstanding the errors in Mr Blake's pamphlet which we have here ventured to point out, and which, if our criticisms be just, are not unimportant, we still think it a very valuable publication, and earnestly recommend it to the attention of our readers, particularly the first and last sections.

Mr Huskisson's pamphlet has been published since the Report of the Committee, and was written, as he intimates, to satisfy the minds of some of his friends, and to support the conclusions which he had formed upon so interesting a question, against the clamours of those who were inimical to the Report. There was not, indeed, much that remained to be done after the publication of the Report itself, and the body of evidence with which it was accompanied. But what Mr Huskisson has done, he has done, on the whole, exceedingly well; and we have little doubt that his authority, as a practical statesman bred in the school of Mr Pitt, will be of essential service to the cause of truth on the present occasion; both by giving a wider circulation to the discussion, and by calming, in some degree, the fears of those who strangely imagine, that the present deranged system of our currency is necessary to the collection of our revenue. We are disposed, therefore, to give Mr Huskisson very great credit, both for the liberal and manly spirit which prompted him to undertake the task, and which pervades the whole performance, and for the general ability with which it is executed; though we think it necessary to begin with some corrections, which appear to us to be material, of his elementary doctrine.

As a very proper and sufficient reason for some explanations relating to the fundamental principles of money, with which Mr Huskisson opens his pamphlet, he intimates, that it is of great importance that the ground should be properly cleared for a discussion of this kind; and that those who engage in it, should be agreed in their first principles. The same reason makes it necessary for us to offer a few remarks on these explanations.

Mr Huskisson, in stating that it is of the very essence of *money* to possess intrinsic value, on account of its being the *common and universal equivalent*, observes, that 'the quality, of being a *common measure*, does not necessarily imply such value, any more than the possession of a foot-rule implies the power of acquiring whatever it enables us to measure.' In this observation, we neither see how the illustration applies, nor are we disposed to acknowledge the truth of the position which it is intended to establish. To us it appears absolutely necessary, that the commodity which measures exchangeable *value*, must itself possess *value* in exchange; in the same manner as a foot-rule, which measures length, must itself possess length. A pound of gold might be said to measure the nominal value, or value in gold, of all the commodities in the country, by stating how many pounds they would exchange for at their market prices: – but it does not follow, that the possessor of a pound of gold, although it has intrinsic value, should be able to acquire *all* the articles of value with which it might be successively compared.

One of the most important functions of the precious metals, is that of acting as a measure of value in exchanges; and if paper, or any other article possessing little or no intrinsic value, appears sometimes to usurp this important function, it is solely and exclusively on account of its constant reference to the intrinsic value of the precious metals. Nor do we conceive it *possible*, that a paper currency could be established, and perform the part of measuring the exchangeable value of commodities, without imminent risk of the most tremendous convulsions of property, if there were not some article of intrinsic value in exchange, with which it was constantly compared; and which, therefore, and not the paper, would be the real measure of value.

We have no great objection to the term, *universal equivalent*, which Mr Huskisson considers as the quality which most pre-eminently distinguishes the precious metals from all other commodities; but we doubt whether it advantageously supplies the place of the term *medium of exchange*, or *instrument of commerce*; because it is precisely on account of their being adopted by the common consent of society as the general medium of exchange, that they are received as a universal equivalent. Were it not for this consent, it is quite clear, that they would only be accepted as an equivalent for other commodities, of equal exchangeable value, by those who wished to make use of them as plate.

Mr Huskisson further states, that paper currency 'is so much circulating credit,' that 'whoever buys, gives – whoever sells, receives – such a quantity of pure gold, as is equivalent to the article bought or sold: – or, if he gives or receives paper instead of money, he gives or receives that which is valuable only as it stipulates the payment of a given quantity of gold or silver … that money alone is the universal equivalent; paper currency the representative of that money.' This account appears to us exactly to suit the state of circulation which is represented to have prevailed in Holland before the revolution, arising from a Bank of Deposit; but it does not apply to the system of banking, and of paper currency, which has been adopted in this and most other countries. In Holland, it was really true, that every Bank credit represented a certain weight of coins, or of bullion of a known fineness; that no part of these coins or bullion was exported in consequence of the substitution of Bank money for bullion; and that, if all the creditors of the Bank required at once what those credits represented, the whole of the bullion and coins that had been deposited would be forthcoming at a moment's notice. But every person who is acquainted with the system of banking in this country, knows perfectly well, that such a realization could never have taken place here; he knows perfectly well, that the peculiar advantages which we derive from this system, depend chiefly upon the substitution of a very cheap instrument for a very dear one; and that, consequently, when this substitution has once taken place, there seldom has been, nor ever will be, a sufficient quantity of coin in the country to realize in the precious metals the whole of its paper currency. It is true, that, in the healthy state of our circulation, Bank notes are, and always should be, exchangeable for coin at the option of the holder; but it is found by experience, that, in all ordinary times, the option of the holder is satisfied with a very moderate portion of coin, compared with the whole currency. It is found by experience, that a bank-note is not considered as valuable, only because it enables him to obtain a given quantity of the precious metals. The holder is in general satisfied, if he feels quite sure of always obtaining for his note a quantity of commodities *equal in value* to the quantity of the precious metals specified in it. This is, in fact, what, ninety-nine times out of a hundred, he really wants; and what alone, in reference to the whole body of notes in circulation, the country possesses the means of effecting.

The reason why his wants are, for the most part, directed to the value, rather than the substance, of the precious metals, depends upon a quality which peculiarly distinguishes that commodity, whatever it is, which has once been constituted by the common consent of society the general medium of exchange. This is, that every person is a dealer in it; and that men want it most frequently, not for its intrinsic uses, but in order to obtain other commodities for it; in the same manner as a dealer in corn, as far as he is only a dealer, wants it, not on account of its intrinsic use in supporting human creatures, but in order to obtain the necessaries, conveniences, and comforts of life in exchange for it. And if such a person dealt in pieces of paper marked with bushels and quarters of corn, provided that, by any process, they could be kept always on a level with the varying market prices of real corn, he would carry on his trade with exactly the same advantage to himself as he does at present. But it is quite clear, that, with regard to corn, no possible process could preserve the level of value here supposed; and precisely, because very few, comparatively, are dealers in corn, and the great majority of mankind want it to eat, not to sell; whereas the very simple process of making every bank which issues notes, perform its promise of paying them in specie, at the option of the holder, under the penalty of complete loss of credit in case of failure, is known to be sufficient to effect a level of value between bank-notes and the precious metals; and precisely because, with regared to the precious metals, in their character of a circulating medium, every man is a dealer, and wants them to sell – not to use.

This is a view of the subject which has not been sufficiently attended to, although it appears to us to afford the only satisfactory explanation of the great quantity of paper which may be substituted for the precious metals, in the common systems of banking. In fact, we believe, that the circumstance of our being chiefly dealers in the medium of exchange, not consumers of it, is the very foundation of all those systems of paper currency, the great advantage of which consists in the substitution of a cheap for a dear instrument of commerce.

It will be observed, that this circumstance does not, in any degree, tend to impeach the necessity of the obligation upon all bankers to pay their notes in specie, whenever they are called upon; as in no other way would it be *possible* so to regulate the quantity of bank notes, as *uniformly* and *certainly* to maintain them of the same value as coin. It is merely a somewhat different, and, in our opinion, a more correct view of what actually takes place in those countries where banking establishments prevail, than that which considers the usual kinds of paper-currency in the light of the bank money of Amsterdam, as representing so much coin or bullion at all times forthcoming, and which affirms, that whoever buys, gives, whoever sells, receives, such a quantity of pure gold or silver as is equivalent to the article bought or sold; when it is perfectly well known that the fact is not, and cannot be so, according to the principle of substitution. The precious metals, therefore, in our opinion, perform a more important part in society, and are more frequently called into action, as a measure of exchangeable value, than as a universal equivalent.

But, notwithstanding the little elementary inaccuracy which has given rise to these observations, we must again repeat, that Mr Huskisson's doctrines appear to us to be on the whole quite sound and satisfactory. Nothing can be clearer, or more convincing, than the statements in proof of the actual depreciation of our currency, from p. 12. to p. 17, to which we particularly refer our readers. If a pound of gold, which being coined, according to the law of the country, into forty-four guineas and a half, must, in an undegraded state of the currency, be equal in value to 46l. 14s. 6d., cannot now be purchased for less than 56l of our actual currency: – if a *light* guinea, which, by being legally convertible into bullion, represents the value of the currencies of surrounding countries, be worth above 24s. in our currency, while the few heavy guineas which are current, being forced to partake of the degradation of the general currency, are worth only 21s.: – if the only reason why a solitary guinea here and there remains in our circulation, and purchases only the same quantity of goods as a one pound note and a shilling, is, that the law will punish, by fine and imprisonment, every man who dares to sell his commodity for what it is really worth: – if, by the act of 1774, gold, which for many years had been the practical measure of value in this country, was made the only legal tender for payments above a certain sum; and if no repeal or alteration in this act took place in consequence of the restriction bill in 1797: – if our foreign exchanges have been, for a considerable period, permanently against us, to the amount of between 15 and 20 per cent., which, when the highest expense of transmitting gold was about 7 per cent., could not possibly have happened if gold could have been had in exchange for notes at the Bank, and our currency had been of the same value as the currencies of surrounding countries: – if what alone can be meant by the term 'depreciated currency,' is a depreciation below the value of that metal which has long formed the effective legal tender of the realm, or below the currencies of the different nations of the commercial world, which, being always estimated in one or other of the precious metals, can admit only of the slight variations that affect the relative values of gold and silver: – If, we say, these things are so, whatever may be urged in favour of the benefits to be derived from a redundant currency, or the inconvenience of returning to payments in specie, *the fact* of such redundancy, and the propriety of applying the term 'depreciated' to the present state of our currency, appears to us to be placed beyond the possibility of doubt.

In answer to the decisive argument suggested by the high price of gold when compared with our currency, it has been confidently asserted, that this high price is not occasioned by the depreciation of that currency, but by the unusual demand for gold abroad. These assertions, Mr Huskisson considers in a subsequent part of his pamphlet, and denies their having any foundation either in fact or probability. But he does not seem to be sufficiently aware, that, even if they were admitted, they have nothing to do with the *existence* of the depreciation, though they have with its *cause*. And this is a point of view which ought to be by no means omitted in our consideration of the subject.

The precious metals are the currency of the commercial world; and whatever variations may take place in their value, either from a greater or less supply of them from the mines, or a greater or less use of them in commerce, it is clear, that all the nations which have a mutual intercourse with each other, must partake of them. If any have currencies, consisting partly of coin and partly of paper, convertible, at the will of the holder, into coin, it is equally clear, that this paper must partake in all the changes that affect the coin. Let us suppose, now, the case of a more abundant supply from the mines. – An influx of the precious metals would evidently take place, which, for a short time, would sink the market price of bullion below the mint price; but more bullion would be immediately converted into coin, and each bank would find that it might issue more of its notes without risk. The consequence would be, that the whole of the currency, retaining probably the same proportions of paper and coin, would be enlarged; the market price of bullion would quickly be raised to the mint price; the exchanges which had been very favourable, would return to their usual state; and no other effect would be experienced, than a general rise of prices throughout the commercial world.

On the other hand, in the case of a diminished supply from the mines, or a greater consumption of the precious metals in some of the principal states of Europe, an immediate demand would be felt in the rest for bullion to be exported; the market price of bullion would be raised for a time above the mint price; the notes of the different banks would return upon them, to be exchanged for coin, which would be sent abroad. The consequence would be, that the whole currency, consisting still of the same proportion of paper to coin, would be diminished in quantity, and raised in value; the market price of bullion would soon sink to the mint price; the exchanges, which had been unusually unfavourable, would be restored to their accustomed state; and no other effect would be felt, than a general fall of prices throughout the commercial world.

Now, if, in the case last supposed, the paper of one of these countries were not convertible into coin, and very little specie remained in circulation, it is quite clear, that the currency would not have the means of assimilating itself to the currencies of the nations with which it was connected. The market price of bullion would rise very greatly above its mint price; all the gold which could be readily collected would be exported. But as this would be inconsiderable, and as the great mass of paper would remain undiminished, or perhaps be slightly increased, to supply the vacancies occasioned by the gold exported, the great excess of the market price of bullion above the mint price, and the very unfavourable exchanges, would become permanent, (subject however, still, to variations occasioned by the balance of trade, and payments); and the currency of such a country would be to all intents and purposes depreciated, when compared with gold and silver and the currencies of other countries, just as it would be from an original excess of paper issues; although, on the whole, taking paper and guineas together, the amount of the currency might not be increased by a single pound.

It is material to observe, that, under all possible variations in the value of the precious metals, whether they are increased in quantity tenfold, or diminished to one tenth, the defect or excess of the market price of the precious metals, compared with the mint price, always ceases as soon as the level is effected; and *nothing* but a depreciated currency *can* render gold in bullion permanently of greater value than gold in coin.

Whether any rise has really taken place in the value of the precious metals on the Continent during the last few years, and has contributed, in a slight degree, to the present state of our currency, we will not take upon ourselves to determine. We certainly do not think it quite so improbable as Mr Huskisson does; as we conceive, that the great shock which mercantile credit has suffered, by the difficulties thrown in the way of commercial intercourse, may have operated something like a return to a less advanced period of civilization, and occasioned the necessity of employing a greater quantity of the precious metals, in proportion to the number of exchanges to be transacted. We think, also, that in the evidence before the Bullion Committee, there are some symptoms of a rise of this kind, which are not sufficiently noticed in that Report.

As, however, the effect derived from this cause, appears, at any rate, to be very inconsiderable, compared with the degree of actual depreciation, an attempt to ascertain its proportion to the whole would certainly be very difficult, and could not be very important. But it appears to us to be extremely important to know, that the Bank directors cannot, with any degree of property, urge the argument of a great demand for gold on the Continent, to justify the comparative depreciation of their notes. Whatever may be the variations in the value of the precious metals, their business is to regulate the issue of their notes, so as always to maintain them of the same value. To this course the course they would be forced, by considerations of personal interest, if the restriction bill had not passed; and, after its enactment, to this course they ought to be impelled, by a sense of their duty to the public, and a proper estimate of the high responsibility that must attach to a set of men, to whose discretion, during the continuance of this act, the entire regulation of the national currency is entrusted.

We had intended to point out to our readers, many parts of Mr Huskisson's pamphlet in which we think he has been very successsul; and a few, in which we do not agree with him, besides his doctrine of equivalents in trade.* But our limits oblige us to hasten to Mr Bosanquet, whose various alleged facts and desultory observations, we confess, excited in us, at first, a considerable degree of alarm; – not, however, on account of their formidable nature – for, though he very correctly describes himself as 'a partizan,' we cannot help thinking that he is a little incorrect in adding that he is 'a succesful' one; but on account of their mere number, and the consequent time and space which the shortest remarks upon them would take up. Fortunately, however, the second edition of his pamphlet fell into our hands; and, in reading his supplementary observations, we found ourselves relieved from the task we had undertaken, by the *concessions* of Mr Bosanquet himself.

We had conceived, that the great object of the various facts and observations which he had brought forward, was to show, that the present phenomena relating to the market price of gold bullion, and the course of our foreign exchanges, were of the same temporary nature as those of a similar kind which

---

* We trust that we shall not be suspected, because we disapprove of the doctrine of equivalents, of adopting the old mercantile notion, that the profits of foreign trade are derived from a balance paid in the precious metals; which Mr Huskisson very oddly seems to think is the alternative. Our opinion is, that, in all commercial transactions, both parties gain what, in the estimation of each, is decidedly more than an equivalent for what it has given; and that it is out of this excess, that the gains of the merchants concerned are taken, who, it appears to us would be very badly off, and would be little disposed to continue their business, if what they imported were not worth more to the purchasers of it, and would consequently sell for more, than what had been exported.

had often occurred before, – though, from an unusual concurrence of circumstances, they had been aggravated, both in degree and duration; and that the Report of the Bullion Committee was not justified in representing them as indications of a permanent depreciation of our currency below the legal tender of the realm, and the currencies of surrounding countries. What then was our surprise to find him, on second thoughts, *giving up completely the question of depreciation*, in reference to our legal tender, – *acknowledging fairly* that the gold contained in a guinea is now of more value than $^{21}/_{40}$th parts of a two pound note, and, without any allusion to it as a temporary occurrence, proposing an entirely new standard of value, from a comparison with which it appears that our currency is not depreciated!

When this standard is, we are quite sure that our readers would never guess; and we cannot but consider it as one of the most curious instances of self-deception that we have ever met with, and a most unlucky specimen of the reasoning of practical men, that *the interest of 33l. 6s. 8d. in the 3 per cent. stocks*, should be gravely proposed as the standard measure of the value of our currency; that is, that a *one pound note of the Bank of England*, which is the interest of this sum, and the kind of currency in which it is paid, should be the criterion by which we are to judge of the depreciation of – *a one pound note of the Bank of England!*

It may be true, as suggested in the Report of the Committee, that, ever since 1797, Bank of England notes have been the practical medium of exchange, and the measure of relative value in all our sales and purchases at home. But the public has always flattered itself, that during the temporary suspension of payments in specie, the quantity and value of these notes would be regulated by a constant comparison with the legal tender of the realm. Let the reader for a moment consider, in what a dreadfully critical state must the property and contracts of a country be placed, which has a paper currency not referrible to *any commodity of intrinsic worth* for the correction of its quantity, and the maintenance of its value, and which might consequently sink, in the course of a few months, 50 or 100 per cent. below the value of the precious metals, and deprive individuals of half their fortunes, and yet appear to be unchangeable. The moment we quit the precious metals as the constant standard of reference, there is no fancy so wild, respecting a paper circulation, which may not be indulged, and no limit to the degree of depreciation which may not in time be expected. Yet, *of this standard*, to our utter surprise and grief, the Bank Directors, and their friends, have openly avowed their neglect before a Committee of the House of Commons. What they mean to substitute, we are not informed; nor do we know whether or not Mr Bosanquet is sanctioned by their authority in the new standard which *he* has brought forward. But it is unquestionable, that, except in regard to the integrity of a few individuals, on which the great mass of the property of a country ought never to be made to depend, even the assignats of France rested upon a better foundation than that on which it is now proposed to place the paper circulation of Great Britain. In fact, what security have we, except in this integrity, that the Bank Directors may not agree to create and divide 24 millions in notes among them for their private fortunes? Or, to put a less strong, and not so improbable a case; What security have we that the Bank, when released from all obligation to keep their notes of the value of the precious metals, may not alter their mode of conducting business, and lend money for longer terms than they do at present, and on any fair personal security? Mr Bosanquet, in the course of his work, has given us an elaborate explanation of the manner in which the demand for discounts at the Bank naturally limits itself; for which we are really much obliged to him, though we do not think that it proves sufficiently what he intends; and , in one respect, it is rather unfortunate for his general argument, as he appears to have been led by it, unintentionally, to let out some of the secrets of his 'prison house,' by talking of a recurrence of demand for notes by the *first class* of discounters; which he explains to be 'those which the Directors distinguish as solid paper for real transactions;' from which we may fairly conclude, that there are other classes well known, and not always rejected at the Bank, which are probably distinguished as accommodation paper. But whatever faith Mr Bosanquet may attach to his natural limit, we are quite sure, that neither he, nor any man of business, will venture to deny, that there are thousands and thousands of traders in the kingdom, who would eagerly seize the opportunity of borrowing capital on their personal security at 5 percent.; and that the immense profits of the Bank, in lending such sums, would beyond all comparison counterbalance the risk: Yet, while the country was thus absolutely inundated with paper, a one pound note would be still worth the interest of 33l. 6s. 8d. 3 per cents.

We cannot believe that Mr Bosanquet would have resorted to so very strange a solution of his difficulties, if he had felt any real confidence in his practical observations against the doctrines of the Report. We do not therefore think it necessary to combat arguments which the author himself gives up. But, to those who have only read the first edition of his pamphlet, or have a greater faith in the correctness and efficacy of his facts than he has himself, we would recommend the careful perusal of the able reply of Mr Ricardo, accompanied by the remarks of Mr Blake, on the real, nominal, and computed exchange, and corrected by the few observations which we have ventured to suggest in a former part of this article. With these helps, we are persuaded, that an impartial and attentive inquirer after truth will see, that the facts of Mr Bosanquet, as far as they are stated correctly, may be easily explained, in perfect accordance with the main doctrines of the Report.

We do not, however, think, that these facts are at all satisfactorily explicable upon the principles of Mr Ricardo alone, who, in his Reply, still perseveres in the confined view which he had before taken of the causes that operate upon exchange, and in considering redundancy or deficiency of currency as the mainspring of all commercial movements. According to this view of the subject, it is certainly not easy to explain an improving exchange under an obviously increasing issue of notes; an event that not unfrequently happens, and was much insisted upon by the Deputy-governor of the Bank, as a proof that our foreign exchanges had no connexion with the state of our currency. Nothing, however, is more easy of explanation, if we take into our consideration the effects produced upon the real exchange by the payments necessary to be made, for the supply of past or present wants; which effects, in such instances, will always be found operating in a direction exactly opposite to the effects of redundancy of currency. If the Bank were paying in specie, the precise period when it could keep the greatest quantity of its notes in circulation, would be that in which the state of mercantile transactions was occasioning a current of payments in bullion into the country. The increased issue of notes, under such circumstances, would for a time be imperceptible; though its tendency would undoubtedly be to raise prices at home, and thus to shorten the duration of the favourable exchange; and, when it turned, to increase the strength of the current in the opposite direction. The real state of the case seems to be, that though the effects of a redundancy of currency upon the exchange are sure, they are slow, compared with the effects of those mercantile transactions not connected with the question of currency; and, while the former of these causes is proceeding in its operations with a steady and generally uniform pace, the more rapid movements of the latter are opposing, aggravating or modifying these operations in various ways, and producing all those complex, and seemingly inconsistent appearances, which are to be found in the computed exchange.

We agree, therefore, entirely in opinion with the Report of the Bullion Committee, that the great and sudden depression of the exchange in the summer and autumn of 1809, is to be traced principally to mercantile causes. A depreciation of the currency to a certain degree, had existed for many years before; because, of all the symptoms of such depreciation, there is none so completely unequivocal as an excess of the market price above the mint price of that metal which is the standard measure of the country, accompanied by a favourable state of foreign exchanges, which, we believe, took place for six years, from 1802 to 1808. But this depreciation, a considerable part of which was probably concealed from view by the favourable exchange, was not sufficient to excite alarm, till it operated in conjunction with an unfavourable one, occasioned by mercantile difficulties and great purchases; and till the restoration of the exchange in the usual way was prevented, by the impossibility of getting specie at the Bank, and the fresh issues of notes for mercantile speculations. Since this time, however, the exchanges have occasionally improved, from the debts for our great exports being in the course of payment, and our bills consequently in request. And now, again, we understand they have rapidly fallen, owing perhaps to the diminished competition for our bills, from the loss of funds occasioned by the late severe decrees of Bonaparte, and his occupation of Hamburgh and Holstein; while, during the whole of the time the depreciation of our currency may have been proceeding with a steady and uniform pace, or, if it has occasionally been stationary or retrograde, has certainly not been subject to those great fluctuations which have been observed in our exchanges.

One of the principal faults which we have remarked in almost all the writers that are unfavourable to the Bank restriction, is, that they have not made sufficient concessions to the mercantile classes in some points where they appear to have truth on their side. We have already adverted to the error (confined, however, principally to Mr Ricardo, and from which the Report is entirely free) of denying the existence of a balance of trade or of payments, not connected with some original redundancy or deficiency of currency. A practical merchant must, to be sure, be extremely surprised at such a denial, and feel more than ever confirmed in his preference of practice to theory. But there is another point in which also almost all the writers on this side of the question concur, where, notwithstanding, we cannot agree with them, and feel more inclined to the mercantile view of the subject. Though they acknowledge that bullion occasionally passes from one country to another, from causes connected with the exchange, yet they represent these transactions as quite inconsiderable in degree. Mr Huskisson observes, that 'the operations in the trade of bullion originate almost entirely in the fresh supplies which are yearly poured in from the mines of the New World, and are chiefly confined to the distribution of those supplies through the different parts of Europe. If this supply were to cease altogether, the dealings in gold and silver, as objects of foreign trade, would be very few, and those of short duration.'

Mr Ricardo, in his reply to Mr Bosanquet, refers to this passage with particular approbation. Mr Blake seems inclined to separate the dealer in bills of exchange, from the dealers in bullion; and the latter he considers as exclusively employed in supplying the manufacturers, though he says that the purchases made for this purpose are sometimes seized upon by the bill-merchants to pay an unfavourable balance.

Now, though we are perfectly ready to acknowledge, that an unfavourable exchange has a tendency to right itself, without the transmission of the precious metals, and that the transmission of a moderate quantity has a considerable effect; yet we cannot believe that these transactions are altogether, either few in number, or small in amount. If the precious metals did not pass from one country to another, in consequence of the state of the exchange, the varying necessities of these countries would frequently raise the rate of the exchange very far above the expense of transport; and it would be impossible for the debtor country to make its payments at the time promised. But if the precious metals *do* pass readily from one country to another, from this cause, we cannot help thinking, that the same varying desires and necessities must render these transactions not very unfrequent. Every peculiar failure, or peculiar abundance of produce, in any of the states of the great mercantile republic; every subsidy to be paid or received; and every movement of a considerable army from one country to another, must almost inevitably give some employment to the bullion trade: and when the level of the precious metals has been in some degree destroyed by these necessary operations, the bullion dealer is again called into action to restore the balance. But, not only on such occasions as these, does bullion pass from one country to another, but it is well known that most states, in their usual relations of commercial intercourse, have an almost constantly favourable exchange with some countries, and an almost constantly unfavourable one with others. And Dr A. Smith has justly observed, that bullion forms, in general, the most convenient medium for carrying on the various roundabout foreign trades of consumption which a country finds it necessary to engage in; and is, in consequence, greatly used for this purpose. It appears, then, that in the most permanent and ordinary relations of countries with each other, the bullion trader will always have something to do.

The quantity of the precious metals employed in supplying and maintaining the coins of different nations, and making payments in the currency of the commercial world, far exceeds, we conceive, the quantity used in manufactures. Though the intrinsic value of these metals was first founded, and is still supported, by their use for plate and ornaments; yet, their much more general use, as a medium of exchange, has rendered the supply of the manufacturer a subordinate branch of the bullion trade. But, for whatever purpose the precious metals may be wanted, as the only variations in the prices at which they can be purchased are those which show themselves in the exchange, it is to this quarter that the bullion dealer always directs his attention. He imports or exports, according as the exchange is sufficiently favourable, or sufficiently unfavourable, to afford him an adequate profit in the transaction. And, in so doing, his main operations, we believe, will be found to consist in facilitating the purchases of those nations which have not, at the moment, any other commodities that they can give, or that will be readily accepted in return; and in restoring that level of the precious metals which has been temporarily destroyed by the unequal desires and necessities, and the unequal advantages and disadvantages of the different nations between which the trade of the world is carried on. In this view of the effect of the exchange upon the bullion trade, we think we shall be supported by the practical merchants; and it seems to us to have been confirmed by the evidence before the Bullion Commttee, where it appears that the quantity of the precious metals sold for home consumption in manufactures, is quite inconsiderable, compared with the quantity imported and exported by the bullion merchants.

There is yet another point, still more important, where the experience of the merchant will be apt to lead him to a conclusion quite different from that which is generally maintained by the writers in question. A merchant, or manufacturer, obtains a loan in paper from a bank; and, with this loan, he is able to command materials to work upon, tools to work with, and wherewithal to pay the wages of labour; and yet, he is told that this transaction does not tend, in the slightest degree, to increase the capital of the country.

The question, of how far, and in what manner, an increase of currency tends to increase capital, appears to us so very important, as fully to warrant our attempt to explain it. No writer that we are acquainted with, has ever seemed sufficiently aware of the influence which a different distribution of the circulating medium of a country must have on those accumulations which are destined to facilitate future productions; although it follows, as a direct consequence, from the most correct and legitimate view of capital that can be taken.

Dr A. Smith justly observes, that 'though the whole annual produce of the land and labour of every country is, no doubt, ultimately destined for supplying the consumption of its inhabitants, and for procuring a revenue to them; yet, when it first comes, either from the ground, or from the hands of the productive labourers, it naturally divides itself into two parts. One of them is, in the first place, destined for replacing a capital, and for renewing the materials, provisions and finished work, which had been withdrawn from a capital; the other for constituting a revenue;' which, of course, is destined to be spent without any view to reproduction.

Now, it is quite certain, that any thing like an equal distribution of the circulating medium among all the members of the society, would almost destroy the power of collecting any considerable quantity of materials; – of constructing proper machinery, warehouses, shipping, &c.; – and of maintaining a sufficient quantity of hands, to introduce an effective division of labour. The proportion between capital and revenue would evidently, by this distribution, be altered greatly to the disadvantage of capital; and in a few years, the produce of the country would experience a rapid diminution. On the other hand, if such a distribution of the circulating medium were to take place, as to throw the command of the produce of the country chiefly into the hands of the productive classes, – that is, if considerable portions of the currency were taken from the idle, and those who live upon fixed incomes, and transferred to farmers, manufacturers and merchants, – the proportion between capital and revenue would be greatly altered to the advantage of capital; and in a short time, the produce of the country would be greatly augmented.

Whenever, in the actual state of things, a fresh issue of notes comes into the hands of those who mean to employ them in the prosecution and extension of a profitable business, a difference in the distribution of the circulating medium takes place, similar in kind to that which has been last supposed; and produces similar, though of course comparatively inconsiderable effects, in altering the proportion between capital and revenue in favour of the former. The new notes go into the market, as so much additional capital, to purchase what is necessary for the conduct of the concern. But before the produce of the country has been increased, it is impossible for one person to have more of it, without diminishing the shares of some others. This diminution is effected by the rise of prices, occasioned by the competition of the new notes, which puts it out of the power of those who are only buyers, and not sellers, to purchase as much of the annual produce as before: While all the industrious classes, – all those that fell as well as buy, are, during the progressive rise of prices, making unusual profits; and, even when this progression stops, are left with the command of a greater portion of the annual produce than they possessed previous to the new issues.

It must always be recollected, that it is not the *quantity* of the circulating medium which produces the effect here described, but the *different distribution* of it. If a thousand millions of notes were added to the circulation, and distributed to the various classes of society exactly in the same proportions as before, neither the capital of the country, nor the facility of borrowing, would be in the slightest degree increased. But, on every fresh issue of notes, not only is the quantity of the circulating medium increased, but the distribution of the whole mass is altered. A larger proportion falls into the hands of those who consume and produce, and a smaller proportion into the hands of those who only consume. And as we have always considered capital as that portion of the national accumulations and annual produce, which is at the command of those who mean to employ it with a view to reproduction, we are bound to acknowledge, that an increased issue of notes tends to increase the national capital, and by an almost, though not strictly necessary consequence, to lower the rate of interest.

It may perhaps fairly be questioned, whether the late unusual facility of obtaining discounts, though it has undoubtedly tended to increase the capital of the country, may not have given it so unsafe a direction, as to subject it to losses which may more than counterbalance its first gains; – whether, in short, it has not obliged some of the most respectable mercantile capitalists, who in the way in which they were in the habit of carrying on their trade, scarcely ever failed of increasing the national accumulation, to yield the competition to a new and very different set of merchants, who may be said to gamble in trade, – who, in the hope of great profits, will risk any quantity of capital that they can command. – and in whose hands, therefore, the national accumulation is quite uncertain. Much, we think, might be said on this view of the subject.

But the grand and paramount objection to the stimulus which is applied to the productive powers of a country, by an excessive increase of currency, is, that it is accomplished at the expense of a manifest injustice. The observations we have made may afford a rational explanation of the facts, that countries are often increasing in riches amidst an increasing quantity of individual misery; that a rise of prices is generally found conjoined with public prosperity; and a fall of prices with national decline. But whatever phenomena they may assist to explain, they cannot alter the foundations of right and wrong, or give the slightest sanction to unjust transfers of property.

When the paper currency of a country is regulated in such a manners as to maintain it of the same value as the precious metals, the evil which the possessor of a fixed income may still suffer from depreciation occasioned by banking, is so inconsiderable, and so strictly limited, as probably to be more than counterbalanced, even to him, by the advantage which the country derives from it. It is true, however, that, upon the issue of every fresh quantity of notes, prices rise sufficiently to send a quantity of coin out of the circulation, though not, certainly, a quantity equal in amount to the notes; and the currency is at first left greater in quantity, and consequently lower in value, compared with the commodities which it has to circulate, than before. But it frequently happens, we conceive, that the beneficial employment of the coin set free, and the increased command of the produce transferred to the industrious classes by the increase of prices, gives such a stimulus to the productive powers of the country, that, in a short time, the balance between commodities and currency is restored, by the great multiplication of the former. – and prices return to their former level.

We cannot help thinking, that an effect of this kind took place in Scotland in the interval of two periods alluded to by Hume and Smith. In 1751 and 1752, when Hume published his Political Discourses, and soon after the great multiplication of paper money in Scotland, there was a very sensible rise in the price of provisions; and this was naturally, and probably justly, attributed by him, in part, to the abundance of paper. In 1759, when the paper currency had probably not been diminished, Dr Smith notices a different state of prices; and observes that, for a long period, provisions had never been cheaper. The dearness at the time that Hume wrote, he attributes carelessly, and without any inquiry about the fact, to the badness of the seasons; and intimates, that it could not be occasioned by the multiplication of paper money. The probability, however, seems to be, that the high prices of 1751 and 1752 were influenced by the paper, – as we do not see how it is possible for the substitution of paper for coin to take place, without an increase of prices; but that the new stimulus given to industry by this increase of capital, had so increased the quantity of commodities in the interval between 1752 and 1759, as to restore them to a level with the increased currency.

Independently, however, of the chance of the prices of commodities being restored by the influence of increased capital, the possessor of a fixed income cannot consider himself as unjustly treated, while the currency in which his revenue is paid is maintained on a level with the precious metals. These metals are indeed liable to change in their power of commanding the necessaries and conveniences of life; but the principal changes to which they are subject, depend upon causes so entirely beyond control, that the evils which he may suffer from these changes must be considered as necessarily belonging to the kind of property which he possesses. And if his revenue continues to be paid in the same quantity of coin, or in paper of equal value, however he may occasionally complain of increased prices, he will not feel himself warranted in complaining of injustice. As long, therefore, as the currency of a country is maintained on a level with the precious metals, the increase of national capital, and of national industry, derived from banking establishments, is unaccompanied by any essential drawbacks; but as soon as a positive depreciation takes place, the injustice committed towards one portion of the society is so unquestionable, that, though it may be concealed for a time, it cannot, when known, admit of excuse. If, for all the commodities in this country, two prices were established, one in bullion and one in paper, and if the paper price were fifteen or twenty per cent. higher than the bullion price, we can hardly conceive that our Legislature, so famed as it is for its justice, would think it consistent with its good faith, to pay the numerous servants of the government, and the public creditors, with the same nominal amount of a currency, so obviously below the value of that in which it has contracted to pay them. And yet this is really and truly what it is now doing; and the only reason why the fact is in some degree concealed, is, that a bullion price of commodities not being as yet regularly established, the difference between the value of our legal tender and of our actual currency, is not daily forced on the attention: And, in order to be fully aware of its existence and extent, the evidence of the merchants examined before the Bullion Committee must be consulted; where, it must be allowed, that the difference is as clearly established, as if it appeared in sales and purchases from morning to night. The circumstance of there being no current bullion price of commodities, does not, in the slightest degree, tend to affect the prices in our actual currency. These prices would not be rendered higher by the establishment of another price which was lower; and, consequently, the real injury at present sustained by the classes of society before alluded to, is precisely the same as if it were rendered more obvious by the establishment of a bullion price and a paper price for every article sold.

The fact, however, of there being only one price, has been much insisted upon as a decisive proof that there is no depreciation. But the reasons why no distinction has as yet been openly made, are sufficiently obvious. They are, first and chiefly, the law of the land, which, applied to the present unlooked-for state of things, has the most singular and unjust operation: which forces a heavy guinea to pass for less than a light one, and would oblige any person who could obtain coin for his commodities, to forego all advantage from it, and part with it again for fifteen per cent. less than it was fairly worth: And, secondly, the natural unwillingness of all people in trade, if the depreciation of the currency arises merely from excess, and not from want of confidence, to alter, in any degree, a state of things, and a progression of prices, from which, as being sellers as well as buyers, they are known to receive considerable advantages. And this feeling will of course be powerfully increased and confirmed by the consciousness, that the first person who was to ask two prices for his goods, would, as the law now stands, be considered as intending to make an illegal use of the coin which he might obtain, and would, in consequence, incur such odium, and deter so many customers, that the attempt would probably end in his ruin.

Yet, notwithstanding these reasons, if the Bank Directors continue to conduct their establishment upon the principles which they have openly avowed before the Committee, we do not entertain the slightest doubt, that, in a short time, two prices *must* be established, or the country will be entirely deprived of the power of making its smaller payments. In every state in Europe where a depreciated currency has circulated, it has been found absolutely necessary to allow of an open difference of price between bullion and paper, as the only mean of retaining any coin in the country. The expulsion of the legitimate coin of the realm, has, we really believe, proceeded further in this country than it ever did in any other, before this only remedy for the evil was applied. Gold may be said to be already quite banished from our circulation; and nothing but the very extraordinary degraded state of our silver coin, and the high premium which is daily given even for this, in spite of the law, by bankers and merchants who want small change, could retain an ounce of it in circulation. We touch upon the period, when it will be no longer possible to avoid an open discount upon paper, without such a degree of embarrassment to commerce, as will much more than counterbalance the late advantages which it has derived from a redundant currency. If our silver coin had approximated, in any tolerable degree, to its mint value, there is no doubt that it would long since have disappeared; and all ranks of society would have joined in petitioning the Legislature, if it still thought the Bank unable to pay in specie, either to repeal the law which prohibits an open discount upon paper, or to enjoin the issuing of shilling notes. And the question now is, Whether the Bank Directors, by continuing to act upon their present principles, will submit to one of these two disgraceful alternatives, under the merited reproach of having created the necessity for them by their own mismanagement; or consent to tread back their steps, and return to payments in specie; which may unquestionably be done, without any other evil, either to themselves or their mercantile connexions, than that of foregoing an unfair advantage; which, as it ought never to have been possessed, ought, in honour and justice, as soon as possible to be relinquished.

The principles of banking avowed before the Bullion Committee, belong to so bold a class of projectors, and to times of such questionable authority with regard to the proper foundation of paper credit, that we were never more surprised than to find them brought forward by the Directors of the Bank of England. It is well known, that the celebrated Mr Law proposed to supply Scotland with money, by means of notes to be coined by certain commissoners appointed by Parliament; which notes were to be given out to all who demanded them upon the security of land. In answer to the supposition, that they might be depreciated by excess of quantity, Mr Law observes, that 'the commissioners giving out what sums are demanded, and taking back what sums are offered to be returned, this paper money will keep its value, and there will always be as much money as there is occasion or employment for, and no more.'* This, we conceive, is precisely the language of the present Bank Directors; and they in no respect fall short of Mr Law in the grand mistake, of confounding the quantity of good security in the country, and the quantity of money which people may want to borrow at the legal interest, particularly during a time of mercantile speculation or distress, with the quantity necessary for the circulation, so as to keep it on a level with the precious metals, and the currencies of surrounding countries.

The school of Mr Law is certainly not that in which we should either have wished or expected the Directors to learn their principles of banking. But the real truth, we believe, is, that principles have very little to do with the regulation of the bank concerns; that every thing is done by a kind of practical

---

* *Money and Trade considered*: With a Proposal for supplying the Nation with Money. By John Law esq. p. 167. Glasgow, 1750

routine; and that, most fortunately for the country, and for the credit of the Directors themselves, this practice is still very much influenced by the habits of those wholesome times, when the Bank paid in specie, and was obliged to attend to the safety of its establishment. In no other way can we account for our not having a still greater excess of paper, under the function of principles which lead to almost unlimited issues. But, greatly as we have reason to rejoice, that the practice of the Bank does not accord with its principles, it is of the utmost importance to recollect, that the salutary influence of a practice formed and established while the Bank was at all times liable to pay its notes in specie, will, in the very nature of things, gradually cease to act, under other, and very different circumstances. In fact, the weakening of this influence is already but too manifest, and must be expected to be daily and hourly progressive; and if the Legislature, by declining to enforce the recommendation of the Committee, should relieve the Bank from all immediate prospect of a return to cash payments, the disorder in our currency which we have at present experienced, will be absolutely nothing, compared with that which we must then look forward to. Of course, the longer the term is protracted, and the greater is the previous depreciation of the currency, the greater will be the difficulty to the Bank, and the greater the hardship to the persons who benefit by the present system, of a return to the old one.

We were, at first, inclined to approve of the recommendation of the Committee, to leave to the knowledge and discretion of the Bank Directors the mode of preparing themselves to resume their payments in cash at the time proposed. But it has been suggested, and the language and conduct of their friends have not sufficiently repelled the suspicion, that, under cover of this liberty, they might purposely keep the same, or a greater quantity of notes in circulation, with a view of compelling the legislature to continue the Restriction Act, as there would, of course, be a great unwillingness in all quarters to enforce a law which at the time could not be obeyed, and the attempt to obey which, in such a state of things, would produce very serious inconveniences to the public, as well as to the Bank. We really think, that if any disposition of this kind should be discoverable in the Bank direction, it would be the bounded duty of the legislature to take immediate steps for *the establishment of one or more other banks;* and it cannot be doubted, that both the business of the government and of the public might be carried on, as in America, with equal convenience, and less chance of restriction acts, without the assistance, and very improper influence, of so overgrown an establishment as the Bank of England. It is, indeed, a monstrous deformity in the state, that an incorporated body of individuals should have the power of holding out a threat to the legislature, that if it does not persevere in sanctioning the nonfulfilment of their engagements, they would find the means of embarrassing and punishing the government and the public. We cannot, however, conceive it possible that such an idea should be seriously entertained. At the same time, it is certain, that the Bank Directors have openly shown an unconquerable reluctance to acknowledge that there is any connexion between the market price of bullion, and an excessive paper circulation; and it may be necessary, in consequence, to direct their attention specifically to this main point. There is certainly some objection to a positive limitation of the number of notes; because the only proper criterion of excess, is depreciation below the value of the precious metals, and not any particular amount of notes. But as, from the fact of depreciation, we are quite sure that there is at present excess, though it is impossible to say to what precise amount; perhaps, it might be the best mode of proceeding, in the present state of the knowledge and temper of the Bank Directors, to oblige them, every successive half year, to diminish the average quantity of their notes in circulation by half a million, and to continue this diminution till the market price of bullion was restored to its mint price; and then the resumption of cash payments might take place with perfect safety and convenience, both to the Bank and the public; and the evil of any great and sudden diminution of the currency be completely avoided. We should be inclined to prefer this mode to another, which we have heard suggested, that of beginning by obliging the Bank to pay a small per centage in cash upon its notes, at the option of the holder, and increasing this per centage gradually; as we believe that great difficulties and losses would attend the execution of this plan, from the great scarcity of change in the present state of our silver coinage, and the certainty of the rapid disappearance from the circulation, of all the gold issued, till the number of notes were sufficiently reduced to bring the market and mint prices of gold nearly to a level.

We cannot conclude, without adverting, for a moment, to what has been often urged, both in print and conversation, that the Bullion Committee ought to have attended more to the opinions of those able and experienced merchants and men of business whom they examined. We decidedly think, that, in this respect, they did precisely what it was their duty to do. It was their duty to get at as large and correct a body of facts as possible, from the evidence of the best authorities which could be consulted. It was also their duty to hear the *opinions* of all those who were examined, in order that they might see the subject in the different lights in which it would naturally present itself to different understandings, and under different circumstances. But, having so done, it was most unquestionably their duty to form their own conclusions, without further deference to mercantile authorities. And we have no hesitation in saying, that the gentlemen who composed the Committee, both from their general characters, and the advantageous situation in which they stood, after having heard the evidence and opinions before mentioned, were very much better qualified to come to a just conclusion, than any body of practical merchants that could be chosen. The habits of practical detail have a natural and almost necessary tendency to direct the view to particular, rather than to general consequences, and to identify the interests of the few, with the interests of the many. If, in addition to this almost unavoidable effect of constant habits of business we take into our consideration, that the mercantile classes are greatly interested, both in the facility of obtaining paper loans, and in the progressive rise of prices which this facility occasions, it is quite impossible to affirm, with truth, that they are either the most capable, or the most impartial judges in the present question. And if, when it comes to be determined by the legislature, the authority of merchants shall have more weight in the decision, than that of those who, from a more elevated seat of judgment, and free from the possible influence of interested motives, have taken a more commanding and impartial view of the subject, the consequences will not fail to show that the trust reposed in the great Assembly of the nation, to dispense impartial justice, and attend equally to the happiness of all the classes of the community, has been, in one instance at least, unfulfilled.

David Ricardo (1772–1823)

High Price of Bullion, a Proof of the Depreciation of Bank Notes (1811).

INTRODUCTION

THE writer of the following pages has already submitted some reflections to the attention of the public, on the subject of paper-currency, through the medium of the Morning Chronicle. He has thought proper to republish his sentiments on this question in a form more calculated to bring it to fair discussion; and his reasons for so doing, are, that he has seen, with the greatest alarm, the progressive depreciation of the paper-currency. His fears have been augmented by observing, that by a great part of the public this depreciation is altogether denied, and that by others, who admit the fact, it is imputed to any cause but that which to him appears the real one. Before any remedy can be successfully applied to an evil of such magnitude, it is essential that there should be no doubt as to its cause. The writer proposes, from the admitted principles of political economy, to advance reasons, which, in his opinion, prove, that the paper-currency of this country has long been, and now is, at a considerable discount, proceeding from a superabundance in its quantity, and not from any want of confidence in the Bank of England, or from any doubts of their ability to fulfil their engagements. He does this without reluctance, being fully persuaded that the country is yet in possession of the means of restoring the paper-currency to its professed value, viz. the value of the coins, for the payment of which it purports to be a pledge.

He is aware that he can add but little to the arguments which have been so ably urged by Lord King, and which ought long before this to have carried conviction to every mind; but he trusts, that as the evil has become more glaring, the public will not continue to view, without interest, a subject which yields to no other in importance, and in which the general welfare is so materially concerned.

Dec. 1, 1809.

HIGH PRICE OF BULLION,

A PROOF OF

THE DEPRECIATION OF BANK NOTES.

THE precious metals employed for circulating the commodities of the world, previous to the establishment of banks, have been supposed by the most approved writers on political economy to have been divided into certain proportions among the different civilized nations of the earth, according to the state of their commerce and wealth, and therefore according to the number and frequency of the payments which they had to perform. While so divided they preserved every where the same value, and as each country had an equal necessity for the quantity actually in use, there could be no temptation offered to either for their importation or exportation.

Gold and silver, like other commodities, have an intrinsic value, which is not arbitrary, but is dependent on their scarcity, the quantity of labour bestowed in procuring them, and the value of the capital employed in the mines which produce them.

'The quality of utility, beauty, and scarcity,' says Dr. Smith, 'are the original foundation of the high price of those metals, or of the great quantity of other goods for which they can every where be exchanged. This value was antecedent to, and independent of their being employed as coin, and was the quality which fitted them for that employment.'

If the quantity of gold and silver in the world employed as money was exceedingly small, or abundantly great, it would not in the least affect the proportions in which they would be divided among the different nations – the variation in their quantity would have produced no other effect than to make the commodities for which they were exchanged comparatively dear or cheap. The smaller quantity of money would perform the functions of a circulating medium, as well as the larger. Ten millions would be as effectual for that purpose as one hundred millions. Dr. Smith observes, 'that the most abundant mines of the precious metals would add little to the wealth of the world. A

60

produce of which the value is principally derived from its scarcity is necessarily degraded by its abundance.'

If in the progress towards wealth, one nation advanced more rapidly than the others, that nation would require and obtain a greater proportion of the money of the world. Its commerce, its commodities, and its payments, would increase, and the general currency of the world would be divided according to the new proportions. All countries therefore would contribute their share to this effectual demand.

In the same manner if any nation wasted part of its wealth, or lost part of its trade, it could not retain the same quantity of circulating medium which it before possessed. A part would be exported, and divided among the other nations till the usual proportions were re-established.

While the relative situation of countries continued unaltered, they might have abundant commerce with each other, but their exports and imports would on the whole be equal. England might possibly import more goods from, than she would export to, France, but she would in consequence export more to some other country, and France would import more from that country; so that the exports and imports of all countries would balance each other; bills of exchange would make the necessary payments, but no money would pass, because it would have the same value in all countries.

If a mine of gold were discovered in either of these countries, the currency of that country would be lowered in value in consequence of the increased quantity of the precious metals brought into circulation, and would therefore no longer be of the same value as that of other countries. Gold and silver, whether in coin or in bullion, obeying the law which regulates all other commodities, would immediately become articles of exportation; they would leave the country where they were cheap, for those countries where they were dear, and would continue to do so, as long as the mine should prove productive, and till the proportion existing between capital and money in each country before the discovery of the mine, was again established, and gold and silver restored every where to one value. In return for the gold exported, commodities would be imported; and though what is usually termed the balance of trade would be against the country exporting money or bullion, it would be evident that she was carrying on a most advantageous trade, exporting that which was no way useful to her, for commodities which might be employed in the extension of her manufactures, and the increase of her wealth.

If instead of a mine being discovered in any country, a bank were established, such as the Bank of England, with the power of issuing its notes for a circulating medium; after a large amount had been issued either by way of loan to merchants, or by advances to government, thereby adding considerably to the sum of the currency, the same effect would follow as in the case of the mine. The circulating medium would be lowered in value, and goods would experience a proportionate rise. The equilibrium between that and other nations would only be restored by the exportation of part of the coin.

The establishment of the bank and the consequent issue of its notes therefore, as well as the discovery of the mine, operates as a stimulus to the exportation either of bullion or of coin, and are beneficial only in as far as that object may be accomplished. The bank substitutes a currency of no value for one most costly, and enables us to turn the precious metals (which, though a very necessary part of our capital, yield no revenue,) into a capital which will yield one. Dr. A. Smith compares the advantages attending the establishment of a bank to those which would be obtained by converting our highways into pastures and corn-fields, and procuring a road through the air. The highways, like the coin, are highly useful, but neither yield any revenue. Some people might be alarmed at the specie leaving the country, and might consider that as a disadvantageous trade which required us to part with it; indeed the law so considers it by its enactments against the exportation of specie; but a very little reflection will convince us that it is our choice, and not our necessity, that sends it abroad; and that it is highly beneficial to us to exchange that commodity which is superfluous, for others which may be made productive.

The exportation of the specie may at all times be safely left to the discretion of individuals, it will not be exported more than any other commodity, unless its exportation should be advantageous to the country. If it be advantageous to export it, no laws can effectually prevent its exportation. Happily in this case, as well as in most others in commerce where there is free competition, the interests of the individual and that of the community are never at variance.

Were it possible to carry the law against the exportation of coin into strict execution, at the same time that the exportation of gold bullion were freely allowed, no advantage could accrue from it, but great injury must arise to those who might have to pay, possibly, two ounces or more of coined gold for one of uncoined gold. This would be a real depreciation of our currency, raising the prices of all other commodities in the same proportion as it increased that of gold bullion. The owner of money would in this case suffer an injury equal to what a proprietor of corn would suffer, were a law to be passed prohibiting him from selling his corn for more than half its market value. The law against the exportation of the coin has this tendency, but is so easily evaded, that gold in bullion has always been nearly of the same value as gold in coin.

Thus then it appears that the currency of one country can never for any length of time be much more valuable, as far as equal quantities of the precious metals are concerned, than that of another; that excess of currency is but a relative term; that if the circulation of England were ten millions, that of France five millions, that of Holland four millions, &c. &c. whilst they kept their proportions, though the currency of each country were doubled or trebled, neither country would be conscious of an excess of currency. The prices of commodities would every where rise, on account of the increase of currency, but there would be no exportation of money from either. But if these proportions be destroyed by England alone doubling her currency, while that of France, Holland, &c. &c. continued as before, we should then be conscious of an excess in our currency, and for the same reason the other countries would feel a deficiency in theirs, and part of our excess would be exported till the proportions of ten, five, four, &c. were again established.

If in France an ounce of gold were more valuable than in England, and would therefore in France purchase more of any commodity common to both countries, gold would immediately quit England for such purpose, and we should send gold in preference to any thing else, because it would be the cheapest exchangeable commodity in the English market; for if gold be dearer in France than in England, goods must be cheaper; we should not therefore send them from the dear to the cheap market, but, on the contrary, they would come from the cheap to the dear market, and would be exchanged for our gold.

The Bank might continue to issue their notes, and the specie be exported with advantage to the country, while their notes were payable in specie on demand, because they could never issue more notes than the value of the coin which would have circulated had there been no bank.[*]

If they attempted to exceed this amount, the excess would be immediately returned to them for specie, because our currency being superfluous, there could be no better employment for the superfluity, than the sending it to a better market abroad. These are the means, as I have already explained, by which our currency endeavours to equalize itself with the currencies of other countries. As soon as this equality was attained, all advantage arising from exportation would cease; but if the Bank assuming, that because a given quantity of circulating medium had been necessary last year, therefore the same quantity must be necessary this, or for any other reason, continued to re-issue the returned notes, the stimulus which a redundant currency first gave to the exportation of the coin would be again renewed with similar effects; gold would be again demanded, the exchange would become unfavourable, and gold bullion would rise above its mint price, because it is legal to export bullion, but illegal to export the coin, and the difference would be about equal to the fair compensation for the risk.

---

[*] They might, strictly speaking, rather exceed that quantity, because as the Bank would add to the currency of the world, England would retain its share of the increase.

In this manner if the Bank persisted in returning their notes into circulation, every guinea might be drawn out of their coffers.

If to supply the deficiency of their stock of gold they were to purchase gold bullion at the advanced price, and have it coined into guineas, this would not remedy the evil, guineas would be still demanded, but instead of being exported would be melted and sold to the Bank as bullion at the advanced price. 'The operations of the Bank,' observed Dr. Smith, alluding to an analogous case, 'were upon this account somewhat like the web of Penelope, the work that was done in the day was undone in the night.' The same sentiment is expressed by Mr. Thornton: – 'Finding the guineas in their coffers to lessen every day, they must naturally be supposed to be desirous of replacing them by all effectual and not extravagantly expensive means. They will be disposed, to a certain degree, to buy gold, though at a losing price, and to coin it into new guineas; but they will have to do this at the very moment when many are privately melting what is coined. The one party will be melting and selling while the other is buying and coining. And each of these two contending businesses will now be carried on, not on account of an actual exportation of each melted guinea to Hamburgh, but the operation or at least a great part of it will be confined to London; the coiners and the melters living on the same spot, and giving constant employment to each other.

'The Bank,' continues Mr. Thornton, 'if we suppose it, as we now do, to carry on this sort of contest with the melters, is obviously waging a very unequal war; and even though it should not be tired early, it will be likely to be tired sooner than its adversaries.'

The Bank would be obliged therefore ultimately to adopt the only remedy in their power to put a stop to the demand for guineas. They would withdraw part of their notes from circulation, till they should have increased the value of the remainder to that of gold bullion, and consequently to the value of the currencies of other countries. All advantage from the exportation of gold bullion would then cease, and there would be no temptation to exchange bank-notes for guineas.

Mr. Thornton, who has considered this subject very much at large, supposes that a very unfavourable balance of trade may be occasioned to this country by a bad harvest, and the consequent importation of corn; and that there may be at the same time an unwillingness in the country, to which we are indebted, to receive our goods in payment; the balance due to the foreign country must therefore be paid out of that part of our currency, consisting of coin, and that hence arises the demand for gold bullion and its increased price. He considers the Bank as affording considerable accommodation to the merchants, by supplying with their notes the void occasioned by the exportation of the specie.

Mr. Thornton has not explained to us, why any unwillingness should exist in the foreign country to receive our goods in exchange for their corn; and it would be necessary for him to shew, that if such an unwillingness were to exist, we should agree to indulge it so far as to consent to part with our coin.

If we consent to give coin in exchange for goods, it must be from choice, not necessity. We should not import more goods than we export, unless we had a redundancy of currency, which it therefore suits us to make a part of our exports. The exportation of the coin is caused by its cheapness, and is not the effect, but the cause of an unfavourable balance: we should not export it, if we did not send it to a better market, or if we had any commodity which we could export more profitably. It is a salutary remedy for a redundant currency; and as I have already endeavoured to prove, that redundancy or excess is only a relative term, it follows, that the demand for it abroad arises only from the comparative deficiency of the currency of the importing country, which there causes its superior value.

It resolves itself entirely into a question of interest. If the sellers of the corn to England, to the amount I will suppose of a million, could import goods which cost a million in England, but would produce, when sold abroad, more than if the million had been sent in money, goods would be preferred; if otherwise, money would be demanded.

It is only after a comparison of the value in their markets and in our own, of gold and other commodities, and because gold is cheaper in the London market than in their's, that foreigners prefer gold in exchange for their corn. If we diminish the quantity of currency, we give an additional value to it: this will induce them to alter their election, and prefer the commodities. If I owed a debt in Hamburgh of 100*l.*, I should endeavour to find out the cheapest mode of paying it. If I send money, the expence attending its transportation being, I will suppose, 5*l.* to discharge my debt will cost me 105*l.* If I purchase cloth here, which, with the expences attending its exportation, will cost me 106*l.*, and which will, in Hamburgh, sell for 100*l.*, it is evidently more to my advantage to send the money. If the purchase and expences of sending hardware to pay my debt, will take 107*l.*, I should prefer sending cloth to hardware, but I would send neither in preference to money, because money would be the cheapest exportable commodity in the London market. The same reasons would operate with the exporter of the corn, if the transaction were on his own account. But if the Bank, 'fearful for the safety of their establishment,' and knowing that the requisite number of guineas would be withdrawn from their coffers at the mint price, should think it necessary to diminish the amount of their notes in circulation, the proportion between the value of the money, of the cloth, and of the hardware, would no longer be as 105, 106, and 107; but the money would become the most valuable of the three, and therefore would be less advantageously employed in discharging the foreign debt.

If, which is a much stronger case, we agreed to pay a subsidy to a foreign power, money would not be exported whilst there were any goods, which could more cheaply discharge the payment. The interest of individuals would render the exportation of the money unnecessary.

Such, then, appear to me to be the laws that regulate the distribution of the precious metals throughout the world, and which cause and limit their circulation from one country to another, by regulating their value in each. But before I proceed to examine on these principles the main object of my enquiry, it is necessary that I should shew what is the standard measure of value in this country, and of which, therefore, our paper currency ought to be the representative, because it can only be by a comparison to this standard that its regularity, or its depreciation, may be estimated.

No permanent* measure of value can be said to exist in any nation, while the circulating medium consists of two metals, because they are constantly subject to vary in value with respect to each other. However exact the conductors of the mint may be, in proportioning the relative value of gold to silver in the coins, at the time when they fix the ratio, they cannot prevent one of these metals from rising, while the other remains stationary, or falls in value. Whenever this happens, one of the coins will be melted to be sold for the other. The great Mr. Locke, Lord Liverpool, and many other writers, have ably considered this subject, and have all agreed, that the only remedy for the evils in the currency proceeding from this source, is the making one of the metals only, the standard measure of value. Mr. Locke considered silver as the most proper metal for this purpose, and proposed that gold coins should be left to find their own value, and pass for a greater or lesser number of shillings, as the market price of gold might vary with respect to silver.

Lord Liverpool, on the contrary, maintained that gold was not only the most proper metal for a general measure of value in this country, but that, by the common consent of the people, it had become so, was so considered by

* Strictly speaking, there can be no permanent measure of value. A measure of value should itself be invariable; but this is not the case with either gold or silver, they being subject to fluctuations as well as other commodities. Experience has indeed taught us, that though the variations in the *value* of gold or silver may be considerable, on a comparison of distant periods, yet for short spaces of time their value is tolerably fixed. It is this property, among their other excellencies, which fits them better than any other commodity for the uses of money. Either gold or silver may therefore, in the point of view in which we are considering them, be called a measure of value.

foreigners, and that it was best suited to the increased commerce and wealth of England.

He, therefore, proposed, that gold coin only should be a legal tender for sums exceeding one guinea, and silver coins for sums not exceeding that amount. As the law now stands, gold coin is a legal tender for all sums; but it was enacted in the year 1774, 'That no tender in payment of money made in the silver coin of this realm, of any sum exceeding the sum of twenty-five pounds at any one time, shall be reputed in law, or allowed to be legal tender within Great Britain or Ireland, for more than according to its value by weight, after the rate of 5s. 2d. for each ounce of silver.' The same regulation was revived in 1798, and is now in force.

For many reasons given by Lord Liverpool, it appears proved beyond dispute, that gold coin has been for near a century the principal measure of value, but this is, I think, to be attributed to the inaccurate determination of the mint proportions. Gold has been valued too highly; no silver, therefore, can remain in circulation which is of its standard weight.

If a new regulation were to take place, and silver to be valued too high, or (which is the same thing) if the market proportions between the prices of gold and silver were to become greater than those of the mint, gold would then disappear, and silver become the standard currency.

Gold has lately experienced a considerable rise compared with silver; an ounce of standard gold, which, on an average of many years, was of equal value to 14¾ oz. of standard silver, being now in the market of the same value as 15½ oz. The proportion in our coin, as regulated by the mint, is as 1 to 15 $^9/_{154}$. It is therefore probable, that if the present market relative value of gold and silver should be permanent, and that we should be so fortunate as to restore our currency to the state in which it was previous to 1797, by the repeal of the Bank Restriction-bill, silver would in effect become the standard measure of value. Silver bullion only would then be carried to the mint to be coined; and as gold coin might be advantageously melted, it would disappear from circulation. This would continue till the mint should adopt more just proportions, or till government should follow the recommendations of Lord Liverpool, and make silver a legal tender for sums not exceeding a guinea[*].

---

[*] Since writing the above, I have seen an act of parliament, passed in the 39th of Geo. III. wherein is the following clause: –

'Whereas inconvenience may arise from any coinage of silver until such regulations may be formed as shall appear necessary; and whereas from the present low price of silver bullion, owing to temporary circumstances, a small quantity of silver bullion has been brought to the mint to be coined, and there is reason to suppose that a still further quantity may be brought; and it is therefore necessary to suspend the coining of silver

While the currency of different countries consists of the precious metals, or of a paper money, which is at all times exchangeable for them; and while the metallic currency is not debased by wearing, or clipping, a comparison of the weight, and degree of fineness of their coins, will enable us to ascertain their par of exchange. Thus the par of exchange between Holland and England is stated to be about eleven florins, because the pure silver contained in eleven florins is equal to the pure silver contained in twenty standard shillings.

This par is not, nor can it be, absolutely fixed; because, gold coin being the standard of commerce in England, and silver coin in Holland, a pound sterling, or $^{20}/_{21}$ of a guinea, may at different times be more or less valuable than twenty standard shillings, and therefore more or less valuable than its equivalent of eleven florins. Estimating the par either by silver or by gold will be sufficiently exact for our purpose.

If I owe a debt in Holland; by knowing the par of exchange, I also know the quantity of our money which will be necessary to discharge it.

If my debt amounts to 1100 florins, and gold has not varied in value, 100*l.* in our pure gold coin will purchase as much Dutch currency as is necessary to pay my debt. By exporting the 100*l.* therefore in coin, or (which is the same thing) paying a bullion merchant the 100*l.* in coin, and allowing him the expences attending its transportation, such as freight, insurance, and his profit, he will sell me a bill which will discharge my debt; at the same time he will export the bullion, to enable his correspondent to pay the bill when it shall become due.

These expences then are the utmost limits of an unfavourable exchange. However great my debt may be, though it equalled the largest subsidy ever given by this country to an ally; while I could pay the bullion-merchant in coin of standard value, he would be glad to export it, and to sell me bills. But if I pay him for his bill in a debased coin, or in a depreciated paper-money, he will not

---

for the present; be it therefore enacted, That from and after the passing of this act, no silver bullion shall be coined at the mint, nor shall any silver coin that may have been coined there be delivered, any law to the contrary notwithstanding.'

This law is now in force.

It would appear, therefore, to have been the intention of the legislature to establish gold as the standard of currency in this country. Whilst this law is in force, silver coin must be confined to small payments only, the quantity in circulation being barely sufficient for that purpose. It might be for the interest of a debtor to pay his large debts in silver coin if he could get silver bullion coined into money; but being prevented by the above law from doing so, he is necessarily obliged to discharge his debt with gold coin, which he could obtain at the mint with gold bullion to any amount. Whilst this law is in force, gold must always continue to be the standard of currency.

be willing to sell me his bill at this rate; because if the coin be debased, it does not contain the quantity of pure gold or silver which ought to be contained in 100*l.*, and he must therefore export an additional number of such debased pieces of money, to enable him to pay my debt of 100*l.*, or its equivalent, 1100 florins. If I pay him in paper-money; as he cannot send it abroad, he will consider whether it will purchase as much gold or silver bullion as is contained in the coin for which it is a substitute: if it will do this, paper will be as acceptable to him as coin; but if it will not, he will expect a further premium for his bill, equal to the depreciation of the paper.

While the circulating medium consists, therefore, of coin undebased, or of paper-money immediately exchangeable for undebased coin, the exchange can never be more above, or more below, par, than the expences attending the transportation of the precious metals. But when it consists of a depreciated paper-money, it necessarily will fall according to the degree of the depreciation.

The exchange will, therefore, be a tolerably accurate criterion by which we may judge of the debasement of the currency, proceeding either from a clipped coinage, or a depreciated paper-money.

It is observed by Sir James Stuart, 'That if the foot measure was altered at once over all England, by adding to it, or taking from it, any proportional part of its standard length, the alteration would be best discovered, by comparing the new foot with that of Paris, or of any other country, which had suffered no alteration.

'Just so, if the pound sterling, which is the English unit, shall be found any how changed; and if the variation it has met with be difficult to ascertain, because of a complication of circumstances; the best way to discover it will be to compare the former and the present value of it, with the money of other nations which has suffered no variation. This the exchange will perform with the greatest exactness.'

The Edinburgh reviewers, in speaking of Lord King's pamphlet, observe, that it does not follow because our imports always consist partly of bullion, that the balance of trade is therefore permanently in our favour. Bullion,' they say, 'is a commodity, for which, as for every other, there is a varying demand; and which, exactly like any other, may enter the catalogue either of imports or exports; and this exportation or importation of bullion will not affect the course of exchange in a different way from the exportation or importation of any other commodities.'

No person ever exports or imports bullion without first considering the rate of exchange. It is by the rate of exchange that he discovers the relative value of bullion in the two countries between which it is estimated. It is therefore consulted by the bullion-merchant in the same manner as the price-current is by other merchants, before they determine on the exportation or importation of other commodities. If eleven florins in Holland contain an equal quantity of pure silver as twenty standard shillings, silver bullion, equal in weight to twenty standard shillings, can never be exported from London to Amsterdam whilst the exchange is at par, or favourable to Holland. Some expence and risk must attend its exportation, and the very term *par*, expresses that a quantity of silver bullion, equal to that weight and purity, is to be obtained in Holland by the purchase of a bill of exchange, free of all expence. Who would send bullion to Holland at an expence of three or four per cent. when, by the purchase of a bill at par, he in fact obtains an order for the delivery to his correspondent in Holland, of the same weight of bullion which he was about to export?

It would be as reasonable to contend, that when the price of corn is higher in England than on the Continent, corn would be sent, notwithstanding all the charges on its exportation, to be sold in the cheaper market.

Thus then specie will be sent abroad to discharge a debt only when it is superabundant; only when it is the cheapest exportable commodity. If the Bank were at such a time paying their notes in specie, gold would be demanded for that purpose. It would be obtained there at its mint price, whereas its price as bullion would be something above its value as coin, because bullion could, and coin could not, be legally exported.

It is evident, then, that a depreciation of the circulating medium is the necessary consequence of its redundance; and that in the common state of the national currency this depreciation is counteracted by the exportation of the ,precious metals: but another very serious injury has been at different times sustained by the public from the depreciating of the circulating medium, by the unlawful practice of clipping the coins.

In proportion as they become debased, so the prices of every commodity for which they are exchangeable rise in nominal value, not excepting gold and silver bullion: accordingly we find, that before the re-coinage in the reign of King William the Third, the silver currency had become so degraded, that an ounce of silver, which ought to be contained in sixty-two pence, sold for seventy-seven pence; and a guinea, which was valued at the mint at twenty shillings, passed in all contracts for thirty shillings. This evil was then remedied by the re-coinage. Similar effects followed from the debasement of the gold currency, which were again corrected in 1774 by the same means.

Our gold coins have, since 1774, continued nearly at their standard purity; but our silver currency has again become debased. By an assay at the mint in 1798, it appears that our shillings were found to be twenty-four per cent., and our sixpences thirty-eight per cent. under their mint value; and I am informed, that by a late experiment they were found considerably more deficient. They do not, therefore, contain as much pure silver as they did in the reign of King William. This debasement, however, did not operate previous to 1798, as on the former occasion. At that time both gold and silver bullion rose in proportion to the debasement of the silver coin. All foreign exchanges were against us full twenty per cent., and many of them still more. But although the debasement of the silver coin had continued for many years, it had neither, previous to 1798, raised the price of gold or silver, nor had it produced any effect on the exchanges. This is a convincing proof, that gold coin was, during that period, considered as the standard measure of value. Any debasement of the gold coin would then have produced the same effects on the price of gold and silver bullion, and on the foreign exchanges, which were formerly caused by the debasement of the silver coins[*].

But the disorders now affecting our currency, although not proceeding either from the debased state of the gold or silver coin, are nevertheless more serious in their ultimate consequences. Our circulating medium is almost wholly composed of paper, and it behoves us to guard against the depreciation of the paper currency with at least as much vigilance as against that of the coins.

This we have neglected to do.

Parliament, by restricting the Bank from paying in specie, have enabled the conductors of that concern to increase or decrease at pleasure the quantity and amount of their notes; and the previously existing checks against an over-issue having been thereby removed, those conductors have acquired the power of increasing or decreasing the value of the paper currency.

In tracing the present evils to their source, and proving their existence by an appeal to the two unerring tests I have before mentioned, namely, the rate of exchange and the price of bullion, I shall avail myself of the account given by Mr. Thornton of the conduct of the Bank before the restriction, to shew how clearly they acted on the principle which he has expressly acknowledged, viz. that the value of their notes is dependent on their amount, and that they ascertained the variation in their value by the tests I have just referred to.

Mr. Thornton tells us, 'That if at any time the exchanges of the country became so unfavourable as to produce a material excess of the market above the mint price of gold,' [here the cause is mistaken for the effect] 'the directors of the Bank, as appears by the evidence of some of their body, given to

---

[*] When the gold coin was debased, previous to the re-coinage in 1774, gold and silver bullion rose above their mint prices, and fell immediately on the gold coin attaining its present perfection. The exchanges were, owing to the same causes, from being unfavourable rendered favourable.

parliament, were disposed to resort to a reduction of their paper, as a means of diminishing or removing the excess, and of *thus providing for the security of their establishment*. They moreover have at all times,' he says, been accustomed to observe some limit as to the quantity of their notes for the same prudential reasons.' And in another place: 'When the price which our coin will fetch in foreign countries, is such as to tempt it out of the kingdom, the directors of the Bank naturally diminish, in some degree, the quantity of their paper *through an anxiety for the safety of their establishment*. By diminishing their paper, they raise its value; and in raising its value, they raise also the value in England, of the current coin which is exchanged for it. Thus the value of our gold coin conforms itself to the value of the current paper, and the current paper is rendered by the Bank-directors, of that value which it is necessary that it should bear in order to prevent large exportations; – a value sometimes rising a little above, and sometimes falling a little below, the price which our coin bears abroad.'

The necessity which the Bank felt itself under to guard the safety of its establishment, therefore, always prevented, before the restriction from paying in specie, a too lavish issue of paper money.

Thus we find that, for a period of twenty-three years previous to the suspension of cash payments in 1797, the average price of gold bullion was 3*l*. 17*s*. 7¾*d*. per oz. about 2¾*d*. under the mint price; and for sixteen years previous to 1774, it never was much above 4*l*. per oz. It should be remembered that during these sixteen years our gold coin was debased by wearing, and it is therefore probable that 4*l*. of such debased money did not weigh as much as the ounce of gold for which it was exchanged.

Dr. A. Smith considers every permanent excess of the market above the mint price of gold, as referrible to the state of the coins. While the coin was of its standard weight and purity, the market price of gold bullion, he thought, could not greatly exceed the mint price.

Mr. Thornton contends that this cannot be the only cause. 'We have,' he says, 'lately experienced fluctuations in our exchanges, and correspondent variations in the market, compared with the mint price of gold, amounting to no less than eight or ten per cent.; the state of our coinage continuing in all respects the same.' Mr. Thornton should have reflected that at the time he wrote, specie could not be demanded at the Bank in exchange for notes; that this was a cause for the depreciation of the currency which Dr. Smith could never have anticipated. If Mr. Thornton had proved that there had been a fluctuation of ten per cent. in the price of gold, while the Bank paid their notes in specie, and the coin was undebased, he would then have convicted Dr.

Smith of 'having treated this important subject in a defective and unsatisfactory manner.'*

But as all checks against the over-issues of the Bank are now removed by the act of parliament, which restricts them from paying their notes in specie, they are no longer bound by *'fears for the safety of their establishment,'* to limit the quantity of their notes to that sum which shall keep them of the same value as the coin which they represent. Accordingly we find that gold bullion has risen from 3*l*. 17*s*. 7¾*d*. the average price previous to 1797, to 4*l*. 10*s*. and has been lately as high as 4*l*. 13*s*. per oz.

We may therefore fairly conclude that this difference in the relative value, or, in other words, that this depreciation in the actual value of bank-notes has been caused by the too abundant quantity which the Bank has sent into circulation. The same cause which has produced a difference of from fifteen to twenty per cent. in bank-notes when compared with gold bullion, may increase it to fifty per cent. There can be no limit to the depreciation which may arise from a constantly increasing quantity of paper. The stimulus which a redundant currency gives to the exportation of the coin, has acquired new force, but cannot, as formerly, relieve itself. We have paper money only in circulation, which is necessarily confined to ourselves. Every increase in its quantity degrades it below the value of gold and silver bullion, below the value of the currencies of other countries.

The effect is the same as that which would have been produced from clipping our coins.

* An excess in the market above the mint price of gold or silver bullion, may, whilst the coins of both metals are legal tender, be caused by a variation in the relative value of those metals; – but an excess of the market above the mint price proceeding from this cause will be at once perceived by its affecting only the price of one of the metals. Thus gold would be at or below, while silver was above, its mint price, or silver at or below its mint price, whilst gold was above.

In the latter end of 1795, when the Bank had considerably more notes in circulation than either the preceding or the subsequent year, when their embarrassments had already commenced, when they appear to have resigned all prudence in the management of their concerns, and to have constituted Mr. Pitt sole director, the price of gold bullion did for a short time rise to 4*l*. 3*s*. or 4*l*. 4*s*. per oz.; but the directors were not without their fears for the consequences. In a remonstrance sent by them to Mr. Pitt, dated October 1795, after stating, 'that the demand for gold not appearing likely soon to cease,' and 'that it had excited great apprehension in the court of directors,' they observe, 'The present price of gold being 4*l*. 3*s*. to 4*l*. 4*s*. per ounce, and our guineas being to be purchased at 3*l*. 17*s*. 10½*d*., clearly demonstrates the grounds of our fears; *it being only necessary to state those facts to the Chancellor of the Exchequer.*' It is remarkable that no price of gold above the mint price is quoted during the whole year in Wetenhall's list. In December it is there marked 3*l*. 17*s*. 6*d*.

If one-fifth were taken off from every guinea, the market price of gold bullion would rise one-fifth above the mint price. Forty-four guineas and a half (the number of guineas weighing a pound, and therefore called the mint price,) would no longer weigh a pound, therefore a fifth more than that quantity, or about 56*l.*, would be the price of a pound of gold, and the difference between the market and the mint price, between 56*l.* and 46*l.* 14*s.* 6*d.*, would measure the depreciation.

'It is,' says Mr. Thornton, 'the maintenance of our general exchanges, or, in other words, it is the agreement of the mint price with the bullion price of gold, which seems to be the true proof that the circulating paper is not depreciated.'

When the motive for exporting gold occurs, while the Bank do not pay in specie, and gold cannot therefore be obtained at its mint price, the small quantity that can be procured will be collected for exportation, and bank-notes will be sold at a discount for gold in proportion to their excess. In saying however that gold is at a high price, we are mistaken; it is not gold, it is paper which has changed its value. Compare an ounce of gold, or 3*l.* 7*s.* 10½*d.* to commodities, it bears the same proportion to them which it has before done; and if it do not, it is referrible to increased taxation, or to some of those causes which are so constantly operating on its value. But if we compare the substitute of an ounce of gold, 3*l.* 17*s.* 10½*d.* in bank-notes, with commodities, we shall then discover the depreciation of the bank-notes. In every market of the world I am obliged to part with 4*l.* 10*s.* in bank-notes to purchase the same quantity of commodities which I can obtain for the gold that is in 3*l.* 17*s.* 10½*d.* of coin.

It is said, that, if the Restriction-bill were not in force, every guinea would leave the country.*

This is, no doubt, true; but if the Bank were to diminish the quantity of their notes until they had increased their value fifteen per cent., the restriction might be safely removed, as there would then be no temptation to export specie. However long it may be deferred, however great may be the discount on their notes, the Bank can never resume their payments in specie, until they first reduce the amount of their notes in circulation to these limits.

The law is allowed by all writers on political economy to be a useless barrier against the exportation of guineas; it is so easily evaded, that it is doubted whether it has had the effect of keeping a single guinea more in England than there would have been without such law. Mr. Locke, Sir J. Stuart, Dr. A. Smith, Lord Liverpool, and Mr. Thornton, all agree on this subject. The latter

---

* It must be meant that every guinea in the Bank would leave the country; the temptation of fifteen per cent. is amply sufficient to send those out which can be collected from the circulation.

gentleman observes, 'That the state of the British law unquestionably serves to discourage and limit, though not effectually to hinder, that exportation of guineas which is encouraged by an unfavourable balance of trade, and perhaps scarcely lessens it when the profit on exportation becomes very great.' Yet after every guinea that can in the present state of things be procured by the illicit trader, has been melted and exported, he will hesitate before he openly buys guineas with bank-notes at a premium, because, though considerable profit may attend such speculation, he will thereby render himself an object of suspicion. He may be watched and prevented from effecting his object. As the penalties of the law are severe, and the temptation to informers great, secrecy is essential to his operations. When guineas can be procured by merely sending a bank-note for them to the Bank, the law will be easily evaded; but when it is necessary to collect them openly and from a widely diffused circulation, consisting almost wholly of paper, the advantage attending it must be very considerable before any one will encounter the risk of being detected.

When we reflect that above sixty millions sterling have been coined into guineas during his present Majesty's reign, we may form some idea of the extent to which the exportation of gold must have been carried.– But repeal the law against the exportation of guineas, permit them to be openly sent out of the country, and what can prevent an ounce of standard gold in guineas from selling at as good a price for bank-notes, as an ounce of Portugueze gold coin, or standard gold in bars, when it is known to be equal to them in fineness? And if an ounce of standard gold in guineas would sell in the market, as standard bars do now, at 4*l.* 10*s.* per oz., or as they have lately done at 4*l.* 13*s.* per oz., what shopkeeper would sell his goods at the same price either for gold or bank-notes indifferently? If the price of a coat were 3*l.* 17*s.* 10½*d.*, or an ounce of gold, and if at the same time an ounce of gold would sell for 4*l.* 13*s.*, is it conceivable that it would be a matter of indifference to the tailor whether he were paid in gold or in bank-notes?

It is only because a guinea will not purchase more than a pound-note and a shilling, that many hesitate to allow that bank-notes are at a discount. The Edinburgh Review supports the same opinion; but if my reasoning be correct, I have shewn such objections to be groundless.

Mr. Thornton has told us that an unfavourable trade will account for an unfavourable exchange; but we have already seen that an unfavourable trade, if such be an accurate term, is limited in its effects on the exchange. That limit is probably four or five per cent. This will not account for a depreciation of fifteen or twenty per cent. Moreover Mr. Thornton has told us, and I entirely agree with him, 'That it may be laid down as a general truth, that the commercial exports and imports of a state naturally proportion themselves in some degree to each other, and that the balance of trade therefore cannot continue for a very long time to be either highly favourable, or highly unfavourable to a country.' Now the low exchange, so far from being temporary, existed before Mr. Thornton wrote in 1802, and has since been progressively increasing, and is now from fifteen to twenty per cent. against us. Mr. Thornton must therefore according to his own principles attribute it to some more permanent cause than an unfavourable balance of trade, and will, I doubt not, whatever his opinion may formerly have been, now agree that it is to be accounted for only by the depreciation of the circulating medium.

It can, I think, no longer be disputed that bank-notes are at a discount. While the price of gold bullion is 4*l*. 10*s*. per oz., or in other words, while any man will consent to give that which professes to be an obligation to pay nearly an ounce, and a sixth of an ounce of gold, for an ounce, it cannot be contended that 4*l*. 10*s*. in notes and 4*l*. 10*s*. in gold coin are of the same value.

An ounce of gold is coined into 3*l*. 17*s*. 10½*d*.; by possessing that sum therefore I have an ounce of gold, and would not give 4*l*. 10*s*. in gold coin, or notes which I could immediately exchange for 4*l*. 10*s*., for an ounce of gold.

It is contrary to common sense to suppose that such could be the market value, unless the price were estimated in a depreciated medium.

But it has been contended, that bank-notes are the representatives of silver and not of gold coin.

Bank-notes must necessarily be the representative of that coin which is the standard of currency, and there can be no doubt that for near a century gold has been the standard metal. But if a change have taken place, and silver be now the standard of value, and consequently bank-notes the representative of the silver coins, this will not remove the difficulty. The market price of silver is at the present time 5*s*. 9½*d*. per oz. estimated in bank notes, the mint price being only 5*s*. 2*d*., consequently the standard silver in 100*l*. is worth more than 112*l*. in bank-notes.

But bank-notes, it may be said, are the representatives of our debased silver coin, and not of our standard silver. This is not true, because the law which I have already quoted declares silver to be a legal tender for sums only not exceeding 25*l*. except by weight. If the Bank insisted on paying the holder of a bank-note of 1000*l*. in silver coin, they would be bound either to give him standard silver of full weight, or debased silver of an equal value, with the exception of 25*l*. which they might pay him in debased coin. But the 1000*l*. so consisting of 975*l*. pure money, and 25*l*. debased, is worth more than 1112*l*. at the present market value of silver bullion.

It is said that the amount of bank-notes has not increased in a greater proportion than the augmentation of our trade required, and therefore cannot be excessive. This assertion would be difficult to prove, and if true, no argument but what is delusive could be founded on it. In the first place, the daily improvements which we are making in the art of economizing the use of circu-lating medium, by improved methods of banking, would render the same amount of notes excessive now, which were necessary for the same state of commerce at a former period. Secondly, there is a constant competition between the Bank of England and the country-banks to establish their notes, to the exclusion of those of their rivals, in every district where the country banks are established.

As the latter have more than doubled in number within very few years, is it not probable that their activity may have been crowned with success, in dis-placing with their own notes many of those of the Bank of England?

If this have happened, the same amount of Bank of England notes would now be excessive; which, with a less extended commerce, was before barely sufficient to keep our currency on a level with that of other countries. No just conclusion can therefore be drawn from the actual amount of bank-notes in circulation, though the fact, if examined, would, I have no doubt, be found to be, that the increase in the amount of bank-notes, and the high price of gold, have usually accompanied each other.

It is doubted, whether two or three millions of Bank-notes (the sum which the Bank is supposed to have added to the circulation, over and above the amount which it will easily bear,) could have had such effects as are ascribed to them; but it should be recollected, that the Bank regulate the amount of the circulation of all the country banks, and it is probable, that if the Bank increase their issues three millions, they enable the country banks to add more than twelve millions to the general circulation of England.

The money of a particular country is divided amongst its different provinces by the same rules as the money of the world is divided amongst the different nations of which it is composed. Each district will retain in its circulation such a proportionate share of the currency of the country, as its trade, and conse-quently its payments may require, compared to the trade of the whole; and no increase can take place in the circulating medium of one district, without being generally diffused, or calling forth a proportionable quantity in every other district. It is this which keeps a country-bank note always of the same value as a Bank of England note. If in London, where Bank of England notes only are current, one million be added to the amount in circulation, the cur-rency will become cheaper there than elsewhere, or goods will become dearer. Goods will, therefore, be sent from the country to the London market, to be sold at the high prices, or which is much more probable, the country banks will take advantage of the relative deficiency in the country currency, and increase the amount of their notes in the same proportion as the Bank of England had done; prices would then be generally, and not partially affected.

In the same manner, if Bank of England notes be diminished one million, the comparative value of the currency of London will be increased, and the prices of goods diminished. A Bank of England note will then be more valuable than a country-bank note, because it will be wanted to purchase goods in the cheap market; and as the country banks are obliged to give Bank of England notes for their own when demanded, they would be called upon for them till the quantity of country paper should be reduced to the same proportion which it before bore to the London paper, producing a corresponding fall in the prices of all goods for which it was exchangeable.

The country banks could never increase the amount of their notes, unless to fill up a relative deficiency in the country currency, caused by the increased issues of the Bank of England[*]. If they attempted it, the same check which obliged the Bank of England to withdraw part of their notes from circulation when they were obliged to pay them on demand in specie, would oblige the country banks to adopt the same course. Their notes would, on account of the increased quantity, be rendered of less value than the Bank of England notes, in the same manner as Bank of England notes were rendered of less value than the guineas which they represented. They would therefore be exchanged for Bank of England notes until they were of the same value.

The Bank of England is the great regulator of the country paper. When they increase or decrease the amount of their notes, the country banks do the same; and in no case can country banks add to the general circulation, unless the Bank of England shall have previously increased the amount of their notes.

It is contended, that the rate of interest, and not the price of gold or silver bullion, is the criterion by which we may always judge of the abundance of paper-money; that if it were too abundant, interest would fall, and if not sufficiently so, interest would rise. It can, I think, be made manifest, that the rate of interest is not regulated by the abundance or scarcity of money, but by the abundance or scarcity of that part of capital, not consisting of money.

'Money,' observes Dr. A. Smith, 'the great wheel of circulation, the great instrument of commerce, like all other instruments of trade, though it makes a part, and a very valuable part, of the capital, makes no part of the revenue of the society to which it belongs; and though the metal pieces of which it is composed, in the course of their annual circulation, distribute to every man the revenue which properly belongs to him, they make themselves no part of that revenue.

'When we compute the quantity of industry which the circulating capital of any society can employ, we must always have regard to those parts of it only

---

[*] They might, on some occasions, displace Bank of England notes, but that consideration does not affect the question which we are now discussing.

which consist in provisions, materials, and finished work: the other, which consists in money, and which serves only to circulate those three, must always be deducted. In order to put industry into motion, three things are requisite:– materials to work upon, tools to work with, and the wages or recompense for the sake of which the work is done. Money is neither a material to work upon, nor a tool to work with; and though the wages of the workman are commonly paid to him in money, his real revenue, like that of all other men, consists not in money, but in money's worth; not in the metal pieces, but what can be got for them.'

And in other parts of his work, it is maintained, that the discovery of the mines in America, which so greatly increased the quantity of money, did not lessen the interest for the use of it: the rate of interest being regulated by the profits on the employment of capital, and not by the number or quality of the pieces of metal, which are used to circulate its produce.

Mr. Hume has supported the same opinion. The value of the circulating medium of every country bears some proportion to the value of the commodities which it circulates. In some countries this proportion is much greater than in others, and varies, on some occasions, in the same country. It depends upon the rapidity of circulation, upon the degree of confidence and credit existing between traders, and above all, on the judicious operations of banking. In England so many means of economizing the use of circulating medium have been adopted, that its value, compared with the value of the commodities which it circulates, is probably (during a period of confidence[*]) reduced to as small a proportion as is practicable. What that proportion may be has been variously estimated.

No increase or decrease of its quantity, whether consisting of gold, silver, or paper-money, can increase or decrease its value above or below this proportion. If the mines cease to supply the annual consumption of the precious metals, money will become more valuable, and a smaller quantity will be employed as a circulating medium. The diminution in the quantity will be proportioned to the increase of its value. In like manner, if new mines be discovered, the value of the precious metals will be reduced, and an increased quantity used in the circulation; so that in either case the relative value of money, to the commodities which it circulates, will continue as before.

If, whilst the Bank paid their notes on demand in specie, they were to increase their quantity, they would produce little permanent effect on the value of the currency, because nearly an equal quantity of the coin would be withdrawn from circulation and exported.

* In the following observations, I wish to be understood, as supposing always the same degree of confidence and credit to exist.

If the Bank were restricted from paying their notes in specie, and all the coin had been exported, any excess of their notes would depreciate the value of the circulating medium in proportion to the excess. If twenty millions had been the circulation of England before the restriction, and four millions were added to it, the twenty-four millions would be of no more value than the twenty were before, provided commodities had remained the same, and there had been no corresponding exportation of coins; and if the Bank were successively to increase it to fifty, or a hundred millions, the increased quantity would be all absorbed in the circulation of England, but would be, in all cases, depreciated to the value of the twenty millions.

I do not dispute, that if the Bank were to bring a large additional sum of notes into the market, and offer them on loan, but that they would for a time affect the rate of interest. The same effects would follow from the discovery of a hidden treasure of gold or silver coin. If the amount were large, the Bank, or the owner of the treasure, might not be able to lend the notes or the money at four, nor perhaps, above three per cent.; but having done so, neither the notes, nor the money, would be retained unemployed by the borrowers; they would be sent into every market, and would every where raise the prices of commodities, till they were absorbed in the general circulation. It is only during the interval of the issues of the Bank, and their effect on prices, that we should be sensible of an abundance of money; interest would, during that interval, be under its natural level; but as soon as the additional sum of notes or of money became absorbed in the general circulation, the rate of interest would be as high, and new loans would be demanded with as much eagerness as before the additional issues.

The circulation can never be over-full. If it be one of gold and silver, any increase in its quantity will be spread over the world. If it be one of paper, it will diffuse itself only in the country where it is issued. Its effects on prices will then be only local and nominal, as a compensation by means of the exchange will be made to foreign purchasers.

To suppose that any increased issues of the Bank can have the effect of lowering the rate of interest, and satisfying the demands of all borrowers, so that there will be none to apply for new loans, or that a productive gold or silver mine can have such an effect, is to attribute a power to the circulating medium which it can never possess. Banks would, if this were possible, become powerful engines indeed. By creating paper-money, and lending it at three or two per cent. under the present market rate of interest, the Bank would reduce the profits on trade in the same proportion; and if they were sufficiently patriotic to lend their notes at an interest no higher than necessary to pay the expences of their establishment, profits would be still further reduced; no nation, but by similar means, could enter into competition with us, we should engross the trade of the world. To what absurdities would not such a theory lead us! Profits can only be lowered by a competition of capitals not consisting of circulating medium. As the increase of Bank-notes does not add to this species of capital, as it neither increases our exportable commodities, our machinery, or our raw materials, it cannot add to our profits nor lower interest*.

When any one borrows money for the purpose of entering into trade, he borrows it as a medium by which he can possess himself of 'materials, provisions, &c.' to carry on that trade; and it can be of little consequence to him, provided he obtain the quantity of materials, &c. necessary, whether he be obliged to borrow a thousand, or ten thousand pieces of money. If he borrow ten thousand, the produce of his manufacture will be ten times the nominal value of what it would have been, had one thousand been sufficient for the same purpose. The capital actually employed in the country is necessarily limited to the amount of the 'materials, provisions, &c.' and might be made equally productive, though not with equal facility, if trade were carried on wholly by barter. The successive possessors of the circulating medium have the command over this capital: but however abundant may be the quantity of money or of bank-notes; though it may increase the nominal prices of commodities; though it may distribute the productive capital in different proportions; though the Bank, by increasing the quantity of its notes, may enable A to carry on part of the business formerly engrossed by B and C, nothing will be added to the real revenue and wealth of the country. B and C may be injured, and A and the Bank may be gainers, but they will gain exactly what B and C lose. There will be a violent and an unjust transfer of property, but no benefit whatever will be gained by the community.

For these reasons I am of opinion that the funds are not indebted for their high price to the depreciation of our currency. Their price must be regulated by the general rate of interest given for money. If before the depreciation I gave thirty years' purchase for land, and twenty-five for an annuity in the stocks, I can after the depreciation give a larger sum for the purchase of land, without giving more years' purchase, because the produce of the land will sell for a greater nominal value in consequence of the depreciation; but as the annuity in the funds is paid in the depreciated medium, there can be no reason

---

* I have already allowed that the Bank, as far as they enable us to turn our coin into 'materials, provisions, &c.' have produced a national benefit, as they have thereby increased the quantity of productive capital; but I am here speaking of an excess of their notes, of that quantity which adds to our circulation without effecting any corresponding exportation of coin, and which, therefore, degrades the notes below the value of the bullion contained in the coin which they represent.

why I should give a greater nominal value for it after than before the depreciation.

If guineas were degraded by clipping to half their present value, every commodity as well as land would rise to double its present nominal value; but as the interest of the stocks would be paid in the degraded guineas, they would, on that account, experience no rise.

The remedy which I propose for all the evils in our currency, is that the Bank should gradually decrease the amount of their notes in circulation until they shall have rendered the remainder of equal value with the coins which they represent, or, in other words, till the prices of gold and silver bullion shall be brought down to their mint price. I am well aware that the total failure of paper credit would be attended with the most disastrous consequences to the trade and commerce of the country, and even its sudden limitation would occasion so much ruin and distress, that it would be highly inexpedient to have recourse to it as the means of restoring our currency to its just and equitable value.

If the Bank were possessed of more guineas than they had notes in circulation, they could not, without great injury to the country, pay their notes in specie, while the price of gold bullion continued greatly above the mint price, and the foreign exchanges unfavourable to us. The excess of our currency would be exchanged for guineas at the Bank and exported, and would be suddenly withdrawn from circulation. Before therefore they can safely pay in specie, the excess of notes must be gradually withdrawn from circulation. If gradually done, little inconvenience would be felt; so that the principle were fairly admitted, it would be for future consideration whether the object should be accomplished in one year or in five. I am fully persuaded that we shall never restore our currency to its equitable state, but by this preliminary step, or by the total overthrow of our paper credit.

If the Bank directors had kept the amount of their notes within reasonable bounds; *if they had acted up to the principle which they have avowed to have been that which regulated their issues when they were obliged to pay their notes in specie, namely, to limit their notes to that amount which should prevent the excess of the market above the mint price of gold, we should not have been now exposed to all the evils of a depreciated, and perpetually varying currency.*

Though the Bank derive considerable advantage from the present system, though the price of their capital stock has nearly doubled in price since 1797, and their dividends have proportionally increased, I am ready to admit with Mr. Thornton, that the directors, as monied men, sustain losses in common with others by a depreciation of the currency, much more serious to them than any advantages which they may reap from it. I do therefore acquit them of being influenced by interested motives, but their mistakes, if they are such, are in their effects quite as pernicious to the community.

The extraordinary powers with which they are entrusted, enable them to regulate at their pleasure the price at which those who are possessed of a particular kind of property, called money, shall dispose of it. The Bank directors have imposed upon these, holders of money, all the evils of a maximum. To-day it is their pleasure that 4*l.* 10*s.* shall pass for 3*l.* 17*s.* 10½*d.*, tomorrow they may degrade 4*l.* 15*s.* to the same value, and in another year 10*l.* may not be worth more. By what an insecure tenure is property consisting of money or annuities paid in money held! What security has the public creditor that the interest on the public debt, which is now paid in a medium depreciated fifteen per cent., may not hereafter be paid in one degraded fifty per cent.? The injury to private creditors is not less serious. A debt contracted in 1797, may now be paid with eighty-five per cent. of its amount, and who shall say that the depreciation will go no further?

The following observations of Dr. Smith on this subject are so important, that I cannot but recommend them to the serious attention of all thinking men.

'The raising the denomination of the coin has been the most usual expedient by which a real public bankruptcy has been disguised under the appearance of a pretended payment. If a sixpence, for example, should, either by act of parliament or royal proclamation, be raised to the denomination of a shilling, and twenty sixpences to that of a pound sterling, the person who under the old denomination had borrowed twenty shillings, or near four ounces of silver, would, under the new, pay with twenty sixpences, or with something less than two ounces. A national debt of about a hundred and twenty millions, nearly the capital of the funded debt of Great Britain, might in this manner be paid with about sixty-four millions of our present money. It would indeed be a pretended payment only, and the creditors of the public would be defrauded of ten shillings in the pound of what was due to them. The calamity too would extend much further than to the creditors of the public, and those of every private person would suffer a proportionable loss; and this without any advantage, but in most cases with a great additional loss, to the creditors of the public. If the creditors of the public indeed were generally much in debt to other people, they might in some measure compensate their loss by paying their creditors in the same coin in which the public had paid them. But in most countries the creditors of the public are, the greater part of them, wealthy people, who stand more in the relation of creditors than in that of debtors towards the rest of their fellow-citizens. A pretended payment of this kind, therefore instead of alleviating, aggravates in most cases the loss of the creditors of the public; and without any advantage to the public, extends the calamity to a great number of other innocent people. It occasions a general, and most pernicious subversion of the fortunes of private people; enriching in most cases the idle and profuse debtor at the expence of the industrious and frugal creditor, and transporting a great part of the national capital from the hands which are likely to increase and improve it, to those which are likely to dissipate and destroy it. When it becomes necessary for a state to declare itself bankrupt, in the same manner as when it becomes necessary for an individual to do so, a fair, open, and avowed bankruptcy is always the measure which is both least dishonourable to the debtor, and least hurtful to the creditor. The honour of a state is surely very poorly provided for, when in order to cover the disgrace of a real bankruptcy, it has recourse to a juggling trick of this kind, so easily seen through, and at the same time so extremely pernicious.'

These observations of Dr. Smith on a debased money, are equally applicable to a depreciated paper currency. He has enumerated but a few of the disastrous consequences which attend the debasement of the circulating medium, but he has sufficiently warned us against trying such dangerous experiments. It will be a circumstance ever to be lamented, if this great country, having before its eyes the consequences of a forced paper circulation in America and France, should persevere in a system pregnant with so much disaster. Let us hope that she will be more wise. It is said indeed that the cases are dissimilar: that the Bank of England is independent of government. If this were true, the evils of a superabundant circulation would not be less felt; but it may be questioned whether a Bank lending many millions more to government than its capital and savings, can be called independent of that government.

When the order of council for suspending the cash payments became necessary in 1797, the run upon the Bank was, in my opinion, caused by political alarm alone, and not by a superabundant, or a deficient quantity (as some have supposed) of their notes in circulation[*].

This is a danger to which the Bank, from the nature of its institution, is at all times liable. No prudence on the part of the directors could perhaps have averted it: but if their loans to government had been more limited; if the same amount of notes had been issued to the public through the medium of discounts; they would have been able, in all probability, to have continued their payments till the alarm had subsided. At any rate, as the debtors to the Bank would have been obliged to discharge their debts in the space of sixty days, that being the longest period for which any bill discounted by the Bank has to run. The directors would in that time, if necessary, have been enabled to redeem every note in circulation. It was then owing to the too intimate

* At that period the price of gold kept steadily under its mint price.

connection between the Bank and government, that the restriction became necessary; it is to that cause too that we owe its continuance.

To prevent the evil consequences which may attend the perseverance in this system, we must keep our eyes steadily fixed on the repeal of the Restriction-bill.

The only legitimate security which the public can possess against the indiscretion of the Bank is to oblige them to pay their notes on demand in specie; and this can only be effected by diminishing the amount of bank-notes in circulation till the nominal price of gold be lowered to the mint price.

Here I will conclude; happy if my feeble efforts should awaken the public attention to a due consideration of the state of our circulating medium. I am well aware that I have not added to the stock of information with which the public has been enlightened by many able writers on the same important subject. I have had no such ambition. My aim has been to introduce a calm and dispassionate enquiry into a question of great importance to the state, and the neglect of which may be attended with consequences which every friend of his country would deplore.

David Ricardo (1772–1823)

Extract from *Principles of Political Economy and Taxation* (1817).

CHAPTER XXVII. – ON CURRENCY AND BANKS.

§ 124.

So much has already been written on currency, that of those who give their attention to such subjects, none but the prejudiced are ignorant of its true principles. I shall, therefore, take only a brief survey of some of the general laws which regulate its quantity and value.

Gold and silver, like all other commodities, are valuable only in proportion to the quantity of labour necessary to produce them, and bring them to market. Gold is about fifteen times dearer than silver, not because there is a greater demand for it, nor because the supply of silver is fifteen times greater than that of gold, but solely because fifteen times the quantity of labour is necessary to procure a given quantity of it.

The quantity of money that can be employed in a country must depend on its value: if gold alone were employed for the circulation of commodities, a quantity would be required, one fifteenth only of what would be necessary if silver were made use of for the same purpose.

A circulation can never be so abundant as to overflow; for by diminishing its value, in the same proportion you will increase its quantity, and by increasing its value, diminish its quantity.

While the State coins money, and charges no seignorage, money will be of the same value as any other piece of the same metal of equal weight and fineness; but if the State charges a seignorage for coinage, the coined piece of money will generally exceed the value of the uncoined piece of metal by the whole seignorage charged, because it will require a greater quantity of labour, or, which is the same thing, the value of the produce of a greater quantity of labour to procure it.

While the State alone coins, there can be no limit to this charge of seignorage; for by limiting the quantity of coin, it can be raised to any conceivable value.

§125. It is on this principle that paper money circulates: the whole charge for paper money may be considered as seignorage. Though it has no intrinsic value, yet, by limiting its quantity, its value in exchange is as great as an equal denomination of coin, or of bullion in that coin. On the same principle, too, namely, by a limitation of its quantity, a debased coin would circulate at the value it should bear, if it were of the legal weight and fineness, and not at the value of the quantity of metal which it actually contained. In the history of the British coinage, we find, accordingly, that the currency was never depreciated in the same proportion that it was debased; the reason of which was, that it never was increased in quantity, in proportion to its diminished intrinsic value.*

There is no point more important in issuing paper money, than to be fully impressed with the effects which follow from the principle of limitation of quantity. It will scarcely be believed fifty years hence, that Bank directors and ministers gravely contended in our times, both in parliament, and before committees of parliament, that the issues of notes by the Bank of England, unchecked by any power in the holders of such notes, to demand in exchange either specie, or bullion, had not, nor could have any effect on the prices of commodities, bullion, or foreign exchanges.

After the establishment of Banks, the State has not the sole power of coining or issuing money. The currency may as effectually be increased by paper as by coin; so that if a State were to debase its money, and limit its quantity, it could not support its value, because the Banks would have an equal power of adding to the whole quantity of circulation.

On these principles, it will be seen that it is not necessary that paper money should be payable in specie to secure its value; it is only necessary that its quantity should be regulated according to the value of the metal which is declared to be the standard. If the standard were gold of a given weight and fineness, paper might be increased with every fall in the value of gold, or, which is the same thing in its effects, with every rise in the price of goods.

§126. 'By issuing too great a quantity of paper,' says Dr. Smith, 'of which the excess was continually returning, in order to be exchanged for gold and silver, the Bank of England was, for many years together, obliged to coin gold to the extent of between eight hundred thousand pounds and a million a year, or at an average, about eight hundred and fifty thousand pounds. For this great coinage, the Bank, in consequence of the worn and degraded state into which the gold coin had fallen a few years ago, was frequently obliged to purchase bullion, at the high price of four pounds an ounce, which soon after issued in

---

* Whatever I say of gold coin, is equally applicable to silver coin; but it is not necessary to mention both on every occasion.

coin at £3 17s. 10½d. an ounce, losing in this manner between two and a half and three per cent. upon the coinage of so very large a sum. Though the Bank, therefore, paid no seignorage, though the Government was properly at the expense of the coinage, this liberality of Government did not prevent altogether the expense of the Bank.'

On the principle above stated, it appears to me most clear, that by not reissuing the paper thus brought in, the value of the whole currency, of the degraded as well as the new gold coin, would have been raised, when all demands on the Bank would have ceased.

Mr. Buchanan, however, is not of this opinion, for he says, 'that the great expense to which the Bank was at this time exposed, was occasioned, not, as Dr. Smith seems to imagine, by any imprudent issue of paper, but by the debased state of the currency, and the consequent high price of bullion. The Bank, it will be observed, having no other way of procuring guineas but by sending bullion to the Mint to be coined, was always forced to issue new coined guineas in exchange for its returned notes; and when the currency was generally deficient in weight, and the price of bullion high in proportion, it became profitable to draw these heavy guineas from the Bank in exchange for its paper; to convert them into bullion, and to sell them with a profit for Bank paper, to be again returned to the Bank for a new supply of guineas, which were again melted and sold. To this drain of specie, the Bank must always be exposed while the currency is deficient in weight, as both an easy and a certain profit then arises from the constant interchange of paper for specie. It may be remarked, however, that to whatever inconvenience and expense the Bank was then exposed by the drain of its specie, it never was imagined necessary to rescind the obligation to pay money for its notes.'

Mr. Buchanan evidently thinks that the whole currency must, necessarily, be brought down to the level of the value of the debased pieces; but, surely, by a diminution of the quantity of the currency, the whole that remains can be elevated to the value of the best pieces.

Dr. Smith appears to have forgotten his own principle, in his argument on colony currency. Instead of ascribing the depreciation of that paper to its too great abundance, he asks whether, allowing the colony security to be perfectly good, a hundred pounds, payable fifteen years hence, would be equally valuable with a hundred pounds to be paid immediately?I answer yes, if it be not too abundant.

§127. Experience, however, shows, that neither a State nor a Bank ever have had the unrestricted power of issuing paper money, without abusing that power: in all States, therefore, the issue of paper money ought to be under some check and control; and none seems so proper for that purpose, as that of subjecting the issuers of paper money to the obligation of paying their notes, either in gold coin or bullion.

A currency is in its most perfect state when it consists wholly of paper money, but of paper money of an equal value with the gold which it professes to represent. The use of paper instead of gold, substitutes the cheapest in place of the most expensive medium, and enables the country, without loss to any individual, to exchange all the gold which it before used for this purpose, for raw materials, utensils, and food; by the use of which, both its wealth and its enjoyments are increased.

§128. In a national point of view, it is of no importance whether the issuers of this well regulated paper money be the Government or a Bank, it will, on the whole, be equally productive of riches, whether it be issued by one or by the other; but it is not so with respect to the interest of individuals. In a country where the market rate of interest is 7 per cent., and where the State requires for a particular expense £70,000 per annum, it is a question of importance to the individuals of that country, whether they must be taxed to pay this £70,000 per annum, or whether they could raise it without taxes. Suppose that a million of money should be required to fit out an expedition. If the State issued a million of paper, and displaced a million of coin, the expedition would be fitted out without any charge to the people; but if a Bank issued a million of paper, and lent it to Government at 7 per cent., thereby displacing a million of coin, the country would be charged with a continual tax of £70,000 per annum: the people would pay the tax, the Bank would receive it, and the society would in either case be as wealthy as before; the expedition would have been really fitted out by the improvement of our system, by rendering capital of the value of a million productive in the form of commodities, instead of letting it remain unproductive in the form of coin; but the advantage would always be in favour of the issuers of paper; and as the State represents the people, the people would have saved the tax, if they, and not the Bank, had issued this million.

I have already observed, that if there were perfect security that the power of issuing paper money would not be abused, it would be of no importance with respect to the riches of the country collectively, by whom it was issued; and I have now shown that the public would have a direct interest that the issuers should be the State, and not a company of merchants or bankers. The danger, however, is, that this power would be more likely to be abused, if in the hands of Government, than if in the hands of a banking company. A company would, it is said, be more under the control of law, and although it might be their interest to extend their issues beyond the bounds of discretion, they would be limited and checked by the power which individuals would have of calling for bullion or specie. It is argued that the same check would not be long respected, if Government had the privilege of issuing money; that they would be too apt to consider present convenience, rather than future security, and might, therefore, on the alleged grounds of expediency, be too much inclined to remove the checks, by which the amount of their issues was controlled.

Under an arbitrary Government, this objection would have great force; but, in a free country, with an enlightened legislature, the power of issuing paper money, under the requisite checks of convertibility at the will of the holder, might be safely lodged in the hands of commissioners appointed for that special purpose, and they might be made totally independent of the control of ministers.

The sinking fund is managed by commissioners, responsible only to parliament, and the investment of the money entrusted to their charge, proceeds with the utmost regularity; what reason can there be to doubt that the issues of paper money might be regulated with equal fidelity, if placed under similar management?

§129. It may be said, that although the advantage accruing to the State, and, therefore, to the public, from issuing paper money, is sufficiently manifest, as it would exchange a portion of the national debt, on which interest is paid by the public, into a debt bearing no interest; yet it would be disadvantageous to commerce, as it would preclude the merchants from borrowing money, and getting their bills discounted, the method in which Bank paper is partly issued.

This, however, is to suppose that money could not be borrowed, if the Bank did not lend it, and that the market rate of interest and profit depends on the amount of the issues of money, and on the channel through which it is issued. But as a country would have no deficiency of cloth, of wine, or any other commodity, if they had the means of paying for it, in the same manner neither would there be any deficiency of money to be lent, if the borrowers offered good security, and were willing to pay the market rate of interest for it.

In another part of this work, I have endeavoured to show, that the real value of a commodity is regulated, not by the accidental advantages which may be enjoyed by some of its producers, but by the real difficulties encountered by that producer who is least favoured. It is so with respect to the interest for money; it is not regulated by the rate at which the Bank will lend, whether it be 5, 4, or 3 per cent., but by the rate of profits which can be made by the employment of capital, and which is totally independent of the quantity, or of the value of money. Whether a Bank lent one million, ten million, or

---

* [Though this is true, there is little doubt that the large advances made to the Government by the Bank had tended to its considerable embarrassment. The crisis was brought about by the general feeling of insecurity brought about by the French advance and the rumours of its possible consequence. In view of a still further run, in addition to

a hundred millions, they would not permanently alter the market rate of interest; they would alter only the value of the money which they thus issued. In one case, 10 or 20 times more money might be required to carry on the same business, than what might be required in the other. The applications to the Bank for money, then, depend on the comparison between the rate of profits that may be made by the employment of it, and the rate at which they are willing to lend it. If they charge less than the market rate of interest, there is no amount of money which they might not lend, – if they charge more than that rate, none but spendthrifts and prodigals would be found to borrow of them. We accordingly find, that when the market rate of interest exceeds the rate of 5 per cent. at which the Bank uniformly lend, the discount office is besieged with applicants for money; and, on the contrary, when the market rate is even temporarily under 5 per cent., the clerks of that office have no employment.

The reason, then, why for the last twenty years, the Bank is said to have given so much aid to commerce, by assisting the merchants with money, is, because they have, during that whole period, lent money below the market rate of interest; below that rate at which the merchants could have borrowed elsewhere; but, I confess, that to me this seems rather an objection to their establishment, than an argument in favour of it.

What should we say of an establishment which should regularly supply half the clothiers with wool under the market price? Of what benefit would it be to the community? It would not extend our trade, because the wool would equally have been bought if they had charged the market price for it. It would not lower the price of cloth to the consumer, because the price, as I have said before, would be regulated by the cost of its production to those who were the least favoured. Its sole effect, then, would be, to swell the profits of a part of the clothiers beyond the general and common rate of profits. The establishment would be deprived of its fair profits, and another part of the community would be in the same degree benefited. Now this is precisely the effect of our banking establishments; a rate of interest is fixed by the law below that at which it can be borrowed in the market, and at this rate the Bank are required to lend, or not to lend at all. From the nature of their establishment, they have large funds which they can only dispose of in this way; and a part of the traders of the country are unfairly, and for the country, unprofitably benefited, by

that which they had experienced, the directors, February 26th, 1797, obtained permission to abstain from payment of their notes in cash. On Saturday, 25th, they had only £1,272,000 in coin and bullion to meet their liabilities. Ricardo was probably mistaken as to what might have happened had they continued to pay in cash.]

being enabled to supply themselves with an instrument of trade, at a less charge than those who must be influenced only by market price.

The whole business, which the whole community can carry on, depends on the quantity of its capital, that is, of its raw material, machinery, food, vessels, etc., employed in production. After a well regulated paper money is established, these can neither be increased nor diminished by the operations of banking. If, then, the State were to issue the paper money of the country, although it should never discount a bill, or lend one shilling to the public, there would be no alteration in the amount of trade; for we should have the same quantity of raw materials, of machinery, food, and ships; and it is probable, too, that the same amount of money might be lent, not always at 5 per cent. indeed, a rate fixed by law, when that might be under the market rate, but at 6, 7, or 8 per cent., the result of the fair competition in the market between the lenders and the borrowers.

Adam Smith speaks of the advantages derived by merchants from the superiority of the Scotch mode of affording accommodation to trade, over the English mode, by means of cash accounts. These cash accounts are credits given by the Scotch banker to his customers, in addition to the bills which he discounts for them; but, as the banker, in proportion as he advances money, and sends it into circulation in one way, is debarred from issuing so much in the other, it is difficult to perceive in what the advantage consists. If the whole circulation will bear only one million of paper, one million only will be circulated; and it can be of no real importance either to the banker or merchant, whether the whole be issued in discounting bills, or a part be so issued, and the remainder be issued by means of these cash accounts.

§130. It may perhaps be necessary to say a few words on the subject of the two metals, gold and silver, which are employed in currency, particularly as this question appears to perplex, in many people's minds, the plain and simple principles of currency. 'In England,' says Dr. Smith, 'gold was not considered as a legal tender for a long time after it was coined into money. The proportion between the values of gold and silver money was not fixed by any public law or proclamation, but was left to be settled by the market. If a debtor offered payment in gold, the creditor might either reject such payment altogether, or accept of it at such a valuation of the gold, as he and his debtor could agree upon.'

In this state of things it is evident that a guinea might sometimes pass for 22s. or more, and sometimes for 18s. or less, depending entirely on the alteration in the relative market value of gold and silver. All the variations, too, in the value of gold, as well as in the value of silver, would be rated in the gold coin, – it would appear as if silver was invariable, and as if gold only was subject to rise and fall. Thus, although a guinea passed for 22s. instead of 18s., gold might not have varied in value; the variation might have been wholly confined to the silver, and therefore 22s. might have been of no more value than 18s. were before. And, on the contrary, the whole variation might have been in the gold: a guinea, which was worth 18s., might have risen to the value of 22s.

If now we suppose this silver currency to be debased by clipping, and also increased in quantity, a guinea might pass for 30s.; for the silver in 30s. of such debased money might be of no more value than the gold in one guinea. By restoring the silver currency to its Mint value, silver money would rise: but it would appear as if gold fell, for a guinea would probably be of no more value than 21 of such good shillings.

If now gold be also made a legal tender, and every debtor be at liberty to discharge a debt by the payment of 420 shillings, or twenty guineas for every £21 that he owes, he will pay in one or the other according as he can most cheaply discharge his debt. If with five quarters of wheat he can procure as much gold bullion as the Mint will coin into twenty guineas, and for the same wheat as much silver bullion as the Mint will coin for him into 430 shillings, he will prefer paying in silver, because he would be a gainer of ten shillings by so paying his debt. But if, on the contrary, he could obtain with his wheat as much gold as would be coined into twenty guineas and a half, and as much silver only as would coin into 420 shillings he would naturally prefer paying his debt in gold. If the quantity of gold which he could procure could be coined only into twenty guineas, and the quantity of silver into 420 shillings, it would be a matter of perfect indifference to him in which money, silver or gold, it was that he paid his debt. It is not then a matter of chance; it is not because gold is better fitted for carrying on the circulation of a rich country, that gold is ever preferred for the purpose of paying debts; but, simply, because it is the interest of the debtor so to pay them.

During a long period previous to 1797, the year of the restriction on the Bank payments in coin, gold was so cheap, compared with silver, that it suited the Bank of England, and all other debtors, to purchase gold in the market, and not silver, for the purpose of carrying it to the Mint to be coined, as they could in that coined metal more cheaply discharge their debts. The silver currency was, during a great part of this period, very much debased; but it existed in a degree of scarcity, and, therefore, on the principle which I have before explained, it never sunk in its current value. Though so debased, it was still the interest of debtors to pay in the gold coin. If, indeed, the quantity of this debased silver coin had been enormously great, or if the Mint had issued such debased pieces, it might have been the interest of debtors to pay in this debased money; but its quantity was limited, and it sustained its value, and, therefore, gold was in practice the real standard of currency.

That it was so, is no where denied; but it has been contended, that it was made so by the law, which declared that silver should not be a legal tender for any debt exceeding £25, unless by weight, according to the Mint standard.

But this law did not prevent any debtor from paying his debt, however large its amount, in silver currency fresh from the Mint; that the debtor did not pay in this metal, was not a matter of chance, nor a matter of compulsion, but wholly the effect of choice; it did not suit him to take silver to the Mint, it did suit him to take gold thither. It is probable, that if the quantity of this debased silver in circulation had been enormously great, and also a legal tender, that a guinea would have been again worth thirty shillings; but it would have been the debased shilling that would have fallen in value, and not the guinea that had risen.

It appears, then, that whilst each of the two metals was equally a legal tender for debts of any amount, we were subject to a constant change in the principal standard measure of value. It would sometimes be gold, sometimes silver, depending entirely on the variations in the relative value of the two metals; and at such times the metal, which was not the standard, would be melted, and withdrawn from circulation, as its value would be greater in bullion than in coin. This was an inconvenience, which it was highly desirable should be remedied; but so slow is the progress of improvement, that although it had been unanswerably demonstrated by Mr. Locke, and had been noticed by all writers on the subject of money since his day, a better system was never adopted till the session of Parliament, 1816, when it was enacted that gold only should be a legal tender for any sum exceeding forty shillings.

Dr. Smith does not appear to have been quite aware of the effect of employing two metals as currency, and both a legal tender for debts of any amount; for he says, that 'in reality, during the continuance of any one regulated proportion between the respective values of the different metals in coin, the value of the most precious metal regulates the value of the whole coin.' Because gold was in his day the medium in which it suited debtors to pay their debts, he thought that it had some inherent quality by which it did then, and always would regulate the value of silver coin.

On the reformation of the gold coin in 1774, a new guinea fresh from the Mint, would exchange for only twenty-one debased shillings; but in the reign of King William, when the silver coin was in precisely the same condition, a guinea also new and fresh from the Mint would exchange for thirty shillings. On this Mr. Buchanan observes, 'Here, then, is a most singular fact, of which the common theories of currency offer no account; the guinea exchanging at one time for thirty shillings, its intrinsic worth in a debased silver currency, and afterwards the same guinea exchanged for only twenty-one of those debased shillings. It is clear that some great change must have intervened in the state of the currency between these two different periods, of which Dr. Smith's hypothesis offers no explanation.'

It appears to me, that the difficulty may be very simply solved, by referring this different state of the value of the guinea at the two periods mentioned, to the different *quantities* of debased silver currency in circulation. In King William's reign gold was not a legal tender; it passed only at a conventional value. All the large payments were probably made in silver, particularly as paper currency, and the operations of banking, were then little understood. The quantity of this debased silver money exceeded the quantity of silver money, which would have been maintained in circulation, if nothing but undebased money had been in use; and, consequently, it was depreciated as well as debased. But in the succeeding period when gold was a legal tender, when Bank notes also were used in effecting payments, the quantity of debased silver money did not exceed the quantity of silver coin fresh from the Mint, which would have circulated if there had been no debased silver money; hence, though the money was debased, it was not depreciated. Mr. Buchanan's explanation is somewhat different; he thinks that a subsidiary currency is not liable to depreciation, but that the main currency is. In King William's reign silver was the main currency, and hence was liable to depreciation. In 1774 it was a subsidiary currency, and, therefore, maintained its value. Depreciation, however, does not depend on a currency being the subsidiary or the main currency, it depends wholly on its being in excess of quantity.*

* It has lately been contended in parliament by Lord Lauderdale, that, with the existing Mint regulation, the Bank could not pay their notes in specie, because the relative value of the two metals is such, that it would be for the interest of all debtors to pay their debts with silver and not with gold coin, while the law gives a power to all the creditors of the Bank to demand gold in exchange for Bank notes. This gold, his Lordship thinks, could be profitably exported, and if so, he contends that the Bank, to keep a supply, will be obliged to buy gold constantly at a premium, and sell it at par. If every other debtor could pay in silver, Lord Lauderdale would be right; but he cannot do so if his debt exceed 40s. This, then, would limit the amount of silver coin in circulation; (if Government had not reserved to itself the power to stop the coinage of that metal whenever they might think it expedient,) because if too much silver were coined, it would sink in relative value to gold, and no man would accept it in payment for a debt exceeding 40 shillings, unless a compensation were made for its lower value. To pay a debt of £100, one hundred sovereigns, or Bank notes to the amount of £100 would be necessary, but £105 in silver coin might be required, if there were too much silver in circulation. There are, then, two checks against an excessive quantity of silver coin: first, the direct check which Government may at any time interpose to prevent more from being coined; secondly, no motive of interest would lead any one to take silver to the Mint, if he might do so, for if it were coined, it would not pass current at its Mint, but only at its market value.

To a moderate seignorage on the coinage of money there cannot be much objection, particularly on that currency which is to effect the smaller payments. Money is generally enhanced in value to the full amount of the seignorage, and, therefore, it is a tax which in no way effects those who pay it, while the quantity of money is not in excess. It must, however, be remarked, that in a country where a paper currency is established, although the issuers of such paper should be liable to pay it in specie on the demand of the holder, still, both their notes and the coin might be depreciated to the full amount of the seignorage on that coin, which is alone the legal tender, before the check, which limits the circulation of paper, would operate. If the seignorage of gold coin were 5 per cent. for instance, the currency, by an abundant issue of Bank notes, might be really depreciated 5 per cent. before it would be the interest of the holders to demand coin for the purpose of melting it into bullion; a depreciation to which we should never be exposed, if either there was no seignorage on the gold coin; or, if a seignorage were allowed, the holders of Bank notes might demand bullion, and not coin, in exchange for them, at the Mint price of £3 17s. 10½d. Unless, then, the Bank should be obliged to pay their notes in bullion or coin, at the will of the holder, the late law which allows a seignorage of 6 per cent., or four-pence per oz., on the silver coin, but which directs that gold shall be coined by the Mint without any charge whatever, is perhaps the most proper, as it will most effectually prevent any unnecessary variation of the currency.

John Stuart Mill (1806–73)

Extract from *Principles of Political Economy with Some of their Applications to Social Philosophy* (1848).

CHAPTER VII

OF MONEY

§ 1. HAVING proceeded thus far in ascertaining the general laws of Value, without introducing the idea of Money (except occasionally for illustration,) it is time that we should now superadd that idea, and consider in what manner the principles of the mutual interchange of commodities are affected by the use of what is termed a Medium of Exchange.

In order to understand the manifold functions of a Circulating Medium, there is no better way than to consider what are the principal inconveniences which we should experience if we had not such a medium. The first and most obvious would be the want of a common measure for values of different sorts. If a tailor had only coats, and wanted to buy bread or a horse, it would be very troublesome to ascertain how much bread he ought to obtain for a coat, or how many coats he should give for a horse. The calculation must be recommenced on different data, every time he bartered his coats for a different kind of article; and there could be no current price, or regular quotations of value. Whereas now each thing has a current price in money, and he gets over all difficulties by reckoning his coat at 4l. or 5l., and a four-pound loaf at 6d. or 7d. As it is much easier to compare different lengths by expressing them in a common language of feet and inches, so it is much easier to compare values by means of a common language of pounds, shillings, and pence. In no other way can values be arranged one above another in a scale; in no other can a person conveniently calculate the sum of his possessions; and it is easier to ascertain and remember the relations of many things to one thing, than their innumerable cross relations with one another. This advantage of having a common language in which values may be expressed, is, even by itself, so important, that some such mode of expressing and computing them would probably be used even if a pound or a shilling did not express any real thing, but a mere unit of calculation. It is said that there are African tribes in which this somewhat artificial contrivance actually prevails. They calculate the value of things in a sort of money of account, called macutes. They say one thing is worth ten macutes, another fifteen, another twenty.* There is no real thing called a macute: it is a conventional unit, for the more convenient comparison of things with one another.

This advantage, however, forms but an inconsiderable part of the economical benefits derived from the use of money. The inconveniences of barter are so great, that without some more commodious means of effecting exchanges, the division of employments could hardly have been carried to any considerable extent. A tailor, who had nothing but coats, might starve before he could find any person having bread to sell who wanted a coat: besides, he would not want as much bread at a time as would be worth a coat, and the coat could not be divided. Every person, therefore, would at all times hasten to dispose of his commodity in exchange for anything which, though it might not be fitted to his own immediate wants, was in great and general demand, and easily divisible, so that he might be sure of being able to purchase with it whatever was offered for sale. The primary necessaries of life possess these properties in a high degree. Bread is extremely divisible, and an object of universal desire. Still, this is not the sort of thing required: for, of food, unless in expectation of a scarcity, no one wishes to possess more at once, than is wanted for immediate consumption; so that a person is never sure of finding an immediate purchaser for articles of food; and unless soon disposed of, most of them perish. The thing which people would select to keep by them for making purchases, must be one which, besides being divisible and generally desired, does not deteriorate by keeping. This reduces the choice to a small number of articles.

§ 2. By a tacit concurrence, almost all nations, at a very early period, fixed upon certain metals, and especially gold and silver, to serve this purpose. No other substances unite the necessary qualities in so great a degree, with so many subordinate advantages. Next to food and clothing, and in some climates even before clothing, the strongest inclination in a rude state of society is for personal ornament, and for the kind of distinction which is obtained by rarity or costliness in such ornaments. After the immediate necessities of life were satisfied, every one was eager to accumulate as great a store as possible of things at once costly and ornamental; which were chiefly gold, silver, and jewels. These were the things which it most pleased every one to possess, and which there was most certainty of finding others willing to receive in exchange for any kind of produce. They were among the most imperishable of all substances. They were also portable, and containing great value in small bulk, were easily hid; a consideration of much importance in an age of insecurity. Jewels are inferior to gold and silver in the quality of divisibility; and are of

* Montesquieu, *Esprit des Lois*, liv. xxii. ch. 8.

very various qualities, not to be accurately discriminated without great trouble. Gold and silver are eminently divisible, and when pure, always of the same quality; and their purity may be ascertained and certified by a public authority.

Accordingly, though furs have been employed as money in some countries, cattle in others, in Chinese Tartary cubes of tea closely pressed together, the shells called cowries on the coast of Western Africa, and in Abyssinia at this day blocks of rock salt; though even of metals, the less costly have sometimes been chosen, as iron in Lacedæmon from an ascetic policy, copper in the early Roman republic from the poverty of the people; gold and silver have been generally preferred by nations which were able to obtain them, either by industry, commerce, or conquest. To the qualities which originally recommended them, another came to be added, the importance of which only unfolded itself by degrees. Of all commodities they are among the least influenced by any of the causes which produce fluctuations of value. No commodity is quite free from such fluctuations. Gold and silver have sustained, since the beginning of history, one great permanent alteration of value, from the discovery of the American mines; and some temporary variations, such as that which, in the last great war, was produced by the absorption of the metals in hoards, and in the military chests of the immense armies constantly in the field. In the present age the opening of new sources of supply, so abundant as the Ural mountains, California, and Australia, may be the commencement of another period of decline, on the limits of which it would be useless at present to speculate. But on the whole, no commodities are so little exposed to causes of variation. They fluctuate less than almost any other things in their cost of production. And from their durability, the total quantity in existence is at all times so great in proportion to the annual supply, that the effect on value even of a change in the cost of production is not sudden: a very long time being required to diminish materially the quantity in existence, and even to increase it very greatly not being a rapid process. Gold and silver, therefore, are more fit than any other commodity to be the subject of engagements for receiving or paying a given quantity at some distant period. If the engagement were made in corn, a failure of crops might increase the burthen of the payment in one year to fourfold what was intended, or an exuberant harvest sink it in another to one-fourth. If stipulated in cloth, some manufacturing invention might permanently reduce the payment to a tenth of its original value. Such things have occurred even in the case of payments stipulated in gold and silver; but the great fall of their value after the discovery of America, is, as yet the only authenticated instance; and in this case the change was extremely gradual, being spread over a period of many years.

When gold and silver had become virtually a medium of exchange, by becoming the things for which people generally sold, and with which they generally bought, whatever they had to sell or to buy; the contrivance of coining obviously suggested itself. By this process the metal was divided into convenient portions, of any degree of smallness, and bearing a recognised proportion to one another; and the trouble was saved of weighing and assaying at every change of possessors, an inconvenience which on the occasion of small purchases would soon have become insupportable. Governments found it their interest to take the operation into their own hands, and to interdict all coining by private persons; indeed, their guarantee was often the only one which would have been relied on, a reliance however which very often it ill deserved; profligate governments having until a very modern period seldom scrupled, for the sake of robbing their creditors, to confer on all other debtors a licence to rob theirs, by the shallow and impudent artifice of lowering the standard; that least covert of all modes of knavery, which consists in calling a shilling a pound, that a debt of one hundred pounds may be cancelled by the payment of a hundred shillings. It would have been as simple a plan, and would have answered the purpose as well, to have enacted that 'a hundred' should always be interpreted to mean five, which would have effected the same reduction in all pecuniary contracts, and would not have been at all more shameless. Such strokes of policy have not wholly ceased to be recommended, but they have ceased to be practised; except occasionally through the medium of paper money, in which case the character of the transaction, from the greater obscurity of the subject, is a little less barefaced.

§ 3. Money, when its use has grown habitual, is the medium through which the incomes of the different members of the community are distributed to them, and the measure by which they estimate their possessions. As it is always by means of money that people provide for their different necessities, there grows up in their minds a powerful association leading them to regard money as wealth in a more peculiar sense than any other article; and even those who pass their lives in the production of the most useful objects, acquire the habit of regarding those objects as chiefly important by their capacity of being exchanged for money. A person who parts with money to obtain commodities, unless he intends to sell them, appears to the imagination to be making a worse bargain than a person who parts with commodities to get money; the one seems to be spending his means, the other adding to them. Illusions which, though now in some measure dispelled, were long powerful enough to overmaster the mind of every politician, both speculative and practical, in Europe.

It must be evident, however, that the mere introduction of a particular mode of exchanging things for one another by first exchanging a thing for money, and then exchanging the money for something else, makes no difference in the essential character of transactions. It is not with money that things are really purchased. Nobody's income (except that of the gold or silver miner) is derived from the precious metals. The pounds or shillings which a person receives weekly or yearly, are not what constitutes his income; they are a sort of tickets or orders which he can present for payment at any shop he pleases, and which entitle him to receive a certain value of any commodity that he makes choice of. The farmer pays his labourers and his landlord in these tickets, as the most convenient plan for himself and them; but their real income is their share of his corn, cattle, and hay, and it makes no essential difference whether he distributes it to them directly, or sells it for them and gives them the price; but as they would have to sell it for money if he did not, and as he is a seller at any rate, it best suits the purposes of all, that he should sell their share along with his own, and leave the labourers more leisure for work and the landlord for being idle. The capitalists, except those who are producers of the precious metals, derive no part of their income from those metals, since they only get them by buying them with their own produce: while all other persons have their incomes paid to them by the capitalists, or by those who have received payment from the capitalists; and as the capitalists have nothing, from the first, except their produce, it is that and nothing else which supplies all incomes furnished by them. There cannot, in short, be intrinsically a more insignificant thing, in the economy of society, than money; except in the character of a contrivance for sparing time and labour. It is a machine for doing quickly and commodiously, what would be done, though less quickly and commodiously, without it: and like many other kinds of machinery, it only exerts a distinct and independent influence of its own when it gets out of order.

The introduction of money does not interfere with the operation of any of the Laws of Value laid down in the preceding chapters. The reasons which make the temporary or market value of things depend on the demand and supply, and their average and permanent values upon their cost of production, are as applicable to a money system as to a system of barter. Things which by barter would exchange for one another, will, if sold for money, sell for an equal amount of it, and so will exchange for one another still, though the process of exchanging them will consist of two operations instead of only one. The relations of commodities to one another remain unaltered by money: the only new relation introduced is their relation to money itself; how much or how little money they will exchange for; in other words, how the Exchange Value of money itself is determined. And this is not a question of any difficulty, when the illusion is dispelled, which caused money to be looked upon as a peculiar thing, not governed by the same laws as other things. Money is a commodity, and its value is determined like that of other commodities, temporarily by demand and supply, permanently and on the average by cost of production. The illustration of these principles, considered in their application to money, must be given in some detail, on account of the confusion which, in minds not scientifically instructed on the subject, envelopes the whole matter; partly from a lingering remnant of the misleading associations, and partly from the mass of vapoury and baseless speculation with which this, more than any other topic of political economy, has in latter times become surrounded. I shall therefore treat of the Value of Money in a chapter apart.

CHAPTER VIII

OF THE VALUE OF MONEY, AS DEPENDENT ON DEMAND AND SUPPLY

§ 1. IT is unfortunate that in the very outset of the subject we have to clear from our path a formidable ambiguity of language. The Value of Money is to appearance an expression as precise, as free from possibility of misunderstanding, as any in science. The value of a thing is what it will exchange for: the value of money is what money will exchange for; the purchasing power of money. If prices are low, money will buy much of other things, and is of high value; if prices are high, it will buy little of other things, and is of low value. The value of money is inversely as general prices: falling as they rise, and rising as they fall.

But unhappily the same phrase is also employed, in the current language of commerce, in a very different sense. Money, which is so commonly understood as the synonym of wealth, is more especially the term in use to denote it when it is the subject of borrowing. When one person lends to another, as well as when he pays wages or rent to another, what he transfers is not the mere money, but a right to a certain value of the produce of the country, to be selected at pleasure; the lender having first bought this right by giving for it a portion of his capital. What he really lends is so much capital; money is the mere instrument of transfer. But the capital usually passes from the lender to the receiver through the means either of money, or of an order to receive money, and at any rate it is in money that the capital is computed and estimated. Hence, borrowing capital is universally called borrowing money; the loan market is called the money market: those who have their capital disposable for investment on loan are called the monied class: and the equivalent given for the use of capital, or in other words, interest, is not only called the interest of money, but, by a grosser perversion of terms, the value of money. This misapplication of language, assisted by some fallacious appearances which we shall notice and clear up hereafter,[*] has created a general notion among persons in business, that the Value of Money, meaning the rate of interest, has an intimate connexion with the Value of Money in its proper sense, the value or purchasing power of the circulating medium. We shall return to this subject before long: at present it is enough to say, that by Value I shall always mean Exchange Value, and by money the medium of exchange, not the capital which is passed from hand to hand through that medium.

§ 2. The value or purchasing power of money depends, in the first instance, on demand and supply. But demand and supply, in relation to money, present themselves in a somewhat different shape from the demand and supply of other things.

The supply of a commodity means the quantity offered for sale. But it is not usual to speak of offering money for sale. People are not usually said to buy or sell money. This, however, is merely an accident of language. In point of fact, money is bought and sold like other things, whenever other things are bought and sold *for* money. Whoever sells corn, or tallow, or cotton, buys money. Whoever buys bread, or wine, or clothes, sells money to the dealer in those articles. The money with which people are offering to buy is money offered for sale. The supply of money, then, is the quantity of it which people are wanting to lay out; that is, all the money they have in their possession, except what they are hoarding, or at least keeping by them as a reserve for future contingencies. The supply of money, in short, is all the money in *circulation* at the time.

The demand for money, again, consists of all the goods offered for sale. Every seller of goods is a buyer of money, and the goods he brings with him constitute his demand. The demand for money differs from the demand for other things in this, that it is limited only by the means of the purchaser. The demand for other things is for so much and no more; but there is always a demand for as much money as can be got. Persons may indeed refuse to sell, and withdraw their goods from the market, if they cannot get for them what they consider a sufficient price. But this is only when they think that the price will rise, and that they shall get more money by waiting. If they thought the low price likely to be permanent, they would take what they could get. It is always a *sine quâ non* with a dealer to dispose of his goods.

As the whole of the goods in the market compose the demand for money, so the whole of the money constitutes the demand for goods. The money and the goods are seeking each other for the purpose of being exchanged. They are reciprocally supply and demand to one another. It is indifferent whether, in

* Infra, chap. xxiii.

characterizing the phenomena, we speak of the demand and supply of goods, or the supply and the demand of money. They are equivalent expressions.

We shall proceed to illustrate this proposition more fully. And in doing this, the reader will remark a great difference between the class of questions which now occupy us, and those which we previously had under discussion respecting Values. In considering Value, we were only concerned with causes which acted upon particular commodities apart from the rest. Causes which affect all commodities alike do not act upon values. But in considering the relation between goods and money, it is with the causes that operate upon all goods whatever that we are specially concerned. We are comparing goods of all sorts on one side, with money on the other side, as things to be exchanged against each other.

Suppose, everything else being the same, that there is an increase in the quantity of money, say by the arrival of a foreigner in a place, with a treasure of gold and silver. When he commences expending it (for this question it matters not whether productively or unproductively), he adds to the supply of money, and, by the same act, to the demand for goods. Doubtless he adds, in the first instance, to the demand only for certain kinds of goods, namely, those which he selects for purchase; he will immediately raise the price of those, and so far as he is individually concerned, of those only. If he spends his funds in giving entertainments, he will raise the prices of food and wine. If he expends them in establishing a manufactory, he will raise the prices of labour and materials. But at the higher prices, more money will pass into the hands of the sellers of these different articles; and they, whether labourers or dealers, having more money to lay out, will create an increased demand for all the things which they are accustomed to purchase: these accordingly will rise in price, and so on until the rise has reached everything. I say everything, though it is of course possible that the influx of money might take place through the medium of some new class of consumers, or in such a manner as to alter the proportions of different classes of consumers to one another, so that a greater share of the national income than before would thenceforth be expended in some articles, and a smaller in others; exactly as if a change had taken place in the tastes and wants of the community. If this were the case, then until production had accommodated itself to this change in the comparative demand for different things, there would be a real alteration in values, and some things would rise in price more than others, while some perhaps would not rise at all. These effects, however, would evidently proceed, not from the mere increase of money, but from accessory circumstances attending it. We are now only called upon to consider what would be the effect of an increase of money, considered by itself. Supposing the money in the hands of individuals to be increased, the want and inclinations of the community collectively in respect to consumption remaining exactly the same; the increase of demand would reach all things equally, and there would be an universal rise of prices. We might suppose, with Hume, that some morning, every person in the nation should wake and find a gold coin in his pocket: this example, however, would involve an alteration of the proportions in the demand for different commodities; the luxuries of the poor would, in the first instance, be raised in price in a much greater degree than other things. Let us rather suppose, therefore, that to every pound, or shilling, or penny, in the possession of any one, another pound, shilling, or penny, were suddenly added. There would be an increased money demand, and consequently an increased money value, or price, for things of all sorts. This increased value would do no good to any one; would make no difference, except that of having to reckon pounds, shillings, and pence, in higher numbers. It would be an increase of values only as estimated in money, a thing only wanted to buy other things with; and would not enable any one to buy more of them than before. Prices would have risen in a certain ratio, and the value of money would have fallen in the same ratio.

It is to be remarked that this ratio would be precisely that in which the quantity of money had been increased. If the whole money in circulation was doubled, prices would be doubled. If it was only increased one-fourth, prices would rise one-fourth. There would be one-fourth more money, all of which would be used to purchase goods of some description. When there had been time for the increased supply of money to reach all markets, or (according to the conventional metaphor) to permeate all the channels of circulation, all prices would have risen one-fourth. But the general rise of price is independent of this diffusing and equalizing process. Even if some prices were raised more, and others less, the average rise would be one-fourth. This is a necessary consequence of the fact that a fourth more money would have been given for only the same quantity of goods. *General* prices, therefore, would in any case be a fourth higher.

The very same effect would be produced on prices if we suppose the goods diminished, instead of the money increased: and the contrary effect if the goods were increased or the money diminished. If there were less money in the hands of the community, and the same amount of goods to be sold, less money altogether would be given for them, and they would be sold at lower prices; lower, too, in the precise ratio in which the money was diminished. So that the value of money, other things being the same, varies inversely as its quantity; every increase of quantity lowering the value, and every diminution raising it, in a ratio exactly equivalent.

This, it must be observed, is a property peculiar to money. We did not find it to be true of commodities generally, that every diminution of supply raised the value exactly in proportion to the deficiency, or that every increase lowered it in the precise ratio of the excess. Some things are usually affected in a greater ratio than that of the excess or deficiency, others usually in a less: because, in ordinary cases of demand, the desire, being for the thing itself, may be stronger or weaker: and the amount of what people are willing to expend on it, being in any case a limited quantity, may be affected in very unequal degrees by difficulty or facility of attainment. But in the case of money, which is desired as the means of universal purchase, the demand consists of everything which people have to sell; and the only limit to what they are willing to give is the limit set by their having nothing more to offer. The whole of the goods being in any case exchanged for the whole of the money which comes into the market to be laid out, they will sell for less or more of it, exactly according as less or more is brought.

§ 3. From what precedes, it might for a moment be supposed that all the goods on sale in a country, at any one time, are exchanged for all the money existing and in circulation at that same time: or, in other words, that there is always in circulation in a country a quantity of money equal in value to the whole of the goods then and there on sale. But this would be a complete misapprehension. The money laid out is equal in value to the goods it purchases; but the quantity of money laid out is not the same thing with the quantity in circulation. As the money passes from hand to hand, the same piece of money is laid out many times, before all the things on sale at one time are purchased and finally removed from the market: and each pound or dollar must be counted for as many pounds or dollars, as the number of times it changes hands in order to effect this object. The greater part of the goods must also be counted more than once, not only because most things pass through the hands of several sets of manufacturers and dealers before they assume the form in which they are finally consumed, but because in times of speculation (and all times are so, more or less) the same goods are often bought repeatedly, to be resold for a profit, before they are bought for the purpose of consumption at all.

If we assume the quantity of goods on sale, and the number of times those goods are resold, to be fixed quantities, the value of money will depend upon its quantity, together with the average number of times that each piece changes hands in the process. The whole of the goods sold (counting each resale of the same goods as so much added to the goods) have been exchanged for the whole of the money, multiplied by the number of purchases made on the average by each piece. Consequently, the amount of goods and of transactions being the same, the value of money is inversely as its quantity multiplied by what is called the rapidity of circulation. And the quantity of money in circulation is equal to the money value of all the goods sold, divided by the number which expresses the rapidity of circulation.

The phrase, rapidity of circulation, requires some comment. It must not be understood to mean the number of purchases made by each piece of money in a given time. Time is not the thing to be considered. The state of society may be such that each piece of money hardly performs more than one purchase in a year: but if this arises from the small number of transactions – from the small amount of business done, the want of activity in traffic, or because what traffic there is, mostly takes place by barter – it constitutes no reason why prices should be lower, or the value of money higher. The essential point is, not how often the same money changes hands in a given time, but how often it changes hands in order to perform a given amount of traffic. We must compare the number of purchases made by the money in a given time, not with the time itself, but with the goods sold in that same time. If each piece of money changes hands on an average ten times while goods are sold to the value of a million sterling, it is evident that the money required to circulate those goods is 100,000*l*. And conversely, if the money in circulation is 100,000*l*., and each piece changes hands by the purchase of goods ten times in a month, the sales of goods for money which take place every month must amount on the average to 1,000,000*l*.

Rapidity of circulation being a phrase so ill adapted to express the only thing which it is of any importance to express by it, and having a tendency to confuse the subject by suggesting a meaning extremely different from the one intended, it would be a good thing if the phrase could be got rid of, and another substituted, more directly significant of the idea meant to be conveyed. Some such expression as 'the efficiency of money,' though not unexceptionable, would do better; as it would point attention to the quantity of work done, without suggesting the idea of estimating it by time. Until an appropriate term can be devised, we must be content, when ambiguity is to be apprehended, to express the idea by the circumlocution which alone conveys it adequately, namely, the average number of purchases made by each piece in order to effect a given pecuniary amount of transactions.

§ 4. The proposition which we have laid down respecting the dependence of general prices upon the quantity of money in circulation, must be understood as applying only to a state of things in which money, that is, gold or silver, is the exclusive instrument of exchange, and actually passes from hand to hand at every purchase, credit in any of its shapes being unknown. When credit comes into play as a means of purchasing, distinct from money in hand, we shall hereafter find that the connexion between prices and the amount of the circulating medium is much less direct and intimate, and that such connexion as does exist no longer admits of so simple a mode of expression. But on a subject so full of complexity as that of currency and prices, it is necessary to lay the foundation of our theory in a thorough understanding of the most simple cases, which we shall always find lying as a groundwork or substratum under those which arise in practice. That an increase of the quantity of money raises prices, and a diminution lowers them, is the most elementary proposition in the theory of currency, and without it we should have no key to any of the others. In any state of things, however, except the simple and primitive one which we have supposed, the proposition is only true other things being the same: and what those other things are, which must be the same, we are not yet ready to pronounce. We can, however, point out, even now, one or two of the cautions with which the principle must be guarded in attempting to make use of it for the practical explanation of phenomena; cautions the more indispensable, as the doctrine, though a scientific truth, has of late years been the foundation of a greater mass of false theory, and erroneous interpretation of facts, than any other proposition relating to interchange. From the time of the resumption of cash payments by the Act of 1819, and especially since the commercial crisis of 1825, the favourite explanation of every rise or fall of prices has been the 'currency;' and like most popular theories, the doctrine has been applied with little regard to the conditions necessary for making it correct.

For example, it is habitually assumed that whenever there is a greater amount of money in the country, or in existence, a rise of prices must necessarily follow. But this is by no means an inevitable consequence. In no commodity is it the quantity in existence, but the quantity offered for sale, that determines the value. Whatever may be the quantity of money in the country, only that part of it will affect prices which goes into the market of commodities, and is there actually exchanged against goods. Whatever increases the amount of this portion of the money in the country, tends to raise prices. But money hoarded does not act on prices. Money kept in reserve by individuals to meet contingencies which do not occur, does not act on prices. The money in the coffers of the Bank, or retained as a reserve by private bankers, does not act on prices until drawn out, nor even then unless drawn out to be expended in commodities.

It frequently happens that money, to a considerable amount, is brought into the country, is there actually invested as capital, and again flows out, without having ever once acted upon the markets of commodities, but only upon the market of securities, or, as it is commonly though improperly called, the money market. Let us return to the case already put for illustration, that of a foreigner landing in the country with a treasure. We supposed him to employ his treasure in the purchase of goods for his own use, or in setting up a manufactory and employing labourers; and in either case he would, *cæteris paribus*, raise prices. But instead of doing either of these things, he might very probably prefer to invest his fortune at interest; which we shall suppose him to do in the most obvious way, by becoming a competitor for a portion of the stock, exchequer bills, railway debentures, mercantile bills, mortgages, &c., which are at all times in the hands of the public. By doing this he would raise the prices of those different securities, or in other words would lower the rate of interest; and since this would disturb the relation previously existing between the rate of interest on capital in the country itself, and that in foreign countries, it would probably induce some of those who had floating capital seeking employment, to send it abroad for foreign investment rather than buy securities at home at the advanced price. As much money might thus go out as had previously come in, while the prices of commodities would have shown no trace of its temporary presence. This is a case highly deserving of attention: and it is a fact now beginning to be recognised, that the passage of the precious metals from country to country is determined much more than was formerly supposed by the state of the loan market in different countries, and much less by the state of prices.

Another point must be adverted to, in order to avoid serious error in the interpretation of mercantile phenomena. If there be, at any time, an increase in the number of money transactions, a thing continually liable to happen from differences in the activity of speculation, and even in the time of year (since certain kinds of business are transacted only at particular seasons); an increase of the currency which is only proportional to this increase of transactions, and is of no longer duration, has no tendency to raise prices. At the quarterly periods when the public dividends are paid at the Bank, a sudden increase takes place of the money in the hands of the public; an increase estimated at from a fifth to two-fifths of the whole issues of the Bank of England. Yet this never has any effect on prices; and in a very few weeks, the currency has again shrunk into its usual dimensions, by a mere reduction in the demands of the public (after so copious a supply of ready money) for accommodation from the Bank in the way of discount or loan. In like manner the currency of the agricultural districts fluctuates in amount at different seasons of the year. It is always lowest in August: 'it rises generally towards Christmas, and obtains its greatest elevation about Lady-day, when the farmer commonly lays in his stock, and has to pay his rent and summer taxes,' and when he therefore makes his principal applications to country bankers for loans. 'Those variations occur with the same regularity as the season, and with just as little disturbance of the markets as the quarterly fluctuations of the notes of the Bank of England. As soon as the extra payments have been completed, the superfluous' currency, which is estimated at half a million, 'as certainly and immediately is reabsorbed and disappears.'[*]

If extra currency were not forthcoming to make these extra payments, one of three things must happen. Either the payments must be made without money, by a resort to some of those contrivances by which its use is dispensed with; or there must be an increase in the rapidity of circulation, the same sum of money being made to perform more payments; or, if neither of these things took place, money to make the extra payments must be withdrawn from the market for commodities, and prices, consequently, must fall. An increase of the circulating medium, conformable in extent and duration to the temporary stress of business, does not raise prices, but merely prevents this fall.

The sequel of our investigation will point out many other qualifications with which the proposition must be received, that the value of the circulating medium depends on the demand and supply, and is in the inverse ratio of the quantity; qualifications which, under a complex system of credit like that existing in England, render the proposition an extremely incorrect expression of the fact.

---

* Fullarton, *Regulation of Currencies*, 2nd edit. pp. 87–9.

CHAPTER IX

OF THE VALUE OF MONEY, AS DEPENDENT ON COST OF PRODUCTION

§ 1. BUT money, no more than commodities in general, has its value definitely determined by demand and supply. The ultimate regulator of its value is Cost of Production.

We are supposing, of course, that things are left to themselves. Governments have not always left things to themselves. They have undertaken to prevent the quantity of money from adjusting itself according to spontaneous laws, and have endeavoured to regulate it at their pleasure; generally with a view of keeping a greater quantity of money in the country, than would otherwise have remained there. It was, until lately, the policy of all governments to interdict the exportation and the melting of money; while, by encouraging the exportation and impeding the importation of other things, they endeavoured to have a stream of money constantly flowing in. By this course they gratified two prejudices; they drew, or thought that they drew, more money into the country, which they believed to be tantamount to more wealth; and they gave, or thought that they gave, to all producers and dealers, high prices, which, though no real advantage, people are always inclined to suppose to be one.

In this attempt to regulate the value of money artificially by means of the supply, governments have never succeeded in the degree, or even in the manner, which they intended. Their prohibitions against exporting or melting the coin have never been effectual. A commodity of such small bulk in proportion to its value is so easily smuggled, and still more easily melted, that it has been impossible by the most stringent measures to prevent these operations. All the risk which it was in the power of governments to attach to them, was outweighed by a very moderate profit.* In the more indirect mode of aiming at the

---

* The effect of the prohibition cannot, however, have been so entirely insignificant as it has been supposed to be by writers on the subject. The facts adduced by Mr. Fullarton, in the note to page 7 of his work on the *Regulation of Currencies*, shows that it required a greater percentage of difference in value between coin and bullion than has commonly been imagined, to bring the coin to the melting-pot.

same purpose, by throwing difficulties in the way of making the returns for exported goods in any other commodity than money, they have not been quite so unsuccessful. They have not, indeed, succeeded in making money flow continuously into the country; but they have to a certain extent been able to keep it at a higher than its natural level; and have, thus far, removed the value of money from exclusive dependence on the causes which fix the value of things not artificially interfered with.

We are, however, to suppose a state, not of artificial regulation, but of freedom. In that state, and assuming no charge to be made for coinage, the value of money will conform to the value of the bullion of which it is made. A pound weight of gold or silver in coin, and the same weight in an ingot, will precisely exchange for one another. On the supposition of freedom, the metal cannot be worth more in the state of bullion than of coin; for as it can be melted without any loss of time, and with hardly any expense, this would of course be done until the quantity in circulation was so much diminished as to equalize its value with that of the same weight in bullion. It may be thought however that the coin, though it cannot be of less, may be, and being a manufactured article will naturally be, of greater value than the bullion contained in it, on the same principle on which linen cloth is of more value than an equal weight of linen yarn. This would be true, were it not that Government, in this country, and in some others, coins money gratis for anyone who furnishes the metal. The labour and expense of coinage, when not charged to the possessor, do not raise the value of the article. If Government opened an office where, on delivery of a given weight of yarn, it returned the same weight of cloth to any one who asked for it, cloth would be worth no more in the market than the yarn it contained. As soon as coin is worth a fraction more than the value of the bullion, it becomes the interest of the holders of bullion to send it to be coined. If Government, however, throws the expense of coinage, as is reasonable, upon the holder, by making a charge to cover the expense (which is done by giving back rather less in coin than has been received in bullion, and is called levying a seignorage), the coin will rise, to the extent of the seignorage, above the value of the bullion. If the Mint kept back one per cent to pay the expense of coinage, it would be against the interest of the holders of bullion to have it coined, until the coin was more valuable than the bullion by at least that fraction. The coin, therefore, would be kept one per cent higher in value, which could only be by keeping it one per cent less in quantity, than if its coinage were gratuitous.

The Government might attempt to obtain a profit by the transaction, and might lay on a seignorage calculated for that purpose; but whatever they took for coinage beyond its expenses, would be so much profit on private coining. Coining, though not so easy an operation as melting, is far from a difficult one, and, when the coin produced is of full weight and standard fineness, is very

119

difficult to detect. If, therefore, a profit could be made by coining good money, it would certainly be done: and the attempt to make seignorage a source of revenue would be defeated. Any attempt to keep the value of the coin at an artificial elevation, not by a seignorage, but by refusing to coin, would be frustrated in the same manner.*

§ 2. The value of money, then, conforms, permanently, and, in a state of freedom, almost immediately, to the value of the metal of which it is made; with the addition, or not, of the expenses of coinage, according as those expenses are borne by the individual or by the state. This simplifies extremely the question which we have here to consider: since gold and silver bullion are commodities like any others, and their value depends, like that of other things, on their cost of production.

To the majority of civilized countries, gold and silver are foreign products: and the circumstances which govern the values of foreign products, present some questions which we are not yet ready to examine. For the present, therefore, we must suppose the country which is the subject of our inquiries, to be supplied with gold and silver by its own mines, reserving for future consideration how far our conclusions require modification to adapt them to the more usual case.

Of the three classes into which commodities are divided – those absolutely limited in supply, those which may be had in unlimited quantity at a given cost of production, and those which may be had in unlimited quantity, but at an increasing cost of production – the precious metals, being the produce of mines, belong to the third class. Their natural value, therefore, is in the long run proportional to their cost of production in the most unfavourable existing circumstances, that is, at the worst mine which it is necessary to work in order to obtain the required supply. A pound weight of gold will, in the gold-producing countries, ultimately tend to exchange for as much of every other commodity as is produced at a cost equal to its own; meaning by its own cost the cost in labour and expense, at the least productive sources of supply which the then existing demand makes it necessary to work. The average value of

* In England, though there is no seignorage on gold coin, (the Mint returning in coin the same weight of pure metal which it receives in bullion,) there is a delay of a few weeks after the bullion is deposited, before the coin can be obtained, occasioning a loss of interest, which, to the holder, is equivalent to a trifling seignorage. From this cause, the value of coin is in general slightly above that of the bullion it contains. An ounce of gold, according to the quantity of metal in a sovereign, should be worth 3*l.* 17*s.* 10½*d.*; but it was usually quoted at 3*l.* 17*s.* 6*d.*, until the Bank Charter Act of 1844 made it imperative on the Bank to give its notes for all bullion offered to it at the rate of 3*l.* 17*s.* 9*d.*

gold is made to conform to its natural value in the same manner as the values of other things are made to conform to their natural value. Suppose that it were selling above its natural value; that is, above the value which is an equiv- alent for the labour and expense of mining, and for the risks attending a branch of industry in which nine out of ten experiments have usually been fail- ures. A part of the mass of floating capital which is on the look out for investment, would take the direction of mining enterprise; the supply would thus be increased, and the value would fall. If, on the contrary, it were selling below its natural value, miners would not be obtaining the ordinary profit; they would slacken their works; if the depreciation was great, some of the infe- rior mines would perhaps stop working altogether: and a falling off in the annual supply, preventing the annual wear and tear from being completely compensated, would by degrees reduce the quantity, and restore the value.

When examined more closely, the following are the details of the process. If gold is above its natural or cost value – the coin, as we have seen, conforming in its value to the bullion – money will be of high value, and the prices of all things, labour included, will be low. These low prices will lower the expenses of all producers; but as their returns will also be lowered, no advantage will be obtained by any producer, except the producer of gold: whose returns from his mine, not depending on price, will be the same as before, and his expenses being less, he will obtain extra profits, and will be stimulated to increase his production. *E converso* if the metal is below its natural value: since this is as much as to say that prices are high, and the money expenses of all producers unusually great: for this, however, all other producers will be compensated by increased money returns: the miner alone will extract from his mine no more metal than before, while his expenses will be greater: his profits therefore being diminished or annihilated, he will diminish his production, if not abandon his employment.

In this manner it is that the value of money is made to conform to the cost of production of the metal of which it is made. It may be well, however, to repeat (what has been said before) that the adjustment takes a long time to effect, in the case of a commodity so generally desired and at the same time so durable as the precious metals. Being so largely used not only as money but for plate and ornament, there is at all times a very large quantity of these metals in existence: while they are so slowly worn out, that a comparatively small annual production is sufficient to keep up the supply, and to make any addition to it which may be required by the increase of goods to be circulated, or by the increased demand for gold and silver articles by wealthy consumers. Even if this small annual supply were stopt entirely, it would require many years to reduce the quantity so much as to make any very material difference in prices. The quantity may be increased much more rapidly than it can be diminished;

but the increase must be very great before it can make itself much felt over such a mass of the precious metals as exists in the whole commercial world. And hence the effects of all changes in the conditions of production of the precious metals are at first, and continue to be for many years, questions of quantity only, with little reference to cost of production. More especially is this the case when, as at the present time, many new sources of supply have been simultaneously opened, most of them practicable by labour alone, without any capital in advance beyond a pickaxe and a week's food; and when the operations are as yet wholly experimental, the comparative permanent productiveness of the different sources being entirely unascertained.

§ 3. Since, however, the value of money really conforms, like that of other things, though more slowly, to its cost of production, some political economists have objected altogether to the statement that the value of money depends on its quantity combined with the rapidity of circulation; which, they think, is assuming a law for money that does not exist for any other commodity, when the truth is that it is governed by the very same laws. To this we may answer, in the first place, that the statement in question assumes no peculiar law. It is simply the law of demand and supply, which is acknowledged to be applicable to all commodities, and which, in the case of money as of most other things, is controlled, but not set aside, by the law of cost of production, since cost of production would have no effect on value if it could have none on supply. But, secondly, there really is, in one respect, a closer connexion between the value of money and its quantity, than between the values of other things and their quantity. The value of other things conforms to the changes in the cost of production, without requiring, as a condition, that there should be any actual alteration of the supply: the potential alteration is sufficient; and if there even be an actual alteration, it is but a temporary one, except in so far as the altered value may make a difference in the demand, and so require an increase or diminution of supply, as a consequence, not a cause, of the alteration in value. Now this is also true of gold and silver, considered as articles of expenditure for ornament and luxury; but it is not true of money. If the permanent cost of production of gold were reduced one-fourth, it might happen that there would not be more of it bought for plate, gilding, or jewellery, than before; and if so, though the value would fall, the quantity extracted from the mines for these purposes would be no greater than previously. Not so with the portion used as money; that portion could not fall in value one-fourth, unless actually increased one-fourth; for, at prices one-fourth higher, one-fourth more money would be required to make the accustomed purchases; and if this were not forthcoming, some of the commodities would be without purchasers, and prices could not be kept up. Alterations, therefore, in the cost of production of the precious metals, do not act upon the value of money except just in proportion as they increase or diminish its quantity; which cannot be said of any other commodity. It would therefore, I conceive, be an error, both scientifically and practically, to discard the proposition which asserts a connexion between the value of money and its quantity.

It is evident, however, that the cost of production, in the long run, regulates the quantity; and that every country (temporary fluctuations excepted) will possess, and have in circulation, just that quantity of money which will perform all the exchanges required of it, consistently with maintaining a value conformable to its cost of production. The prices of things will, on the average, be such that money will exchange for its own cost in all other goods: and, precisely because the quantity cannot be prevented from affecting the value, the quantity itself will (by a sort of self-acting machinery) be kept at the amount consistent with that standard of prices – at the amount necessary for performing, at those prices, all the business required of it.

'The quantity wanted will depend partly on the cost of producing gold, and partly on the rapidity of its circulation. The rapidity of circulation being given, it would depend on the cost of production: and the cost of production being given, the quantity of money would depend on the rapidity of its circulation.'[*] After what has been already said, I hope that neither of these propositions stands in need of any further illustration.

Money, then, like commodities in general, having a value dependent on, and proportional to, its cost of production; the theory of money is, by the admission of this principle, stript of a great part of the mystery which apparently surrounded it. We must not forget, however, that this doctrine only applies to the places in which the precious metals are actually produced; and that we have yet to enquire whether the law of the dependence of value on cost of production applies to the exchange of things produced at distant places. But however this may be, our propositions with respect to value will require no other alteration, where money is an imported commodity, than that of substituting for the cost of its production the cost of obtaining it in the country. Every foreign commodity is bought by giving for it some domestic production; and the labour and capital which a foreign commodity costs to us is the labour and capital expended in producing the quantity of our own goods which we give in exchange for it. What this quantity depends upon, – what determines the proportions of interchange between the productions of one country and those of another, – is indeed a question of somewhat greater

---

* From some printed, but not published, Lectures of Mr. Senior: in which the great differences in the business done by money, as well as in the rapidity of its circulation, in different states of society and civilization, are interestingly illustrated.

complexity than those we have hitherto considered. But this at least is indisputable, that within the country itself the value of imported commodities is determined by the value, and consequently by the cost of production, of the equivalent given for them; and money, where it is an imported commodity, is subject to the same law.

CHAPTER X

OF A DOUBLE STANDARD, AND SUBSIDIARY COINS

§ 1. THOUGH the qualities necessary to fit any commodity for being used as money are rarely united in any considerable perfection, there are two commodities which possess them in an eminent, and nearly an equal degree; the two precious metals, as they are called; gold and silver. Some nations have accordingly attempted to compose their circulating medium of these two metals indiscriminately.

There is an obvious convenience in making use of the more costly metal for larger payments and the cheaper one for smaller: and the only question relates to the mode in which this can best be done. The mode most frequently adopted has been to establish between the two metals a fixed proportion; to decide, for example, that a gold coin called a sovereign should be equivalent to twenty of the silver coins called shillings: both the one and the other being called, in the ordinary money of account of the country, by the same denomination, a pound: and it being left free to every one who has a pound to pay, either to pay it in the one metal or in the other.

At the time when the valuation of the two metals relatively to each other, say twenty shillings to the sovereign, or twenty-one shillings to the guinea, was first made, the proportion probably corresponded, as nearly as it could be made to do, with the ordinary relative values of the two metals grounded on their cost of production: and if those natural or cost values always continued to bear the same ratio to one another, the arrangement would be unobjectionable. This, however, is far from being the fact. Gold and silver, though the least variable in value of all commodities, are not invariable, and do not always vary simultaneously. Silver, for example, was lowered in permanent value more than gold, by the discovery of the American mines; and those small variations of value which take place occasionally do not affect both metals alike. Suppose such a variation to take place: the value of the two metals relatively to one another no longer agreeing with their rated proportion, one or other of them will now be rated below its bullion value, and there will be a profit to be made by melting it.

Suppose, for example, that gold rises in value relatively to silver, so that the quantity of gold in a sovereign is now worth more than the quantity of silver in twenty shillings. Two consequences will ensue. No debtor will any longer find it his interest to pay in gold. He will always pay in silver, because twenty shillings are a legal tender for a debt of one pound, and he can procure silver convertible into twenty shillings for less gold than that contained in a sovereign. The other consequence will be, that unless a sovereign can be sold for more than twenty shillings, all the sovereigns will be melted, since as bullion they will purchase a greater number of shillings than they exchange for as coin. The converse of all this would happen if silver, instead of gold, were the metal which had risen in comparative value. A sovereign would not now be worth so much as twenty shillings, and whoever had a pound to pay would prefer paying it by a sovereign; while the silver coins would be collected for the purpose of being melted, and sold as bullion for gold at their real value, that is, above the legal valuation. The money of the community, therefore, would never really consist of both metals, but of the one only which, at the particular time, best suited the interest of debtors; and the standard of the currency would be constantly liable to change from the one metal to the other, at a loss, on each change, of the expense of coinage on the metal which fell out of use.

It appears, therefore, that the value of money is liable to more frequent fluctuations when both metals are a legal tender at a fixed valuation, than when the exclusive standard of the currency is either gold or silver. Instead of being only affected by variations in the cost of production of one metal it is subject to derangement from those of two. The particular kind of variation to which a currency is rendered more liable by having two legal standards, is a fall of value, or what is commonly called a depreciation; since practically that one of the two metals will always be the standard, of which the real has fallen below the rated value. If the tendency of the metals be to rise in value, all payments will be made in the one which has risen least; and if to fall, then in that which has fallen most.

§ 2. The plan of a double standard is still occasionally brought forward by here and there a writer or orator as a great improvement in currency. It is probable that, with most of its adherents, its chief merit is its tendency to a sort of depreciation, there being at all times abundance of supporters for any mode, either open or covert, of lowering the standard. Some, however, are influenced by an exaggerated estimate of an advantage which to a certain extent is real, that of being able to have recourse, for replenishing the circulation, to the united stock of gold and silver in the commercial world, instead of being confined to one of them, which, from accidental absorption, may not be obtainable with sufficient rapidity. The advantage without the disadvantages of a double standard, seems to be best obtained by those nations with whom one only of the two metals is a legal tender, but the other also is coined, and allowed to pass for whatever value the market assigns to it.

When this plan is adopted, it is naturally the more costly metal which is left to be bought and sold as an article of commerce. But nations which, like England, adopt the more costly of the two as their standard, resort to a different expedient for retaining them both in circulation, namely, to make silver a legal tender, but only for small payments. In England, no one can be compelled to receive silver in payment for a larger amount than forty shillings. With this regulation there is necessarily combined another, namely, that silver coin should be rated, in comparison with gold, somewhat above its intrinsic value; that there should not be, in twenty shillings, as much silver as is worth a sovereign: for if there were, a very slight turn of the market in its favour would make it worth more than a sovereign, and it would be profitable to melt the silver coin. The over-valuation of the silver coin creates an inducement to buy silver and send it to the Mint to be coined, since it is given back at a higher value than properly belongs to it: this, however, has been guarded against, by limiting the quantity of the silver coinage, which is not left, like that of gold, to the discretion of individuals, but is determined by the government, and restricted to the amount supposed to be required for small payments. The only precaution necessary is, not to put so high a valuation upon the silver, as to hold out a strong temptation to private coining.

CHAPTER XI

OF CREDIT, AS A SUBSTITUTE FOR MONEY

§ 1. THE functions of credit have been a subject of as much misunderstanding and as much confusion of ideas, as any single topic in Political Economy. This is not owing to any peculiar difficulty in the theory of the subject, but to the complex nature of some of the mercantile phenomena arising from the forms in which credit clothes itself; by which attention is diverted from the properties of credit in general, to the peculiarities of its particular forms.

As a specimen of the confused notions entertained respecting the nature of credit, we may advert to the exaggerated language so often used respecting its national importance. Credit has a great, but not, as many people seem to suppose, a magical power; it cannot make something out of nothing. How often is an extension of credit talked of as equivalent to a creation of capital, or as if credit actually were capital. It seems strange that there should be any need to point out, that credit being only permission to use the capital of another person, the means of production cannot be increased by it, but only transferred. If the borrower's means of production and of employing labour are increased by the credit given him, the lender's are as much diminished. The same sum cannot be used as capital both by the owner and also by the person to whom it is lent: it cannot supply its entire value in wages, tools, and materials, to two sets of labourers at once. It is true that the capital which A has borrowed from B, and makes use of in his business, still forms part of the wealth of B for other purposes: he can enter into arrangements in reliance on it, and can borrow, when needful, an equivalent sum on the security of it; so that to a superficial eye it might seem as if both B and A had the use of it at once. But the smallest consideration will show that when B has parted with his capital to A, the use of it as capital rests with A alone, and that B has no other service from it than in so far as his ultimate claim upon it serves him to obtain the use of another capital from a third person C. All capital (not his own) of which any person

128

has really the use, is, and must be, so much subtracted from the capital of some one else.*

§ 2. But though credit is but a transfer of capital from hand to hand, it is generally, and naturally, a transfer to hands more competent to employ the capital efficiently in production. If there were no such thing as credit, or if, from general insecurity and want of confidence, it were scantily practised, many persons who possess more or less of capital, but who, from their occupations, or for want of the necessary skill and knowledge, cannot personally superintend its employment, would derive no benefit from it: their funds would either lie idle, or would be, perhaps, wasted and annihilated in unskilful attempts to make them yield a profit. All this capital is now lent at interest, and made available for production. Capital thus circumstanced forms a large portion of the productive resources of any commercial country; and is naturally attracted to those producers or traders who, being in the greatest business, have the means of employing it to most advantage; because such are both the most desirous to obtain it, and able to give the best security. Although, therefore, the productive funds of the country are not increased by credit, they are called into a more complete state of productive activity. As the confidence on which credit is grounded extends itself, means are developed by which even the smallest portions of capital, the sums which each person keeps

* To make the proposition in the text strictly true, a corrective, though a very slight one, requires to be made. The circulating medium existing in a country at a given time, is partly employed in purchases for productive, and partly for unproductive consumption. According as a larger proportion of it is employed in the one way or in the other, the real capital of the country is greater or less. If, then, an addition were made to the circulating medium in the hands of unproductive consumers exclusively, a larger portion of the existing stock of commodities would be bought for unproductive consumption, and a smaller for a productive, which state of things, while it lasted, would be equivalent to a diminution of capital; and on the contrary, if the addition made be to the portion of the circulating medium which is in the hands of producers, and destined for their business, a greater portion of the commodities in the country will for the present be employed as capital, and a less portion unproductively. Now an effect of this latter character naturally attends some extensions of credit, especially when taking place in the form of bank notes, or other instruments of exchange. The additional bank notes are, in ordinary course, first issued to producers or dealers, to be employed as capital; and though the stock of commodities in the country is no greater than before, yet as a greater share of that stock now comes by purchase into the hands of producers and dealers, to that extent what would have been unproductively consumed is applied to production, and there is a real increase of capital. The effect ceases, and a counter-process takes place, when the additional credit is stopped, and the notes called in.

by him to meet contingencies, are made available for productive uses. The principal instruments for this purpose are banks of deposit. Where these do not exist, a prudent person must keep a sufficient sum unemployed in his own possession, to meet every demand which he has even a slight reason for thinking himself liable to. When the practice, however, has grown up of keeping this reserve not in his own custody but with a banker, many small sums, previously lying idle, becoming aggregated in the banker's hands; and the banker, being taught by experience what proportion of the amount is likely to be wanted in a given time, and knowing that if one depositor happens to require more than the average, another will require less, is able to lend the remainder, that is, the far greater part, to producers and dealers: thereby adding the amount, not indeed to the capital in existence, but to that in employment, and making a corresponding addition to the aggregate production of the community.

While credit is thus indispensable for rendering the whole capital of the country productive, it is also a means by which the industrial talent of the country is turned to better account for purposes of production. Many a person who has either no capital of his own, or very little, but who has qualifications for business which are known and appreciated by some possessors of capital, is enabled to obtain either advances in money, or more frequently goods on credit, by which his industrial capacities are made instrumental to the increase of the public wealth; and this benefit will be reaped far more largely, whenever, through better laws and better education, the community shall have made such progress in integrity, that personal character can be accepted as a sufficient guarantee not only against dishonestly appropriating, but against dishonestly risking, what belongs to another.

Such are, in the most general point of view, the uses of credit to the productive resources of the world. But these considerations only apply to the credit given to the industrious classes – to producers and dealers. Credit given by dealers to unproductive consumers is never an addition, but always a detriment, to the sources of public wealth. It makes over in temporary use, not the capital of the unproductive classes to the productive, but that of the productive to the unproductive. If A, a dealer, supplies goods to B, a landowner or annuitant, to be paid for at the end of five years, as much of the capital of A as is equal to the value of these goods remains for five years unproductive. During such a period, if payment had been made at once, the sum might have been several times expended and replaced, and goods to the amount might have been several times produced, consumed, and reproduced: consequently B's withholding 100*l.* for five years, even if he pays at last, has cost to the labouring classes of the community during that period an absolute loss of probably several times that amount. A, individually, is compensated, by putting a higher price upon his goods, which is ultimately paid by B: but there is no compensation made to the labouring classes, the chief sufferers by every diversion of capital, whether permanently or temporarily, to unproductive uses. The country has had 100*l*. less of capital during those five years, B having taken that amount from A's capital, and spent it unproductively, in anticipation of his own means, and having only after five years set apart a sum from his income and converted it into capital for the purpose of indemnifying A.

§ 3. Thus far of the general function of Credit in production. It is not a productive power in itself, though, without it, the productive powers already existing could not be brought into complete employment. But a more intricate portion of the theory of Credit is its influence on prices; the chief cause of most of the mercantile phenomena which perplex observers. In a state of commerce in which much credit is habitually given, general prices at any moment depend much more upon the state of credit than upon the quantity of money. For credit, though it is not productive power, is purchasing power; and a person who, having credit, avails himself of it in the purchase of goods, creates just as much demand for the goods, and tends quite as much to raise their price, as if he made an equal amount of purchases with ready money.

The credit which we are now called upon to consider, as a distinct purchasing power, independent of money, is of course not credit in its simplest form, that of money lent by one person to another, and paid directly into his hands; for when the borrower expends this in purchases, he makes the purchases with money, not credit, and exerts no purchasing power over and above that conferred by the money. The forms of credit which create purchasing power are those in which no money passes at the time, and very often none passes at all, the transaction being included with a mass of other transactions in an account, and nothing paid but a balance. This takes place in a variety of ways, which we shall proceed to examine, beginning, as is our custom, with the simplest.

First: Suppose A and B to be two dealers, who have transactions with each other both as buyers and as sellers. A buys from B on credit. B does the like with respect to A. At the end of the year, the sum of A's debts to B is set against the sum of B's debts to A, and it is ascertained to which side a balance is due. This balance, which may be less than the amount of many of the transactions singly, and is necessarily less than the sum of the transactions, is all that is paid in money; and perhaps even this is not paid, but carried over in an account current to the next year. A single payment of a hundred pounds may in this manner suffice to liquidate a long series of transactions, some of them to the value of thousands.

But secondly: The debts of A to B may be paid without the intervention of money, even though there be no reciprocal debts of B to A. A may satisfy B by making over to him a debt due to himself from a third person, C. This is conveniently done by means of a written instrument, called a bill of exchange, which is, in fact, a transferable order by a creditor upon his debtor, and when accepted by the debtor, that is, authenticated by his signature, becomes an acknowledgment of debt.

§ 4. Bills of exchange were first introduced to save the expense and risk of transporting the precious metals from place to place. 'Let it be supposed,' says Mr. Henry Thornton,* 'that there are in London ten manufacturers who sell their article to ten shopkeepers in York, by whom it is retailed; and that there are in York ten manufacturers of another commodity, who sell it to ten shopkeepers in London. There would be no occasion for the ten shopkeepers in London to send yearly to York guineas for the payment of the York manufacturers, and for the ten York shopkeepers to send yearly as many guineas to London. It would only be necessary for the York manufacturers to receive from each of the shopkeepers at their own door the money in question, giving in return letters which should acknowledge the receipt of it; and which should also direct the money, lying ready in the hands of their debtors in London, to be paid to the London manufacturers, so as to cancel the debt in London in the same manner as that at York. The expense and the risk of all transmission of money would thus be saved. Letters ordering the transfer of the debt are termed, in the language of the present day, bills of exchange. They are bills by which the debt of one person is exchanged for the debt of another; and the debt, perhaps, which is due in one place, for the debt due in another.'

Bills of exchange having been found convenient as means of paying debts at distant places without the expense of transporting the precious metals, their use was afterwards greatly extended from another motive. It is usual in every trade to give a certain length of credit for goods bought: three months, six months, a year, even two years, according to the convenience or custom of the particular trade. A dealer who has sold goods, for which he is to be paid in six months, but who desires to receive payment sooner, draws a bill on his debtor payable in six months, and gets the bill discounted by a banker or other money-lender, that is, transfers the bill to him, receiving the amount, minus interest for the time it has still to run. It has become one of the chief functions of bills of exchange to serve as a means by which a debt due from one person can thus be made available for obtaining credit from another. The conve-

* *Enquiry into the Nature and Effects of the Paper Credit of Great Britain*, p. 24. This work, published in 1802, is even now the clearest exposition that I am acquainted with, in the English language, of the modes in which credit is given and taken in a mercantile community.

nience of the expedient has led to the frequent creation of bills of exchange not grounded on any debt previously due to the drawer of the bill by the person on whom it is drawn. These are called *accommodation* bills; and sometimes, with a tinge of disapprobation, *fictitious* bills. Their nature is so clearly stated, and with such judicious remarks, by the author whom I have just quoted, that I shall transcribe the entire passage.*

'A, being in want of 100*l*., requests B to accept a note or bill drawn at two months, which B, therefore, on the face of it, is bound to pay; it is understood, however, that A will take care either to discharge the bill himself, or to furnish B with the means of paying it. A obtains ready money for the bill on the joint credit of the two parties. A fulfils his promise of paying it when due, and thus concludes the transaction. This service rendered by B to A is, however, not unlikely to be requited, at a more or less distant period, by a similar acceptance of a bill on A, drawn and discounted for B's convenience.

'Let us now compare such a bill with a real bill. Let us consider in what points they differ, or seem to differ; and in what they agree.

'They agree, inasmuch as each is a discountable article; each has also been created for the purpose of being discounted; and each is, perhaps, discounted in fact. Each, therefore, serves equally to supply means of speculation to the merchant. So far, moreover, as bills and notes constitute what is called the circulating medium, or paper currency of the country, and prevent the use of guineas, the fictitious and the real bill are upon an equality; and if the price of commodities be raised in proportion to the quantity of paper currency, the one contributes to that rise exactly in the same manner as the other.

'Before we come to the points in which they differ, let us advert to one point in which they are commonly supposed to be unlike; but in which they cannot be said always or necessarily to differ.

'Real notes (it is sometimes said) represent actual property. There are actual goods in existence, which are the counterpart to every real note. Notes which are not drawn in consequence of a sale of goods, are a species of false wealth, by which a nation is deceived. These supply only an imaginary capital; the others indicate one that is real.

'In answer to this statement it may be observed, first, that the notes given in consequence of a real sale of goods cannot be considered as on that account *certainly* representing any actual property. Suppose that A sells 100*l*. worth of goods to B at six months' credit, and takes a bill at six months for it; and that B, within a month after, sells the same goods, at a like credit, to C, taking a like bill; and again, that C, after another month, sells them to D, taking a like bill, and so on. There may then, at the end of six months, be six bills of 100*l*. each,

* Pp. 29–33.

existing at the same time; and every one of these may possibly have been discounted. Of all these bills, then, only one represents any actual property.

'In order to justify the supposition that a real bill (as it is called) represents actual property, there ought to be some power in the bill-holder to prevent the property which the bill represents, from being turned to other purposes than that of paying the bill in question. No such power exists; neither the man who holds the real bill, nor the man who discounts it, has any property in the specific goods for which it was given: he as much trusts to the general ability to pay of the giver of the bill, as the holder of any fictitious bill does. The fictitious bill may, in many cases, be a bill given by a person having a large and known capital, a part of which the fictitious bill may be said in that case to represent. The supposition that real bills represent property, and that fictitious bills do not, seems, therefore, to be one by which more than justice is done to one of these species of bills, and something less than justice to the other.

'We come next to some points in which they differ.

'First, the fictitious note, or note of accommodation, is liable to the objection that it professes to be what it is not. This objection, however, lies only against those fictitious bills which are passed as real. In many cases it is sufficiently obvious what they are. Secondly, the fictitious bill is, in general, less likely to be punctually paid than the real one. There is a general presumption, that the dealer in fictitious bills is a man who is a more adventurous speculator than he who carefully abstains from them. It follows, thirdly, that fictitious bills, besides being less safe, are less subject to limitation as to their quantity. The extent of a man's actual sales forms some limit to the amount of his real notes; and as it is highly desirable in commerce that credit should be dealt out to all persons in some sort of regular and due proportion, the measure of a man's actual sales, certified by the appearance of his bills drawn in virtue of those sales, is some rule in the case, though a very imperfect one in many respects.

'A fictitious bill, or bill of accommodation, is evidently in substance the same as any common promissory note; and even better in this respect, that there is but one security to the promissory note, whereas in the case of the bill of accommodation, there are two. So much jealousy subsists lest traders should push their means of raising money too far, that paper, the same in its general nature with that which is given, being the only paper which can be given, by men out of business, is deemed somewhat discreditable when coming from a merchant. And because such paper, when in the merchant's hand, necessarily imitates the paper which passes on the occasion of a sale of goods, the epithet fictitious has been cast upon it; an epithet which has seemed to countenance the confused and mistaken notion, that there is something altogether false and delusive in the nature of a certain part both of the paper and of the apparent wealth of the country.'

A bill of exchange, when merely discounted, and kept in the portfolio of the discounter until it falls due, does not perform the functions or supply the place of money, but is itself bought and sold for money. It is no more currency than the public funds, or any other securities. But when a bill drawn upon one person is paid to another (or even to the same person) in discharge of a debt or a pecuniary claim, it does something for which, if the bill did not exist, money would be required: it performs the functions of currency. This is a use to which bills of exchange are often applied. 'They not only,' continues Mr. Thornton,[*] 'spare the use of ready money; they also occupy its place in many cases. Let us imagine a farmer in the country to discharge a debt of 10*l*. to his neighbouring grocer, by giving him a bill for that sum, drawn on his cornfactor in London for grain sold in the metropolis; and the grocer to transmit the bill, he having previously indorsed it, to a neighbouring sugar-baker, in discharge of a like debt; and the sugar-baker to send it, when again indorsed, to a West India merchant in an outport, and the West India merchant to deliver it to his country banker, who also indorses it, and sends it into further circulation. The bill in this case will have effected five payments, exactly as if it were a 10*l*. note payable to a bearer on demand. A multitude of bills pass between trader and trader in the country, in the manner which has been described; and they evidently form, in the strictest sense, a part of the circulating medium of the kingdom.'

Many bills, both domestic and foreign, are at last presented for payment quite covered with indorsements, each of which represents either a fresh discounting, or a pecuniary transaction in which the bill has performed the functions of money. Within the present generation, the circulating medium of Lancashire, for sums above five pounds, was almost entirely composed of such bills.

§ 5. A third form in which credit is employed as a substitute for currency, is that of promissory notes. A bill drawn upon any one and accepted by him, and a note of hand by him promising to pay the same sum, are, as far as he is concerned, exactly equivalent, except that the former commonly bears interest and the latter generally does not; and that the former is commonly payable only after a certain lapse of time, and the latter payable at sight. But it is chiefly in the latter form that it has become, in commercial countries, an express occupation to issue such substitutes for money. Dealers in money (as lenders by profession are improperly called) desire, like other dealers, to

* P. 40.

stretch their operations beyond what can be carried on by their own means: they wish to lend, not their capital merely, but their credit, and not only such portion of their credit as consists of funds actually deposited with them, but their power of obtaining credit from the public generally, so far as they think they can safely employ it. This is done in a very convenient manner by lending their own promissory notes payable to bearer on demand: the borrower being willing to accept these as so much money, because the credit of the lender makes other people willingly receive them on the same footing, in purchases or other payments. These notes, therefore, perform all the functions of currency, and render an equivalent amount of money which was previously in circulation, unnecessary. As, however, being payable on demand, they may be at any time returned on the issuer, and money demanded for them, he must, on pain of bankruptcy, keep by him as much money as will enable him to meet any claims of that sort which can be expected to occur within the time necessary for providing himself with more: and prudence also requires that he should not attempt to issue notes beyond the amount which experience shows can remain in circulation without being presented for payment.

The convenience of this mode of (as it were) coining credit, having once been discovered, governments have availed themselves of the same expedient, and have issued their own promissory notes in payment of their expenses; a resource the more useful, because it is the only mode in which they are able to borrow money without paying interest, their promises to pay on demand being, in the estimation of the holders, equivalent to money in hand. The practical differences between such government notes and the issues of private bankers, and the further diversities of which this class of substitutes for money are susceptible, will be considered presently.

§ 6. A fourth mode of making credit answer the purposes of money, by which, when carried far enough, money may be very completely superseded, consists in making payments by cheques. The custom of keeping the spare cash reserved for immediate use or against contingent demands, in the hands of a banker, and making all payments, except small ones, by orders on bankers, is in this country spreading to a continually larger portion of the public. If the person making the payment, and the person receiving it, keep their money with the same banker, the payment takes place without any intervention of money, by the mere transfer of its amount in the banker's books from the credit of the payer to that of the receiver. If all persons in London kept their cash at the same banker's, and made all their payments by means of cheques, no money would be required or used for any transactions beginning and terminating in London. This ideal limit is almost attained in fact, so far as regards transactions between dealers. It is chiefly in the retail transactions between

136

dealers and consumers, and in the payment of wages, that money or bank notes now pass, and then only when the amounts are small. In London, even shopkeepers of any amount of capital or extent of business have generally an account with a banker; which, besides the safety and convenience of the practice, is to their advantage in another respect, by giving them an understood claim to have their bills discounted in cases when they could not otherwise expect it. As for the merchants and larger dealers, they habitually make all payments in the course of their business by cheques. They do not, however, all deal with the same banker, and when A gives a cheque to B, B usually pays it not into the same but into some other bank. But the convenience of business has given birth to an arrangement which makes all the banking houses of the City of London, for certain purposes, virtually one establishment. A banker does not send the cheques which are paid into his banking house, to the banks on which they are drawn, and demand money for them. There is a building called the Clearing-house, to which every City banker sends, each afternoon, all the cheques on other bankers which he has received during the day, and they are there exchanged for the cheques on him which have come into the hands of other bankers, the balances only being paid in money; or even these not in money, but in cheques on the Bank of England. By this contrivance, all the business transactions of the City of London during that day, amounting often to millions of pounds, and a vast amount besides of country transactions, represented by bills which country bankers have drawn upon their London correspondents, are [1848] liquidated by payments not exceeding on the average 200,000*l.**

By means of the various instruments of credit which have now been explained, the immense business of a country like Great Britain is transacted with an amount of the precious metals surprisingly small; many times smaller, in proportion to the pecuniary value of the commodities bought and sold, than is found necessary in France, or any other country in which, the habit and the disposition to give credit not being so generally diffused, these 'economizing expedients,' as they have been called, are not practised to the same extent. What becomes of the money thus superseded in its functions, and by what process it is made to disappear from circulation, are questions the discussion of which must be for a short time postponed.

* According to Mr. Tooke (*Inquiry into the Currency Principle*, p. 27) the adjustments of the Clearing-house 'in the year 1839 amounted to 954,401,600*l.*, making an average amount of payments of upwards of 3,000,000*l.* of bills of exchange and cheques daily effected through the medium of little more than 200,000*l.* of bank notes.' – At present a very much greater amount of transactions is daily liquidated, without bank notes at all, cheques on the Bank of England supplying their place.

CHAPTER XII

INFLUENCE OF CREDIT ON PRICES

§ 1. HAVING now formed a general idea of the modes in which credit is made available as a substitute for money, we have to consider in what manner the use of these substitutes affects the value of money, or, what is equivalent, the prices of commodities. It is hardly necessary to say that the permanent value of money – the natural and average prices of commodities – are not in question here. These are determined by the cost of producing or of obtaining the precious metals. An ounce of gold or silver will in the long run exchange for as much of every other commodity, as can be produced or imported at the same cost with itself. And an order, or note of hand, or bill payable at sight, for an ounce of gold, while the credit of the giver is unimpaired, is worth neither more nor less than the gold itself.

It is not, however, with ultimate or average, but with immediate and temporary prices, that we are now concerned. These, as we have seen, may deviate very widely from the standard of cost of production. Among other causes of fluctuation, one we have found to be the quantity of money in circulation. Other things being the same, an increase of the money in circulation raises prices, a diminution lowers them. If more money is thrown into circulation than the quantity which can circulate at a value conformable to its cost of production, the value of money, so long as the excess lasts, will remain below the standard of cost of production, and general prices will be sustained above the natural rate.

But we have now found that there are other things, such as bank notes, bills of exchange, and cheques, which circulate as money, and perform all the functions of it: and the question arises, Do these various substitutes operate on prices in the same manner as money itself? Does an increase in the quantity of transferable paper tend to raise prices, in the same manner and degree as an increase in the quantity of money? There has been no small amount of discussion on this point among writers of currency, without any result so conclusive as to have yet obtained general assent.

I apprehend that bank notes, bills, or cheques, as such, do not act on prices at all. What does act on prices is Credit, in whatever shape given, and whether it gives rise to any transferable instruments capable of passing into circulation or not.

I proceed to explain and substantiate this opinion.

§ 2. Money acts upon prices in no other way than by being tendered in exchange for commodities. The demand which influences the prices of commodities consists of the money offered for them. But the money offered is not the same thing with the money possessed. It is sometimes less, sometimes very much more. In the long run indeed, the money which people lay out will be neither more nor less than the money which they have to lay out: but this is far from being the case at any given time. Sometimes they keep money by them for fear of an emergency, or in expectation of a more advantageous opportunity for expending it. In that case the money is said not to be in circulation: in plainer language, it is not offered, nor about to be offered, for commodities. Money not in circulation has no effect on prices. The converse, however, is a much commoner case; people make purchases with money not in their possession. An article, for instance, which is paid for by a cheque on a banker, is bought with money which not only is not in the payer's possession, but generally not even in the banker's, having been lent by him (all but the usual reserve) to other persons. We just now made the imaginary supposition that all persons dealt with a bank, and all with the same bank, payments being universally made by cheques. In this ideal case, there would be no money anywhere except in the hands of the banker: who might then safely part with all of it, by selling it as bullion, or lending it, to be sent out of the country in exchange for goods or foreign securities. But though there would then be no money in possession, or ultimately perhaps even in existence, money would be offered, and commodities bought with it, just as at present. People would continue to reckon their incomes and their capitals in money, and to make their usual purchases with orders for the receipt of a thing which would have literally ceased to exist. There would be in all this nothing to complain of, so long as the money, in disappearing, left an equivalent value in other things, applicable when required to the reimbursement of those to whom the money originally belonged.

In the case however of payment by cheques, the purchases are at any rate made, though not with money in the buyer's possession, yet with money to which he has a right. But he may make purchases with money which he only expects to have, or even only pretends to expect. He may obtain goods in return for his acceptances payable at a future time; or on his note of hand; or on a simple book credit, that is, on a mere promise to pay. All these purchases have exactly the same effect on price, as if they were made with ready money. The amount of purchasing power which a person can exercise is composed of all the money in his possession or due to him, and of all his credit. For exercising the whole of this power he finds a sufficient motive only under peculiar circumstances; but he always possesses it; and the portion of it which he at any time does exercise, is the measure of the effect which he produces on price.

Suppose that, in the expectation that some commodity will rise in price, he determines, not only to invest in it all his ready money, but to take up on credit, from the producers or importers, as much of it as their opinion of his resources will enable him to obtain. Every one must see that by thus acting he produces a greater effect on price, than if he limited his purchases to the money he has actually in hand. He creates a demand for the article to the full amount of his money and credit taken together, and raises the price proportionally to both. And this effect is produced, though none of the written instruments called substitutes for currency may be called into existence; though the transaction may give rise to no bill of exchange, nor to the issue of a single bank note. The buyer, instead of taking a mere book credit, might have given a bill for the amount; or might have paid for the goods with bank notes borrowed for that purpose from a banker, thus making the purchase not on his own credit with the seller, but on the banker's credit with the seller, and his own with the banker. Had he done so, he would have produced as great an effect on price as by a simple purchase to the same amount on a book credit, but no greater effect. The credit itself, not the form and mode in which it is given, is the operating cause.

§ 3. The inclination of the mercantile public to increase their demand for commodities by making use of all or much of their credit as a purchasing power, depends on their expectation of profit. When there is a general impression that the price of some commodity is likely to rise, from an extra demand, a short crop, obstruction to importation, or any other cause, there is a disposition among dealers to increase their stocks, in order to profit by the expected rise. This disposition tends in itself to produce the effect which it looks forward to, a rise of price: and if the rise is considerable and progressive, other speculators are attracted, who, so long as the price has not begun to fall, are willing to believe that it will continue rising. These, by further purchases, produce a further advance: and thus a rise of price for which there were originally some rational grounds, is often heightened by merely speculative purchases, until it greatly exceeds what the original grounds will justify. After a time this begins to be perceived; the price ceases to rise, and the holders, thinking it time to realize their gains, are anxious to sell. Then the price begins to decline: the holders rush into the market to avoid a still greater loss, and, few being willing to buy in a falling market, the price falls much more suddenly than it rose. Those who have bought at a higher price than reasonable calculation justified, and who have been overtaken by the revulsion before they had realized, are losers in proportion to the greatness of the fall, and to the quantity of the commodity which they hold, or have bound themselves to pay for.

Now all these effects might take place in a community to which credit was unknown: the prices of some commodities might rise from speculation, to an extravagant height, and then fall rapidly back. But if there were no such thing as credit, this could hardly happen with respect to commodities generally. If all purchases were made with ready money, the payment of increased prices for some articles would draw an unusual proportion of the money of the community into the markets for those articles, and must therefore draw it away from some other class of commodities, and thus lower their prices. The vacuum might, it is true, be partly filled up by increased rapidity of circulation; and in this manner the money of the community is virtually increased in a time of speculative activity, because people keep little of it by them, but hasten to lay it out in some tempting adventure as soon as possible after they receive it. This resource, however, is limited: on the whole, people cannot, while the quantity of money remains the same, lay out much more of it in some things, without laying out less in others. But what they cannot do by ready money, they can do by an extension of credit. When people go into the market and purchase with money which they hope to receive hereafter, they are drawing upon an unlimited, not a limited fund. Speculation, thus supported, may be going on in any number of commodities, without disturbing the regular course of business in others. It might even be going on in all commodities at once. We could imagine that in an epidemic fit of the passion of gambling, all dealers, instead of giving only their accustomed orders to the manufacturers or growers of their commodity, commenced buying up all of it which they could procure, as far as their capital and credit would go. All prices would rise enormously, even if there were no increase of money, and no paper credit, but a mere extension of purchases on book credits. After a time those who had bought would wish to sell, and prices would collapse.

This is the ideal extreme case of what is called a commercial crisis. There is said to be a commercial crisis, when a great number of merchants and traders at once, either have, or apprehend that they shall have, a difficulty in meeting their engagements. The most usual cause of this general embarrassment is the recoil of prices after they have been raised by a spirit of speculation, intense in degree, and extending to many commodities. Some accident which excites expectations of rising prices, such as the opening of a new foreign market, or simultaneous indications of a short supply of several great articles of commerce, sets speculation at work in several leading departments at once. The prices rise, and the holders realize, or appear to have the power of realizing, great gains. In certain states of the public mind, such examples of rapid increase of fortune call forth numerous imitators, and speculation not only goes much beyond what is justified by the original grounds for expecting rise of price, but extends itself to articles in which there never was any such ground: these, however, rise like the rest as soon as speculation sets in. At periods of this kind a great extension of credit takes place. Not only do all whom the contagion reaches employ their credit much more freely than usual; but they really have more credit, because they seem to be making unusual gains, and because a generally reckless and adventurous feeling prevails, which disposes people to give as well as take credit more largely than at other times, and give it to persons not entitled to it. In this manner, in the celebrated speculative year 1825, and at various other periods during the present century, the prices of many of the principal articles of commerce rose greatly, without any fall in others, so that general prices might, without incorrectness, be said to have risen. When, after such a rise, the reaction comes, and prices begin to fall, though at first perhaps only through the desire of the holders to realize, speculative purchases cease: but were this all, prices would only fall to the level from which they rose, or to that which is justified by the state of the consumption and of the supply. They fall, however, much lower; for as, when prices were rising, and everybody apparently making a fortune, it was easy to obtain almost any amount of credit, so now, when everybody seems to be losing, and many fail entirely, it is with difficulty that firms of known solidity can obtain even the credit to which they are accustomed, and which it is the greatest inconvenience to them to be without; because all dealers have engagements to fulfil, and nobody feeling sure that the portion of his means which he has entrusted to others will be available in time, no one likes to part with ready money, or to postpone his claim to it. To these rational considerations there is superadded, in extreme cases, a panic as unreasoning as the previous over-confidence; money is borrowed for short periods at almost any rate of interest, and sales of goods for immediate payment are made at almost any sacrifice. Thus general prices, during a commercial revulsion, fall as much below the usual level as during the previous period of speculation they have risen above it: the fall, as well as the rise, originating not in anything affecting money, but in the state of credit; an unusually extended employment of credit during the earlier period, followed by a great diminution, never amounting, however, to an entire cessation of it, in the later.

It is not, however, universally true that the contraction of credit, characteristic of a commercial crisis, must have been preceded by an extraordinary and irrational extension of it. There are other causes; and one of the more recent crises, that of 1847, is an instance, having been preceded by no particular extension of credit, and by no speculations; except those in railway shares, which, though in many cases extravagant enough, yet being carried on mostly with that portion of means which the speculators could afford to lose, were not calculated to produce the wide-spread ruin which arises from vicissitudes of price in the commodities in which men habitually deal, and in which the bulk of their capital is invested. The crisis of 1847 belonged to another class of mercantile phenomena. There occasionally happens a concurrence of circumstances tending to withdraw from the loan market a considerable portion of the capital which usually supplies it. These circumstances, in the present case, were great foreign payments, (occasioned by a high price of cotton and an unprecedented importation of food,) together with the continual demands on the circulating capital of the country by railway calls and the loan transactions of railway companies, for the purpose of being converted into fixed capital and made unavailable for future lending. These various demands fell principally, as such demands always do, on the loan market. A great, though not the greatest, part of the imported food was actually paid for by the proceeds of a government loan. The extra payments which purchasers of corn and cotton, and railway shareholders, found themselves obliged to make, were either made with their own spare cash, or with money raised for the occasion. On the first supposition, they were made by withdrawing deposits from bankers, and thus cutting off a part of the streams which fed the loan market; on the second supposition, they were made by actual drafts on the loan market, either by the sale of securities, or by taking up money at interest. This combination of a fresh demand for loans, with a curtailment of the capital disposable for them, raised the rate of interest, and made it impossible to borrow except on the very best security. Some firms, therefore, which by an improvident and unmercantile mode of conducting business had allowed their capital to become either temporarily or permanently unavailable, became unable to command that perpetual renewal of credit which had previously enabled them to struggle on. These firms stopped payment: their failure involved more or less deeply many other firms which had trusted them; and, as usual in such cases, the general distrust, commonly called a panic, began to set in, and might have produced a destruction of credit equal to that of 1825, had not circumstances, which may almost be called accidental, given to a very simple measure of the government (the suspension of the Bank Charter Act of 1844) a fortunate power of allaying panic, to which, when considered in itself, it had no sort of claim.*

* The commercial difficulties, not however amounting to a commercial crisis, of 1864, had essentially the same origin. Heavy payments for cotton imported at high prices, and large investments in banking and other joint stock projects, combined with the loan operations of foreign governments, made such large drafts upon the loan market as to raise the rate of discount on mercantile bills as high as nine per cent.

§ 4. The general operation of credit upon prices being such as we have described, it is evident that if any particular mode or form of credit is calculated to have a greater operation on prices than others, it can only be by giving greater facility, or greater encouragement, to the multiplication of credit transactions generally. If bank notes, for instance, or bills, have a greater effect on prices than book credits, it is not by any difference in the transactions themselves, which are essentially the same, whether taking place in the one way or in the other: it must be that there are likely to be more of them. If credit is likely to be more extensively used as a purchasing power when bank notes or bills are the instruments used, than when the credit is given by mere entries in an account, to that extent and no more there is ground for ascribing to the former a greater power over the markets than belongs to the latter.

Now it appears that there is some such distinction. As far as respects the particular transactions, it makes no difference in the effect on price whether A buys goods of B on simple credit, or gives a bill for them, or pays for them with bank notes lent to him by a banker C. The difference is in a subsequent stage. If A has bought the goods on a book credit, there is no obvious or convenient mode by which B can make A's debt to him a means of extending his own credit. Whatever credit he has, will be due to the general opinion entertained of his solvency; he cannot specifically pledge A's debt to a third person, as a security for money lent or goods bought. But if A has given him a bill for the amount, he can get this discounted, which is the same thing as borrowing money on the joint credit of A and himself: or he may pay away the bill in exchange for goods, which is obtaining goods on the same joint credit. In either case, here is a second credit transaction, grounded on the first, and which would not have taken place if the first had been transacted without the intervention of a bill. Nor need the transactions end here. The bill may be again discounted, or again paid away for goods, several times before it is itself presented for payment. Nor would it be correct to say that these successive holders, if they had not had the bill, might have attained their purpose by purchasing goods on their own credit with the dealers. They may not all of them be persons of credit, or they may already have stretched their credit as far as it will go. And at all events, either money or goods are more readily obtained on the credit of two persons than of one. Nobody will pretend that it is as easy a thing for a merchant to borrow a thousand pounds on his own credit, as to get a bill discounted to the same amount, when the drawee is of known solvency.

If we now suppose that A, instead of giving a bill, obtains a loan of bank notes from a banker C, and with them pays B for his goods, we shall find the difference to be still greater. B is now independent even of a discounter: A's bill would have been taken in payment only by those who were acquainted with his reputation for solvency, but a banker is a person who has credit with the public generally, and whose notes are taken in payment by every one, at least in his own neighbourhood: insomuch that, by a custom which has grown into law, payment in bank notes is a complete acquittance to the payer, whereas, if he has paid by a bill, he still remains liable to the debt, if the person on whom the bill is drawn fails to pay it when due. B therefore can expend the whole of the bank notes without at all involving his own credit; and whatever power he had before of obtaining goods on book credit, remains to him unimpaired, in addition to the purchasing power he derives from the possession of the notes. The same remark applies to every person in succession, into whose hands the notes may come. It is only A, the first holder, (who used his credit to obtain the notes as a loan from the issuer,) who can possibly find the credit he possesses in other quarters abated by it; and even in his case that result is not probable; for though, in reason, and if all his circumstances were known, every draft already made upon his credit ought to diminish by so much his power of obtaining more, yet in practice the reverse more frequently happens, and his having been trusted by one person is supposed to be evidence that he may safely be trusted by others also.

It appears, therefore, that bank notes are a more powerful instrument for raising prices than bills, and bills than book credits. It does not, indeed, follow that credit *will* be more used because it *can* be. When the state of trade holds out no particular temptation to make large purchases on credit, dealers will use only a small portion of the credit power, and it will depend only on convenience whether the portion which they use will be taken in one form or in another. It is not until the circumstances of the markets, and the state of the mercantile mind, render many persons desirous of stretching their credit to an unusual extent, that the distinctive properties of the different forms of credit display themselves. Credit already stretched to the utmost in the form of book debts, would be susceptible of a great additional extension by means of bills, and of a still greater by means of bank notes. The first, because each dealer, in addition to his own credit, would be enabled to create a further purchasing power out of the credit which he had himself given to others: the second, because the banker's credit with the public at large, coined into notes, as bullion is coined into pieces of money to make it portable and divisible, is so much purchasing power superadded, in the hands of every successive holder, to that which he may derive from his own credit. To state the matter otherwise; one single exertion of the credit-power in the form of book credit is only the foundation of a single purchase: but if a bill is drawn, that same portion of credit may serve for as many purchases as the number of times the bill changes hands: while every bank note issued renders the credit of the banker a purchasing power to that amount in the hands of all the successive holders, without impairing any power they may possess of effecting purchases on their own credit. Credit, in short, has exactly the same purchasing power with money; and as money tells upon prices not simply in proportion to its amount, but to its amount multiplied by the number of times it changes hands, so also does credit; and credit transferable from hand to hand is in that proportion more potent than credit which only performs one purchase.

§ 5. All this purchasing power, however, is operative upon prices only according to the proportion of it which is used; and the effect, therefore, is only felt in a state of circumstances calculated to lead to an unusually extended use of credit. In such a state of circumstances, that is, in speculative times, it cannot, I think, be denied, that prices are likely to rise higher if the speculative purchases are made with bank notes, than when they are made with bills, and when made by bills than when made by book credits. This, however, is of far less practical importance than might at first be imagined; because, in point of fact, speculative purchases are not, in the great majority of cases, made either with bank notes or with bills, but are made almost exclusively on book credits. 'Applications to the Bank for extended discount,' says the highest authority on such subjects,[*] (and the same thing must be true of applications to other banks) 'occur rarely if ever in the origin or progress of extensive speculations in commodities. These are entered into, for the most part if not entirely, in the first instance, on credit, for the length of term usual in the several trades; thus entailing on the parties no immediate necessity for borrowing so much as may be wanted for the purpose beyond their own available capital. This applies particularly to speculative purchases of commodities on the spot, with a view to resale. But these generally form the smaller proportion of engagements on credit. By far the largest of those entered into on the prospect of a rise of prices, are such as have in view importations from abroad. The same remark, too, is applicable to the export of commodities, when a large proportion is on the credit of the shippers or their consignees. As long as circumstances hold out the prospect of a favourable result, the credit of the parties is generally sustained. If some of them wish to realize, there are others with capital and credit ready to replace them; and if the events fully justify the grounds on which the speculative transactions were entered into (thus admitting of sales for consumption in time to replace the capital embarked) there is no unusual demand for borrowed capital to sustain them. It is only when by the vicissitudes of political events, or of the seasons, or other adventitious circumstances, the forthcoming supplies are found to exceed the computed rate of consumption, and a fall of prices ensues, that an increased demand for capi-

* Tooke, *History of Prices*, vol. iv. pp. 125–6.

tal takes place; the market rate of interest then rises, and increased applications are made to the Bank of England for discount.' So that the multiplication of bank notes and other transferable paper does not, for the most part, accompany and facilitate the speculation; but comes into play chiefly when the tide is turning, and difficulties begin to be felt.

Of the extraordinary height to which speculative transactions can be carried upon mere book credits, without the smallest addition to what is commonly called the currency, very few persons are at all aware. 'The power of purchase,' says Mr. Tooke,[*] 'by persons having capital and credit, is much beyond anything that those who are unacquainted practically with speculative markets have any idea of .... A person having the reputation of capital enough for his regular business, and enjoying good credit in his trade, if he takes a sanguine view of the prospect of a rise of price of the article in which he deals, and is favoured by circumstances in the outset and progress of his speculation, may effect purchases to an extent perfectly enormous, compared with his capital.' Mr. Tooke confirms this statement by some remarkable instances, exemplifying the immense purchasing power which may be exercised, and rise of price which may be produced, by credit not represented by either bank notes or bills of exchange.

'Amongst the earlier speculators for an advance in the price of tea, in consequence of our dispute with China in 1839, were several retail grocers and tea-dealers. There was a general disposition among the trade to get in stock: that is, to lay in at once a quantity which would meet the probable demand from their customers for several months to come. Some, however, among them, more sanguine and adventurous than the rest, availed themselves of their credit with the importers and wholesale dealers, for purchasing quantities much beyond the estimated demand in their own business. As the purchases were made in the first instance ostensibly, and perhaps really, for the legitimate purposes and within the limits of their regular business, the parties were enabled to buy without the condition of any deposit; whereas speculators, known to be such, are required to pay 2l. per chest, to cover any probable difference of price which might arise before the expiration of the prompt, which, for this article, is three months. Without, therefore, the outlay of a single farthing of actual capital or currency in any shape, they made purchases to a considerable extent; and with the profit realized on the resale of a part of these purchases, they were enabled to pay the deposit on further quantities when required, as was the case when the extent of the purchases attracted attention. In this way, the speculation went on at advancing prices (100 per cent and upwards) till nearly the expiration of the prompt; and if at that time circumstances had been such as to justify the apprehension which at one time

[*] *Inquiry into the Currency Principle*, pp. 79 and 136–8.

prevailed, that all future supplies would be cut off, the prices might have still further advanced, and at any rate not have retrograded. In this case, the speculators might have realized, if not all the profit they had anticipated, a very handsome sum, upon which they might have been enabled to extend their business greatly, or to retire from it altogether, with a reputation for great sagacity in thus making their fortune. But instead of this favourable result, it so happened that two or three cargoes of tea which had been transhipped were admitted, contrary to expectation, to entry on their arrival here, and it was found that further indirect shipments were in progress. Thus the supply was increased beyond the calculation of the speculators: and, at the same time, the consumption had been diminished by the high price. There was, consequently, a violent reaction on the market; the speculators were unable to sell without such a sacrifice as disabled them from fulfilling their engagements, and several of them consequently failed. Among these, one was mentioned, who having a capital not exceeding 1200*l.* which was locked up in his business, had contrived to buy 4000 chests, value above 80,000*l.*, the loss upon which was about 16,000*l.*

'The other example which I have to give, is that of the operation on the corn market between 1838 and 1842. There was an instance of a person who, when he entered on his extensive speculations, was, as it appeared by the subsequent examination of his affairs, possessed of a capital not exceeding 5000*l.*, but being successful in the outset, and favoured by circumstances in the progress of his operations, he contrived to make purchases to such an extent, that when he stopped payment his engagements were found to amount to between 500,000*l.* and 600,000*l.* Other instances might be cited of parties without any capital at all, who, by dint of mere credit, were enabled, while the aspect of the market favoured their views, to make purchases to a very great extent.

'And be it observed, that these speculations, involving enormous purchases on little or no capital, were carried on in 1839 and 1840, when the money market was in its most contracted state; or when, according to modern phraseology, there was the greatest scarcity of money.'

But though the great instrument of speculative purchases is book credits, it cannot be contested that in speculative periods an increase does take place in the quantity both of bills of exchange and of bank notes. This increase, indeed, so far as bank notes are concerned, hardly ever takes place in the earliest stage of the speculations: advances from bankers (as Mr. Tooke observes) not being applied for in order to purchase, but in order to hold on without selling when the usual term of credit has expired, and the high price which was calculated on has not arrived. But the tea speculators mentioned by Mr. Tooke could not have carried their speculations beyond the three months which are the usual term of credit in their trade, unless they had been able to obtain advances from bankers, which, if the expectation of a rise of price had still continued, they probably could have done.

Since, then, credit in the form of bank notes is a more potent instrument for raising prices than book credits, an unrestrained power of resorting to this instrument may contribute to prolong and heighten the speculative rise of prices, and hence to aggravate the subsequent recoil. But in what degree? and what importance ought we to ascribe to this possibility? It may help us to form some judgment on this point, if we consider the proportion which the utmost increase of bank notes in a period of speculation, bears, I do not say to the whole mass of credit in the country, but to the bills of exchange alone. The average amount of bills in existence at any one time is supposed greatly to exceed [1848] a hundred millions sterling.* The bank note circulation of Great Britain and Ireland seldom exceeds forty millions, and the increase in specula-tive periods at most two or three. And even this, as we have seen, hardly ever comes into play until that advanced period of the speculation at which the tide shows signs of turning, and the dealers generally are rather thinking of the

---

* The most approved estimate is that of Mr. Leatham, grounded on the official returns of bill stamps issued. The following are the results: –

Year.	Bills created in Great Britain and Ireland, founded on returns of Bill Stamps issued from the Stamp Office.	Average amount in circulation at one time in each year.
1832	£356,153,409	£89,038,352
1833	383,659,585	95,914,896
1834	379,155,052	94,788,763
1835	405,403,051	101,350,762
1836	485,943,473	121,485,868
1837	455,084,445	113,771,111
1838	465,504,041	116,376,010
1839	528,493,842	132,123,460

'Mr. Leatham,' says Mr. Tooke, 'gives the process by which, upon the data furnished by the returns of stamps, he arrives at these results; and I am disposed to think that they are as near an approximation to the truth as the nature of the materials admits of arriving at.' – Inquiry into the Currency Principle, p. 26. – Mr. Newmarch (Appendix No. 39 to Report of the Committee on the Bank Acts in 1857, and History of Prices, vol. vi. p. 587) shows grounds for the opinion that the total bill circulation in 1857 was not much less than 180 millions sterling, and that it sometimes rises to 200 millions.

means of fulfilling their existing engagements, than meditating an extension of them: while the quantity of bills in existence is largely increased from the very commencement of the speculations.

§ 6. It is well known that, of late years, an artificial limitation of the issue of bank notes has been regarded by many political economists, and by a great portion of the public, as an expedient of supreme efficacy for preventing, and when it cannot prevent, for moderating, the fever of speculation; and this opinion received the recognition and sanction of the legislature by the Currency Act of 1844. At the point, however, which our inquiries have reached, though we have conceded to bank notes a greater power over prices than is possessed by bills or book credits, we have not found reason to think that this superior efficacy has much share in producing the rise of prices which accompanies a period of speculation, nor consequently that any restraint applied to this one instrument can be efficacious to the degree which is often supposed, in moderating either that rise, or the recoil which follows it. We shall be still less inclined to think so, when we consider that there is a fourth form of credit transactions, by cheques on bankers, and transfers in a banker's books, which is exactly parallel in every respect to bank notes, giving equal facilities to an extension of credit, and capable of acting on prices quite as powerfully. In the words of Mr. Fullarton,[*] 'there is not a single object at present attained through the agency of Bank of England notes, which might not be as effectually accomplished by each individual keeping an account with the bank, and transacting all his payments of five pounds and upwards by cheque.' A bank, instead of lending its notes to a merchant or dealer, might open an account with him, and credit the account with the sum it had agreed to advance: on an understanding that he should not draw out that sum in any other mode than by drawing cheques against it in favour of those to whom he had occasion to make payments. These cheques might possibly even pass from hand to hand like bank notes; more commonly, however, the receiver would pay them into the hands of his own banker, and when he wanted the money, would draw a fresh cheque against it: and hence an objector may urge that as the original cheque would very soon be presented for payment, when it must be paid either in notes or in coin, notes or coin to an equal amount must be provided as the ultimate means of liquidation. It is not so, however. The person to whom the cheque is transferred may perhaps deal with the same banker, and the cheque may return to the very bank on which it was drawn: this is very often the case in country districts; if so, no payment will be called for, but a simple transfer in the banker's books will settle the transaction. If the cheque is paid into a dif-

* *On the Regulation of Currencies*, p. 41.

ferent bank, it will not be presented for payment, but liquidated by set-off against other cheques; and in a state of circumstances favourable to a general extension of banking credits, a banker who has granted more credit, and has therefore more cheques drawn on him, will also have more cheques on other bankers paid to him, and will only have to provide notes or cash for the payment of balances; for which purpose the ordinary reserve of prudent bankers, one-third of their liabilities, will abundantly suffice. Now, if he had granted the extension of credit by means of an issue of his own notes, he must equally have retained, in coin or Bank of England notes, the usual reserve: so that he can, as Mr. Fullarton says, give every facility of credit by what may be termed a cheque circulation, which he could give by a note circulation.

This extension of credit by entries in a banker's books, has all that superior efficiency in acting on prices, which we ascribed to an extension by means of bank notes. As a bank note of 20*l*., paid to any one, gives him 20*l*. of purchasing power based on credit, over and above whatever credit he had of his own, so does a cheque paid to him do the same: for, although he may make no purchase with the cheque itself, he deposits it with his banker, and can draw against it. As this act of drawing a cheque against another which has been exchanged and cancelled, can be repeated as often as a purchase with a bank note, it effects the same increase of purchasing power. The original loan, or credit, given by the banker to his customer, is potentially multiplied as a means of purchase, in the hands of the successive persons to whom portions of the credit are paid away, just as the purchasing power of a bank note is multiplied by the number of persons through whose hands it passes before it is returned to the issuer.

These considerations abate very much from the importance of any effect which can be produced in allaying the vicissitudes of commerce, by so superficial a contrivance as the one so much relied on of late, the restriction of the issue of bank notes by an artificial rule. An examination of all the consequences of that restriction, and an estimate of the reasons for and against it, must be deferred until we have treated of the foreign exchanges, and the international movements of bullion. At present we are only concerned with the general theory of prices, of which the different influence of different kinds of credit is an essential part.

§ 7.There has been a great amount of discussion and argument on the question whether several of these forms of credit, and in particular whether bank notes, ought to be considered as money. The question is so purely verbal as to be scarcely worth raising, and one would have some difficulty in comprehending why so much importance is attached to it, if there were not some authorities who, still adhering to the doctrine of the infancy of society and of political economy, that the quantity of money compared with that of commodities, determines general prices, think it important to prove that bank notes and no other forms of credit are money, in order to support the inference that bank notes and no other forms of credit influence prices. It is obvious, however, that prices do not depend on money, but on purchases. Money left with a banker, and not drawn against, or drawn against for other purposes than buying commodities, has no effect on prices, any more than credit which is not used. Credit which is used to purchase commodities affects prices in the same manner as money. Money and credit are thus exactly on a par, in their effect on prices; and whether we choose to class bank notes with the one or the other, is in this respect entirely immaterial.

Since, however, this question of nomenclature has been raised, it seems desirable that it should be answered. The reason given for considering bank notes as money, is, that by law and usage they have the property, in common with metallic money, of finally closing the transactions in which they are employed; while no other mode of paying one debt by transferring another has that privilege. The first remark which here suggests itself is, that on this showing, the notes at least of private banks are not money; for a creditor cannot be forced to accept them in payment of a debt. They certainly close the transaction if he does accept them; but so, on the same supposition, would a bale of cloth, or a pipe of wine; which are not for that reason regarded as money. It seems to be an essential part of the idea of money that it be legal tender. An inconvertible paper which is legal tender is universally admitted to be money; in the French language the phrase *papiermonnaie* actually *means* inconvertibility, convertible notes being merely *billets à porteur*. It is only in the case of Bank of England notes under the law of convertibility, that any difficulty arises; those notes not being a legal tender from the Bank itself, though a legal tender from all other persons. Bank of England notes undoubtedly do close transactions, so far as respects the buyer. When he has once paid in Bank of England notes, he can in no case be required to pay over again. But I confess I cannot see how the transaction can be deemed complete, as regards the seller, when he will only be found to have received the price of his commodity provided the Bank keeps its promise to pay. An instrument which would be deprived of all value by the insolvency of a corporation, cannot be money in any sense in which money is opposed to credit. It either is not money, or it is money and credit too. It may be most suitably described as coined credit. The other forms of credit may be distinguished from it as credit in ingots.

§ 8. Some high authorities have claimed for bank notes, as compared with other modes of credit, a greater distinction in respect to influence on price, than we have seen reason to allow; a difference, not in degree, but in kind.

They ground this distinction on the fact that all bills and cheques, as well as all book-debts, are from the first intended to be, and actually are, ultimately liquidated either in coin or in notes. The bank notes in circulation, jointly with the coin, are therefore, according to these authorities, the basis on which all the other expedients of credit rest; and in proportion to the basis will be the superstructure; insomuch that the quantity of bank notes determines that of all the other forms of credit. If bank notes are multiplied, there will, they seem to think, be more bills, more payments by cheque, and, I presume, more book credits; and by regulating and limiting the issue of bank notes, they think that all other forms of credit are, by an indirect consequence, brought under a similar limitation. I believe I have stated the opinion of these authorities correctly, though I have nowhere seen the grounds of it set forth with such distinctness as to make me feel quite certain that I understand them. It may be true that, according as there are more or fewer bank notes, there is also in general (though not invariably), more or less of other descriptions of credit; for the same state of affairs which leads to an increase of credit in one shape, leads to an increase of it in other shapes. But I see no reason for believing that the one is the cause of the other. If indeed we begin by assuming, as I suspect is tacitly done, that prices are regulated by coin and bank notes, the proposition maintained will certainly follow; for, according as prices are higher or lower, the same purchases will give rise to bills, cheques, and book credits of a larger or a smaller amount. But the premise in this reasoning is the very proposition to be proved. Setting this assumption aside, I know not how the conclusion can be substantiated. The credit given to any one by those with whom he deals, does not depend on the quantity of bank notes or coin in circulation at the time, but on their opinion of his solvency: if any consideration of a more general character enters into their calculation, it is only in a time of pressure on the loan market, when they are not certain of being themselves able to obtain the credit on which they have been accustomed to rely; and even then, what they look to is the general state of the loan market, and not (preconceived theory apart) the amount of bank notes. So far as to the willingness to *give* credit. And the willingness of a dealer to *use* his credit depends on his expectations of gain, that is, on his opinion of the probable future price of his commodity; an opinion grounded either on the rise or fall already going on, or on his prospective judgment respecting the supply and the rate of consumption. When a dealer extends his purchases beyond his immediate means of payment, engaging to pay at a specified time, he does so in the expectation either that the transaction will have terminated favourably before that time arrives, or that he shall then be in possession of sufficient funds from the proceeds of his other transactions. The fulfilment of these expectations depends upon prices, but not especially upon the amount of bank notes. He may, doubtless, also ask

153

himself, in case he should be disappointed in these expectations, to what quarter he can look for a temporary advance, to enable him, at the worst, to keep his engagements. But in the first place, this prospective reflection on the somewhat more or less of difficulty which he may have in tiding over his embarrassments, seems too slender an inducement to be much of a restraint in a period supposed to be one of rash adventure, and upon persons so confident of success as to involve themselves beyond their certain means of extrication. And further, I apprehend that their confidence of being helped out in the event of ill-fortune, will mainly depend on their opinion of their own individual credit, with, perhaps, some consideration, not of the quantity of the currency, but of the general state of the loan market. They are aware that, in case of a commercial crisis, they shall have difficulty in obtaining advances. But if they thought it likely that a commercial crisis would occur before they had realized, they would not speculate. If no great contraction of general credit occurs, they will feel no doubt of obtaining any advances which they absolutely require, provided the state of their own affairs at the time affords in the estimation of lenders a sufficient prospect that those advances will be repaid.

CHAPTER XIII

OF AN INCONVERTIBLE PAPER CURRENCY

§ 1. AFTER experience had shown that pieces of paper, of no intrinsic value, by merely bearing upon them the written profession of being equivalent to a certain number of francs, dollars, or pounds, could be made to circulate as such, and to produce all the benefit to the issuers which could have been produced by the coins which they purported to represent; governments began to think that it would be a happy device if they could appropriate to themselves this benefit, free from the condition to which individuals issuing such paper substitutes for money were subject, of giving, when required, for the sign, the thing signified. They determined to try whether they could not emancipate themselves from this unpleasant obligation, and make a piece of paper issued by them pass for a pound, by merely calling it a pound, and consenting to receive it in payment of the taxes. And such is the influence of almost all established governments, that they have generally succeeded in attaining this object: I believe I might say they have always succeeded for a time, and the power has only been lost to them after they had compromised it by the most flagrant abuse.

In the case supposed, the functions of money are performed by a thing which derives its power for performing them solely from convention; but convention is quite sufficient to confer the power; since nothing more is needful to make a person accept anything as money, and even at any arbitrary value, than the persuasion that it will be taken from him on the same terms by others. The only question is, what determines the value of such a currency; since it cannot be, as in the case of gold and silver (or paper exchangeable for them at pleasure), the cost of production.

We have seen, however, that even in the case of a metallic currency, the immediate agency in determining its value is its quantity. If the quantity, instead of depending on the ordinary mercantile motives of profit and loss, could be arbitrarily fixed by authority, the value would depend on the fiat of that authority, not on cost of production. The quantity of a paper currency not convertible into the metals at the option of the holder, can be arbitrarily fixed;

especially if the issuer is the sovereign power of the state. The value, therefore, of such a currency is entirely arbitrary.

Suppose that, in a country of which the currency is wholly metallic, a paper currency is suddenly issued, to the amount of half the metallic circulation; not by a banking establishment, or in the form of loans, but by the government, in payment of salaries and purchase of commodities. The currency being suddenly increased by one-half, all prices will rise, and among the rest, the prices of all things made of gold and silver. An ounce of manufactured gold will become more valuable than an ounce of gold coin, by more than that customary difference which compensates for the value of the workmanship; and it will be profitable to melt the coin for the purpose of being manufactured, until as much has been taken from the currency by the subtraction of gold, as had been added to it by the issue of paper. Then prices will relapse to what they were at first, and there will be nothing changed except that a paper currency has been substituted for half of the metallic currency which existed before. Suppose, now, a second emission of paper; the same series of effects will be renewed; and so on, until the whole of the metallic money has disappeared: that is, if paper be issued of as low a denomination as the lowest coin; if not, as much will remain as convenience requires for the smaller payments. The addition made to the quantity of gold and silver disposable for ornamental purposes, will somewhat reduce, for a time, the value of the article; and as long as this is the case, even though paper has been issued to the original amount of the metallic circulation, as much coin will remain in circulation along with it, as will keep the value of the currency down to the reduced value of the metallic material; but the value having fallen below the cost of production, a stoppage or diminution of the supply from the mines will enable the surplus to be carried off by the ordinary agents of destruction, after which, the metals and the currency will recover their natural value. We are here supposing, as we have supposed throughout, that the country has mines of its own, and no commercial intercourse with other countries; for, in a country having foreign trade, the coin which is rendered superfluous by an issue of paper is carried off by a much prompter method.

Up to this point, the effects of a paper currency are substantially the same, whether it is convertible into specie or not. It is when the metals have been completely superseded and driven from circulation, that the difference between convertible and inconvertible paper begins to be operative. When the gold or silver has all gone from circulation, and an equal quantity of paper has taken its place, suppose that a still further issue is superadded. The same series of phenomena recommences: prices rise, among the rest the prices of gold and silver articles, and it becomes an object as before to procure coin in order to convert it into bullion. There is no longer any coin in circulation; but if the paper currency is convertible, coin may still be obtained from the issuers, in exchange for notes. All additional notes, therefore, which are attempted to be forced into circulation after the metals have been completely superseded, will return upon the issuers in exchange for coin; and they will not be able to maintain in circulation such a quantity of convertible paper as to sink its value below the metal which it represents. It is not so, however, with an inconvertible currency. To the increase of that (if permitted by law) there is no check. The issuers may add to it indefinitely, lowering its value and raising prices in proportion; they may, in other words, depreciate the currency without limit.

Such a power, in whomsoever vested, is an intolerable evil. All variations in the value of the circulating medium are mischievous: they disturb existing contracts and expectations, and the liability to such changes renders every pecuniary engagement of long date entirely precarious. The person who buys for himself, or gives to another, an annuity of 100*l.*, does not know whether it will be equivalent to 200*l.* or to 50*l.* a few years hence. Great as this evil would be if it depended only on accident, it is still greater when placed at the arbitrary disposal of an individual or a body of individuals; who may have any kind or degree of interest to be served by an artificial fluctuation in fortunes; and who have at any rate a strong interest in issuing as much as possible, each issue being in itself a source of profit. Not to add, that the issuers may have, and in the case of a government paper, always have, a direct interest in lowering the value of the currency, because it is the medium in which their own debts are computed.

§ 2. In order that the value of the currency may be secure from being altered by design, and may be as little as possible liable to fluctuation from accident, the articles least liable of all known commodities to vary in their value, the precious metals, have been made in all civilized countries the standard of value for the circulating medium; and no paper currency ought to exist of which the value cannot be made to conform to theirs. Nor has this fundamental maxim ever been entirely lost sight of, even by the governments which have most abused the power of creating inconvertible paper. If they have not (as they generally have) professed an intention of paying in specie at some indefinite future time, they have at least, by giving to their paper issues the names of their coins, made a virtual, though generally a false, profession of intending to keep them at a value corresponding to that of the coins. This is not impracticable, even with an inconvertible paper. There is not indeed the self-acting check which convertibility brings with it. But there is a clear and unequivocal indication by which to judge whether the currency is depreciated, and to what extent. That indication is, the price of the precious metals. When holders of paper cannot demand coin to be converted into bullion, and when there is none left in circulation, bullion rises and falls in price like other things; and if it is above the Mint price, if an ounce of gold, which would be coined into the equivalent of 3*l*. 17*s*. 10½*d*., is sold for 4*l*. or 5*l*. in paper, the value of the currency has just sunk that much below what the value of a metallic currency would be. If, therefore, the issue of inconvertible paper were subjected to strict rules, one rule being that whenever bullion rose above the Mint price, the issues should be contracted until the market price of bullion and the Mint price were again in accordance, such a currency would not be subject to any of the evils usually deemed inherent in an inconvertible paper.

But also such a system of currency would have no advantages sufficient to recommend it to adoption. An inconvertible currency, regulated by the price of bullion, would conform exactly, in all its variations, to a convertible one; and the only advantage gained would be that of exemption from the necessity of keeping any reserve of the precious metals; which is not a very important consideration, especially as a government, so long as its good faith is not suspected, needs not keep so large a reserve as private issuers, being not so liable to great and sudden demands, since there never can be any real doubt of its solvency. Against this small advantage is to be set, in the first place, the possibility of fraudulent tampering with the price of bullion for the sake of acting on the currency; in the manner of the fictitious sales of corn, to influence the averages, so much and so justly complained of while the corn laws were in force. But a still stronger consideration is the importance of adhering to a simple principle, intelligible to the most untaught capacity. Everybody can understand convertibility; every one sees that what can be at any moment exchanged for five pounds is worth five pounds. Regulation by the price of bullion is a more complex idea, and does not recommend itself through the same familiar associations. There would be nothing like the same confidence, by the public generally, in an inconvertible currency so regulated, as in a convertible one: and the most instructed person might reasonably doubt whether such a rule would be as likely to be inflexibly adhered to. The grounds of the rule not being so well understood by the public, opinion would probably not enforce it with as much rigidity, and, in any circumstances of difficulty, would be likely to turn against it; while to the government itself a suspension of convertibility would appear a much stronger and more extreme measure, than a relaxation of what might possibly be considered a somewhat artificial rule. There is therefore a great preponderance of reasons in favour of a convertible, in preference to even the best regulated inconvertible currency. The temptation to over-issue, in certain financial emergencies, is so strong, that nothing is admissible which can tend, in however slight a degree, to weaken the barriers that restrain it.

§ 3. Although no doctrine in political economy rests on more obvious grounds than the mischief of a paper currency not maintained at the same value with a metallic, either by convertibility, or by some principle of limitation equivalent to it; and although, accordingly, this doctrine has, though not till after the discussions of many years, been tolerably effectually drummed into the public mind; yet dissentients are still numerous, and projectors every now and then start up, with plans for curing all the economical evils of society by means of an unlimited issue of inconvertible paper. There is, in truth, a great charm in the idea. To be able to pay off the national debt, defray the expenses of government without taxation, and in fine, to make the fortunes of the whole community, is a brilliant prospect, when once a man is capable of believing that printing a few characters on bits of paper will do it. The philosopher's stone could not be expected to do more.

As these projects, however often slain, always resuscitate, it is not superfluous to examine one or two of the fallacies by which the schemers impose upon themselves. One of the commonest is, that a paper currency cannot be issued in excess so long as every note issued *represents* property, or has a *foundation* of actual property to rest on. These phrases, of representing and resting, seldom convey any distinct or well-defined idea: when they do, their meaning is no more than this – that the issuers of the paper must *have* property, either of their own, or entrusted to them, to the value of all the notes they issue: though for what purpose does not very clearly appear; for if the property cannot be claimed in exchange for the notes, it is difficult to divine in what manner its mere existence can serve to uphold their value. I presume, however, it is intended as a guarantee that the holders would be finally reimbursed, in case any untoward event should cause the whole concern to be wound up. On this theory there have been many schemes for 'coining the whole land of the country into money' and the like.

In so far as this notion has any connexion at all with reason, it seems to originate in confounding two entirely distinct evils, to which a paper currency is liable. One is, the insolvency of the issuers; which, if the paper is grounded on their credit – if it makes any promise of payment in cash, either on demand or at any future time – of course deprives the paper of any value which it derives from the promise. To this evil paper credit is equally liable, however moderately used; and against it a proviso that all issues should be 'founded on property,' as for instance that notes should only be issued on the security of some valuable thing expressly pledged for their redemption, would really be efficacious as a precaution. But the theory takes no account of another evil, which is incident to the notes of the most solvent firm, company, or government; that of being depreciated in value from being issued in excessive quantity. The assignats, during the French Revolution, were an example of a currency grounded on these principles. The assignats 'represented' an immense amount of highly valuable property, namely the lands of the crown, the church, the monasteries, and the emigrants; amounting possibly to half the territory of France. They were, in fact, orders or assignments on this mass of land. The revolutionary government had the idea of 'coining' these lands into money; but, to do them justice, they did not originally contemplate the immense multiplication of issues to which they were eventually driven by the failure of all other financial resources. They imagined that the assignats would come rapidly back to the issuers in exchange for land, and that they should be able to reissue them continually until the lands were all disposed of, without having at any time more than a very moderate quantity in circulation. Their hope was frustrated: the land did not sell so quickly as they expected; buyers were not inclined to invest their money in possessions which were likely to be resumed without compensation if the Revolution succumbed: the bits of paper which represented land, becoming prodigiously multiplied, could no more keep up their value than the land itself would have done if it had all been brought to market at once: and the result was that it at last required an assignat of six hundred francs to pay for a pound of butter.

The example of the assignats has been said not to be conclusive, because an assignat only represented land in general, but not a definite quantity of land. To have prevented their depreciation, the proper course, it is affirmed, would have been to have made a valuation of all the confiscated property at its metallic value, and to have issued assignats up to, but not beyond, that limit; giving to the holders a right to demand any piece of land, at its registered valuation, in exchange for assignats to the same amount. There can be no question about the superiority of this plan over the one actually adopted. Had this course been followed, the assignats could never have been depreciated to the inordinate degree they were; for – as they would have retained all their purchasing power in relation to land, however much they might have fallen in respect to other things – before they had lost very much of their market value, they would probably have been brought in to be exchanged for land. It must be remembered, however, that their not being depreciated would pre-suppose that no greater number of them continued in circulation than would have circulated if they had been convertible into cash. However convenient, therefore, in a time of revolution, this currency convertible into land on demand might have been, as a contrivance for selling rapidly a great quantity of land with the least possible sacrifice; it is difficult to see what advantage it would have, as the permanent system of a country, over a currency convertible into coin: while it is not at all difficult to see what would be its disadvantages; since land is far more variable in value than gold and silver; and besides, land, to most persons, being rather an encumbrance than a desirable possession, except to be converted into money, people would submit to a much greater depreciation before demanding land, than they will before demanding gold or silver.*

§ 4. Another of the fallacies from which the advocates of an inconvertible currency derive support, is the notion that an increase of the currency quickens industry. This idea was set afloat by Hume, in his *Essay on Money*, and has had many devoted adherents since; witness the Birmingham currency school, of whom Mr. Attwood was at one time the most conspicuous representative. Mr. Attwood maintained that a rise of prices, produced by an increase of paper currency, stimulates every producer to his utmost exertions, and brings all the capital and labour of the country into complete employment; and that this has invariably happened in all periods of rising prices, when the rise was on a sufficiently great scale. I presume, however, that the inducement which, according to Mr. Attwood, excited this unusual ardour in all persons engaged in production, must have been the expectation of getting more commodities generally, more real wealth, in exchange for the produce of their labour, and not merely more pieces of paper. This expectation, however, must have been, by the very terms of the supposition, disappointed, since, all prices being supposed to rise equally, no one was really better paid for his goods than before. Those who agree with Mr. Attwood could only succeed in winning people on to these unwonted exertions by a prolongation of what would in fact be a delusion; contriving matters so, that by a progressive rise of money prices, every producer shall always seem to be in the very act of obtaining an increased remuneration which he never, in reality, does obtain. It is unnecessary to advert to any other of the objections to this plan than that of its total impracticability. It calculates on finding the whole world persisting for ever in the belief that more pieces of paper are more riches, and never discovering that, with all their paper, they cannot buy more of anything than they could before. No such mistake was made during any of the periods of high prices, on the

---

* Among the schemes of currency to which, strange to say, intelligent writers have been found to give their sanction, one is as follows: that the state should receive, in pledge or mortgage, any kind or amount of property, such as land, stock, &c., and should advance to the owners inconvertible paper money to the estimated value. Such a currency would not even have the recommendations of the imaginary assignats supposed in the text; since those into whose hands the notes were paid by the persons who received them, could not return them to the government, and demand in exchange land or stock which was only pledged, not alienated. There would be no reflux of such assignats as these, and their depreciation would be indefinite.

experience of which this school lays so much stress. At the periods which Mr. Attwood mistook for times of prosperity, and which were simply (as all periods of high prices, under a convertible currency, must be) times of speculation, the speculators did not think they were growing rich because the high prices would last, but because they would not last, and because whoever contrived to realize while they did last, would find himself, after the recoil, in possession of a greater number of pounds sterling, without their having become of less value. If, at the close of the speculation, an issue of paper had been made, sufficient to keep prices up to the point which they attained when at the highest, no one would have been more disappointed than the speculators; since the gain which they thought to have reaped by realizing in time (at the expense of their competitors, who bought when they sold, and had to sell after the revulsion) would have faded away in their hands, and instead of it they would have got nothing except a few more paper tickets to count by.

Hume's version of the doctrine differed in a slight degree from Mr. Attwood's. He thought that all commodities would not rise in price simultaneously, and that some persons therefore would obtain a real gain, by getting more money for what they had to sell, while the things which they wished to buy might not yet have risen. And those who would reap this gain would always be (he seems to think) the first comers. It seems obvious, however, that for every person who thus gains more than usual, there is necessarily some other person who gains less. The loser, if things took place as Hume supposes, would be the seller of the commodities which are slowest to rise; who, by the supposition, parts with his goods at the old prices, to purchasers who have already benefited by the new. This seller has obtained for his commodity only the accustomed quantity of money, while there are already some things of which that money will no longer purchase as much as before. If, therefore, he knows what is going on, he will raise his price, and then the buyer will not have the gain, which is supposed to stimulate his industry. But if, on the contrary, the seller does not know the state of the case, and only discovers it when he finds, in laying his money out, that it does not go so far, he then obtains less than the ordinary remuneration for his labour and capital; and if the other dealer's industry is encouraged, it should seem that his must, from the opposite cause, be impaired.

§ 5. There is no way in which a general and permanent rise of prices, or in other words, depreciation of money, can benefit anybody, except at the expense of somebody else. The substitution of paper for metallic currency is a national gain: any further increase of paper beyond this is but a form of robbery.

An issue of notes is a manifest gain to the issuers, who, until the notes are returned for payment, obtain the use of them as if they were a real capital: and so long as the notes are no permanent addition to the currency, but merely supersede gold or silver to the same amount, the gain of the issuer is a loss to no one; it is obtained by saving to the community the expense of the more costly material. But if there is no gold or silver to be superseded – if the notes are added to the currency, instead of being substituted for the metallic part of it – all holders of currency lose, by the depreciation of its value, the exact equivalent of what the issuer gains. A tax is virtually levied on them for his benefit. It will be objected by some, that gains are also made by the producers and dealers who, by means of the increased issue, are accommodated with loans. Theirs, however, is not an additional gain, but a portion of that which is reaped by the issuer at the expense of all possessors of money. The profits arising from the contribution levied upon the public, he does not keep to himself, but divides with his customers.

But besides the benefit reaped by the issuers, or by others through them, at the expense of the public generally, there is another unjust gain obtained by a larger class, namely by those who are under fixed pecuniary obligations. All such persons are freed, by a depreciation of the currency, from a portion of the burthen of their debts or other engagements: in other words, part of the property of their creditors is gratuitously transferred to them. On a superficial view it may be imagined that this is an advantage to industry; since the productive classes are great borrowers, and generally owe larger debts to the unproductive (if we include among the latter all persons not actually in business) than the unproductive classes owe to them; especially if the national debt be included. It is only thus that a general rise of prices can be a source of benefit to producers and dealers; by diminishing the pressure of their fixed burthens. And this might be accounted an advantage, if integrity and good faith were of no importance to the world, and to industry and commerce in particular. Not many, however, have been found to say that the currency ought to be depreciated on the simple ground of its being desirable to rob the national creditor and private creditors of a part of what is in their bond. The schemes which have tended that way have almost always had some appearance of special and circumstantial justification, such as the necessity of compensating for a prior injustice committed in the contrary direction.

§ 6. Thus in England, for many years subsequent to 1819, it was pertinaciously contended, that a large portion of the national debt and a multitude of private debts still in existence, were contracted between 1797 and 1819, when the Bank of England was exempted from giving cash for its notes; and that it is grossly unjust to borrowers (that is, in the case of the national debt, to all tax-

163

payers) that they should be paying interest on the same nominal sums in a currency of full value, which were borrowed in a depreciated one. The depreciation, according to the views and objects of the particular writer, was represented to have averaged thirty, fifty, or even more than fifty per cent: and the conclusion was, that either we ought to return to this depreciated currency, or to strike off from the national debt, and from mortgages or other private debts of old standing, a percentage corresponding to the estimated amount of the depreciation.

To this doctrine, the following was the answer usually made. Granting that, by returning to cash payments without lowering the standard, an injustice was done to debtors, in holding them liable for the same amount of a currency enhanced in value, which they had borrowed while it was depreciated; it is now too late to make reparation for this injury. The debtors and creditors of to-day are not the debtors and creditors of 1819: the lapse of years has entirely altered the pecuniary relations of the community; and it being impossible now to ascertain the particular persons who were either benefited or injured, to attempt to retrace our steps would not be redressing a wrong, but superadding a second act of wide-spread injustice to the one already committed. This argument is certainly conclusive on the practical question; but it places the honest conclusion on too narrow and too low a ground. It concedes that the measure of 1819, called Peel's Bill, by which cash payments were resumed at the original standard of 3*l*. 17*s*. 10½*d*., was really the injustice it was said to be. This is an admission wholly opposed to the truth. Parliament had no alternative; it was absolutely bound to adhere to the acknowledged standard; as may be shown on three distinct grounds, two of fact, and one of principle.

The reasons of fact are these. In the first place, it is not true that the debts, private or public, incurred during the Bank restriction, were contracted in a currency of lower value than that in which the interest is now paid. It is indeed true that the suspension of the obligation to pay in specie did put it in the power of the Bank to depreciate the currency. It is true also that the Bank really exercised that power, though to a far less extent than is often pretended; since the difference between the market price of gold and the Mint valuation, during the greater part of the interval, was very trifling, and when it was greatest, during the last five years of the war, did not much exceed thirty per cent. To the extent of that difference, the currency was depreciated, that is, its value was below that of the standard to which it professed to adhere. But the state of Europe at that time was such – there was so unusual an absorption of the precious metals, by hoarding, and in the military chests of the vast armies which then desolated the Continent, that the value of the standard itself was very considerably raised: and the best authorities, among whom it is sufficient to name Mr. Tooke, have, after an elaborate investigation, satisfied themselves that the difference between paper and bullion was not greater than the enhancement in value of gold itself, and that the paper, though depreciated relatively to the then value of gold, did not sink below the ordinary value, at other times, either of gold or of a convertible paper. If this be true (and the evidences of the fact are conclusively stated in Mr. Tooke's *History of Prices*) the foundation of the whole case against the fundholder and other creditors on the ground of depreciation is subverted.

But, secondly, even if the currency had really been lowered in value at each period of the Bank restriction, in the same degree in which it was depreciated in relation to its standard, we must remember that a part only of the national debt, or of other permanent engagements, was incurred during the Bank restriction. A large part had been contracted before 1797; a still larger during the early years of the restriction, when the difference between paper and gold was yet small. To the holders of the former part, an injury was done, by paying the interest for twenty-two years in a depreciated currency: those of the second, suffered an injury during the years in which the interest was paid in a currency more depreciated than that in which the loans were contracted. To have resumed cash payments at a lower standard would have been to perpetuate the injury to these two classes of creditors, in order to avoid giving an undue benefit to a third class, who had lent their money during the few years of greatest depreciation. As it is, there was an underpayment to one set of persons, and an overpayment to another. The late Mr. Mushet took the trouble to make an arithmetical comparison between the two amounts. He ascertained, by calculation, that if an account had been made out in 1819, of what the fundholders had gained and lost by the variation of the paper currency from its standard, they would have been found as a body to have been losers; so that if any compensation was due on the ground of depreciation, it would not be from the fundholders collectively, but to them.

Thus it is with the facts of the case. But these reasons of fact are not the strongest. There is a reason of principle, still more powerful. Suppose that, not a part of the debt merely, but the whole, had been contracted in a depreciated currency, depreciated not only in comparison with its standard, but with its own value before and after; and that we were now paying the interest on this debt in a currency fifty or even a hundred per cent more valuable than that in which it was contracted. What difference would this make in the obligation of paying it, if the condition that it should be so paid was part of the original compact? Now this is not only truth, but less than the truth. The compact stipulated better terms for the fundholder than he has received. During the whole continuance of the Bank restriction, there was a parliamentary pledge, by which the legislature was as much bound as any legislature is capable of binding itself, that cash payments should be resumed on the original footing, at farthest in six months after the conclusion of a general peace. This was there-fore an actual condition of every loan; and the terms of the loan were more favourable in consideration of it. Without some such stipulation, the Govern-ment could not have expected to borrow, unless on the terms on which loans are made to the native princes of India. If it had been understood and avowed that, after borrowing the money, the standard at which it was commuted might be permanently lowered, to any extent which to the 'collective wisdom' of a legislature of borrowers might seem fit – who can say what rate of interest would have been a sufficient inducement to persons of common sense to risk their savings in such an adventure? However much the fundholders had gained by the resumption of cash payments, the terms of the contract insured their giving ample value for it. They gave value for more than they received; since cash payments were not resumed in six months, but in as many years, after the peace. So that waiving all our arguments except the last, and conced-ing all the facts asserted on the other side of the question, the fundholders, instead of being unduly benefited, are the injured party; and would have a claim to compensation, if such claims were not very properly barred by the impossibility of adjudication, and by the salutary general maxim of law and policy, 'quod interest reipublicæ ut sit finis litium.'

George Goschen (1831–1907)

Extract from *The Theory of Foreign Exchanges* (1861).

CHAPTER V.

REMARKS ON THE INTERPRETATION OF THE FOREIGN EXCHANGES.

IN the preceding chapters we have been occupied in tracing the origin and development of the transactions which result in the Foreign Exchanges, from their simplest to their more complicated forms, with the special object of discovering the various causes which combine to produce constant and important fluctuations in the prices of foreign bills. Having gained a theoretical insight into the principles of the system, we are now in a position to approach the more practical and interesting portion of the subject, and to examine it in its direct bearing upon commerce in general. Being acquainted with the influences which are proved to determine the fluctuations in question, we are enabled, by a reverse process, to argue back from them to the existence of their determining causes, and to consider the Foreign Exchanges in their peculiarly valuable character as an unerring mercantile and monetary barometer. But they are more than this. Not only do they offer to the trading community the means of ascertaining the state of the commercial atmosphere – indicating when the air is charged with a storm, or when fair weather is likely to set in, – they so clearly point to the disturbing currents, that their study and due comprehension suggest the course by which danger can be avoided, and moderate the precipitate action of panic.

The general feeling with regard to the function of the exchanges, as giving evidence of the mercantile (or rather monetary) situation of any country, is indicated by the usual phrase of a 'favourable' or 'unfavourable state of the exchanges,' a phrase which occurs so frequently in all banking discussions that it cannot be passed over without remark. Of its inaccuracy, in so far as it enters into the domain of political economy and applies to the general prosperity of the country, it is not necessary to speak. It may originally have implied the erroneous theory that the object of commerce is to attract gold, and that that country towards which the tide of bullion sets with the greatest force is *ipso facto* the most prosperous; that, accordingly, a position of the exchanges which points to an influx of specie is favourable, whereas, when bills become

169

so scarce that the precious metals must be exported, the situation is eminently unfavourable. But the phrase is accurate enough from the monetary or banking point of view. Under the present state of legislation all engagements involve payments in gold, or in paper convertible into gold, the merchants engaging to pay in gold or bank notes, at their option, and the Bank of England being bound by law, without option, to pay those bank notes in gold. Consequently it is of the highest importance to the whole banking and mercantile community, with a view to the certain fulfilment of such engagements, that the aggregate stock of bullion in the country should suffice to meet all wants. Whether the law is wise in itself is beside the argument, so long as the currency laws continue as they are. Under present circumstances a merchant or banker will consider that to be an unfavourable state of things which points to a *dangerous* diminution of the stock of gold, and he will consider that a favourable turn of the exchanges which tends in the opposite direction. When the stock of gold is evidently adequate, it is even in a banking point of view erroneous to consider a further accumulation advantageous or desirable. And just fault may be found with the use of the term 'favourable exchange' beyond the limits of the sufficiency of the bullion for the purposes of the currency; for the temporary excess of gold at one point is of no advantage whatever, but rather the reverse. The limit of the phrase should be strictly kept in view as legitimately applied to express the anxiety or confidence of the banking world as to the means of meeting their legal obligations. And accordingly there is no real discrepancy as to the class of facts which, in practice, the words 'favourable and unfavourable' exchanges denote. Political economists, from their point of view, are correct in their statement that, as regards the country at large and the interchange of commodities, exports and imports are always balanced, and that both the words 'unfavourable balance of trade' and 'unfavourable exchanges' involve a fallacy. But merchants and bankers are influenced by the feeling, that at any given moment they may be under greater liabilities for imports than they can temporarily meet, owing to the system of credit which disturbs the coincidence of payments for exports and imports, though their value may actually be equal; and further, by the anxiety as to the possibility of meeting these liabilities in that specific mode of payment to which they are pledged, namely, in gold or convertible notes. A proper understanding on these points is absolutely necessary, as otherwise differences of opinion might be supposed to exist, while the difference does not lie in the opinion or the theory, but simply in the application of a technical phrase. When, therefore, in banking treatises, it is said that the exchanges are favourable to any particular country, it should be understood that the intention is simply to state the fact that bills of that country upon foreign cities are difficult of sale, whilst bills drawn upon it from abroad are at a premium, indicating an eventual influx of specie. So, when it is said that the exchanges are unfavourable, a situation is described in which foreign bills are in great demand, and when, consequently, their value seems likely to be so enhanced as to render the export of bullion an unavoidable alternative.

It is necessary to call attention to another point before we proceed to consider the interpretation of fluctuating rates of exchange. It must be borne in mind that it is the price of short bills, not of those which have some time to run, which determines the course of bullion shipments. Most of the primary elements of value affect long and short bills equally; but the rate of interest and the question of credit exercise an additional influence upon the former, and so modify the fluctuations in their price as to render them unreliable as indications of the currents of gold. If there is a demand for bills upon any particular town, the price of all such bills, whether short or long, will rise. That is the general tendency. If, however, in the city in question, the rate of interest were at a very high point, it is evident that the price of long bills would not rise in the same proportion as that of short; for the purchaser must bear the discount, which has to be deducted from the long bill before it can become equally available with the short bill; and for any increase in this discount he requires to be compensated by a so much cheaper price. He must be compensated in the same manner for the risk which he will run till the bill be ultimately paid.

As an index of the general position of trade, the value of short bills is the more important; whereas the rates given for long paper, as compared with those for bills on demand, point mainly to the rate of interest, and partially to the state of credit.

Bearing in mind the existence of this distinction in those cases where (as, for instance, between London and Paris) the short exchange is the most prominent, and not straining it too much where, owing to various circumstances, long bills only are to be obtained to any amount, as is the case in St. Petersburg, we may now proceed to illustrate the method to be followed when it becomes desirable to interpret the indications afforded at any given moment by the Foreign Exchanges. It results, from the whole tenor of the previous arguments, that it is, above all, essential to remember that fluctuations can arise not only from one cause but *many*, and that till proof is given that actually no other influence is at work than the one which may be selected as possible and plausible, no trustworthy opinion can be formed. It is an error often committed, when scientific subjects are superficially or popularly treated, to consider it enough to point out one cause as sufficiently accounting for any phenomena, regardless of the fact that it is far more important to prove that there are no other causes which could have led to the same results. But on no occasion does this fallacy more frequently blind the judgment than in questions of mercantile finance, possibly because the facts with which they have to deal are so complex and entangled that any clear and intelligible solution of the difficulty is held to be sufficiently satisfactory, without regard to the necessity of applying further tests. Half of the benefit which might be derived by a study of the exchanges is lost in consequence of the tendency to be satisfied with the first plausible explanation. Egregious errors might be committed if an argument were founded on the state of the exchanges between Hamburg and London which relied on the balance of trade alone, without considering the difference of value which would result from a premium on silver, the currencies of the two countries being dissimilar. So it is not sufficient to consider the Russian exchanges simply as indicating the enormous indebtedness to foreign creditors, to the exclusion of the influence of the depreciated currency.

A notable instance of the necessity of never losing sight of any of the various elements of value which enter into the prices paid for bills of exchange, and also a valuable illustration of the question of interpretation generally, was afforded by the extraordinary course of the American exchanges at the beginning of 1861. A large efflux from Europe to the United States took place, and various theories were started as to its cause. But strangely enough, months elapsed before it was clearly acknowledged and understood by the majority of the public that this efflux of bullion was mainly the consequence of indebtedness. Another explanation, grounded on the growing troubles in the States (which were leading to a kind of panic), and on the presumed speculations of English capitalists, had been put forward as sufficiently explaining the prevailing drain; whereas the test of indebtedness should have been applied first of all. The specie shipments were hurried and intensified by peculiar modifications of that indebtedness; for instance, by the Americans drawing sooner than usual against their claims on England, by their suspending their orders for English manufactures, and by the forced and unnatural increase of exportation even of articles not wanted in Europe. But the primary cause of the fall of the exchanges which led to the flow of bullion to America lay in the immense excess of their exports of wheat and flour, following, too, on a cotton crop of unprecedented extent. Independently of the political crisis, Europe would have had to pay a balance to America in gold; and this was surely the cardinal point to keep in view, in considering whether the export of bullion would continue or cease. Such authorities as, at the commencement of the efflux of bullion, insisted on considering it as a simple speculation, and pointed to the folly of the merchants who sent it out, prophesying that probably it would return to them in the same ships, committed the error of looking principally to the stock of gold in New York, to the speculations in American securities, and to the operations of capitalists, rather than to the one broad fact, which was clearly discernible on closer inspection, that England and Europe were simply paying for their importations from America.

Stress was continually laid upon the fact that the stock of gold was accumulating in New York and was decreasing here, and it was argued that consequently the gold must return. It is plain, however, that for this result to take place, one of the following events would have to occur; either the bullion would be returned because the Americans owed money to us, and sent it to pay their debts; or it would be remitted against fresh orders for English manufactures or for American stocks held in English hands; or it would be sent here as a loan to English capitalists, in the expectation that money would, as was certainly probable, become dearer here than in America. Those who maintained that bullion would return, were bound to prove that one of these operations would take place. The first was a question of fact: Did the Americans owe much to Europe? The second was a question of probability: Was it likely that the Americans would regain sufficient confidence to enter upon new mercantile transactions? The third was also a question on which opinions might be divided: Was it probable, or the reverse, that in a time of great national emergency the New York bankers would remit their capital for employment to Europe, because gold accumulated rapidly in their vaults?

These were the questions upon the solution of which the slow or rapid return of bullion depended, and they might fairly have been made the subject of discussion. But to argue that, because in 1857 the bullion which was exported to America was immediately returned, the same result would be witnessed in 1861, was to overlook the fundamental and primary element of value in the Foreign Exchanges – the relative indebtedness. In 1857 the Americans had incurred enormous debts to Europe; in 1863 Europe had incurred enormous debts to them. Here was the key to the whole position. On the former occasion the export of specie to the States was unnatural and artificial. It was lending your debtor more, in the place of exacting payment. On the latter occasion the export of bullion was natural and inevitable, because it was made to discharge a debt; but the payment was somewhat hurried, and the usual rules were a little set aside, because the creditor (the American), finding himself in the midst of a most dangerous political crisis, became suddenly urgent to receive all that was due to him, and to forestall, rather than to delay, the settlement of his claim. He drew his bills, and forced them on the market with the eagerness of panic. Few buyers were to be found requiring them as remittances in discharge of European liabilities; for, trade had been curtailed, no new orders had been given, and, before the crisis commenced, the unusual prosperity of the Western States, in consequence of vast crops of grain, had made it possible for remittances against previous transactions to be sent earlier than usual. Thus, the bills were bought up in New York, not by such as had liabilities to discharge, but by such as were willing to advance the value of the bills till their equivalent in gold could be procured from England. This was the office of the New York banks, and by far the greater quantity of the bullion shipments consisted in what may be called the anticipated proceeds of these bills. Without the influence of panic, a high rate of interest on this side might have delayed the export of the proceeds, at least till the maturity of the bills. If these proceeds had remained longer on this side, they would either have constituted a loan to the banker to whom they were remitted, or they would have been invested in some kind of merchandize, and returned in that form rather than in gold. What other alternative was possible?

It may be asked, Why, if the balance of trade, in its simplest sense, was, to use the popular phrase, in favour of America – that is to say, if they owed less than they had to claim, – why, then, was there any ground for panic in New York? The answer is clearly that, from a monetary point of view, not only was there no reason whatever to induce a panic, but, on the contrary, there were evident grounds for confidence. Sellers of bills might foresee a difficulty in disposing of them above the specie point, and consequently up to that point press their bills upon the market; but the only apprehension that could be felt was, as to whether they would be able to obtain facilities till the time when the equivalent of their bills, if remitted to Europe to be converted into specie, would return into their possession. The aggregate of a community cannot be alarmed at the position of its money-market and of the exchanges, when the whole world is indebted to itself, at least so long as it has every confidence in the solvency of its debtors. The panic, if it may be called so, which occurred in America during that winter, was attributable *solely* to political causes, which rendered all who had bills for sale eager to underbid each other for the sake of immediate payment, and to accept a price far below what they would have realized if they had had their bills exchanged into gold in England. It was this urgency to secure themselves money at any price which induced the New York merchants to export every kind of produce, which normally, owing to the increase of the currency, would have risen in value in the States, to European markets, where prices were sure to fall owing to the decreasing currency. A panic usually occurs in the money-market of any country when the exchanges become unfavourable to it; but it is a rare occurrence to see alarm felt at an unusually favourable situation of the exchanges.

The ambiguity of the term 'favourable exchanges,' unless it be taken within the limits given above, that is to say, as denoting a simple monetary fact, and not as any judgment on the prosperity of trade, can be easily appreciated in this instance. The exchanges, when at such a point that the necessity of specie remittances from England to America was clearly indicated, were, as the phrase is, highly favourable to America, and the very reverse to ourselves. The

American exporters of grain and cotton were, however, the very class who, in the first instance, suffered most from the situation, in so far as the expense of the costly transmission of specie, with all the losses attached to it, would fall upon them. On the other hand, the English debtors may be argued with some plausibility not to have suffered any loss, because to them it was immaterial how they paid their bills at maturity – whether by handing the amount over to their neighbours, to whom the Americans would, in normal times, have remitted bills upon them; or by shipping it in gold by order and for account of their American creditors. But to a certain extent there is a fallacy in this, as the charge on the exporter so often falls on the consumer of the produce exported. To this extent the interests of the exporter become identical with those of the foreign country. For, that which adds to the cost of the article which he exports, must be borne either by him or by the consumer of his produce; and it is their joint interest that no such addition should be made. The cost of the transmission of bullion is an addition of this nature; and therefore it is contrary to the interest of the exporter, and of the country to which he exports, that such an expense should have to be incurred.

Thus we come to the position, that a condition of the exchanges which leads to the importation of specie into any country favours the importers and consumers of that country, but causes an additional charge to the export trade. However, the extra charge upon this export trade having ultimately, on the above supposition, to be paid by foreign countries, it may be maintained that the state of the exchanges indicated is, in a certain sense, favourable to the country in question, and unfavourable to the foreigners with whom it trades. A clearer view may be gained of this position if it be assumed for the moment (what is partially true) that each country *fetches* from the other that which it requires; in other words, that the export trade of a country is managed upon the order system. Cotton and grain may be sent from the States, not for account of American sellers, but of English buyers, who have given their orders. If the article is bought by a foreign buyer in the place of its production, it is plain that any sudden extra charge upon exportation must be borne by him; and thus a sudden fall in the exchanges, which makes his bill upon his London house less valuable, or causes the whole cost of the transmission of bullion from England to pay for his purchases to fall upon him, becomes unfavourable to the country to which he belongs, and for which he is buying, and not to that from which he is buying. Conversely, the Americans who give orders to English manufacturers are able, during the same period of low exchanges, to buy up bills on England which will pay for their goods, at a cheaper rate than usual, and are able to save the expense of the transmission of bullion, which, during normal times, generally falls on a portion of the American importers. As far as facility and economy in paying for the products of other countries are concerned, a state of the exchanges which renders it possible to purchase bills to pay for them, cheaply and easily, may correctly be designated as favourable.

Returning from this digression, which was prompted by the desire of throwing additional light on the use of the words 'favourable and unfavourable exchanges,' and resuming the consideration of the general mode in which the Foreign Exchanges are to be read and interpreted, we shall find in the course of the American Exchanges during 1862–3 further materials for instructive analysis. In 1861 we saw an extraordinary depression in the price of foreign bills in New York. The situation was afterwards reversed. After the lapse of a certain interval a rise of extraordinary extent and rapidity occurred. How was this change to be interpreted? To what phenomena did it point?

No better illustration for the examination of the different influences which affect Foreign Exchanges could be found. Here we have a case where the effects were evidently greater than could be caused solely by a change in that which we have called the primary element of value – international indebtedness; for the rise went far beyond the normal specie limit. The sudden transmission of capital from America to Europe, and the continuance of a demand for importations from abroad, while the exportation of cotton was stopped by the blockade of the southern ports, might account for the phenomenon to a certain extent, but not beyond what we have so often called the specie limit. We are driven to look for another element of value, for one more unlimited in its operation; and that will at once be found in the depreciation of the currency, of which alone, among the various elements of value determining the price of foreign bills, it could be said, that it rendered fluctuations illimitable. The passing of an act suspending specie payments in the United States, and authorising the issue of inconvertible Government paper money, removed the normal specie limit, and the extent to which the prices of foreign bills could rise, at once became an open question. It was to be anticipated that the effects of a depreciated currency would be developed to their full extent, and it became possible for the Foreign Exchanges to rise, not a few per cents., but 50 or 100 or even 200 per cent. In the Southern States the exchange on London actually rose to 400 per cent.

Experience was at fault as to the probable practical limits, and theory could only establish, as a result certain to ensue, that with every issue of inconvertible paper money a progressive rise, proportionate to the depreciation of the currency, would unavoidably take place. Strangely enough, in the Northern States the rise was actually delayed far beyond the time when it was expected to occur, and the Americans began to believe that it was possible to print paper money without losing gold, or depreciating the remainder of the currency.

The causes of this delay well deserve examination, though, from the complexity of the facts, it is difficult to arrive at any certain results. Two causes have been suggested, which are sufficiently plausible: the one that, during the first months of the issue of the Government paper money, the private banks called in their notes to a very great extent, and that thus the aggregate currency was not increased as much as might have been expected; the other, that the area over which the American currency extends is so vast that the effects of an over-issue of paper would be less rapidly felt.[*] It was said, too, that in the West a considerable dearth of currency had previously existed, and that, consequently, there was a gap to be filled up. However this might be, the satisfaction which was felt by the Americans at the issue of paper money without a heavy fall in its value was of short duration, and the theories of political economy were abundantly justified in the end. An unexampled rise in the American Exchanges took place, the exchange advancing by degrees in little more than a year from 110 to 180. In a former chapter, the endeavour was made to gauge, as far as possible, the probable extent of fluctuations in the exchanges arising from a depreciated currency, and it was shown that where a premium in gold was not prohibited by law, the prices of foreign bills would rise in proportion to the extent to which prices of all purchaseable articles, bullion included, are raised by such depreciation; in other words, in proportion to the discount on the paper money, or the premium on gold. Beyond that proportion, the fact of the depreciation of the currency would scarcely cause them to deviate. Accordingly, on examining the price of foreign bills in New York and the price of gold, we shall see that they constantly rose and fell together. Before the depreciation of the currency, the actual par of exchange for bills on England was, as will presently be explained, expressed in the form of 109. When gold rose, the foreign bills rose as much beyond this point of 109, as gold rose above par, leaving the same margin (and the same variations within that margin), between the premium on gold and the price of sterling bills, as that which, in normal times, existed between the nominal par of exchange and the actual mean premium on English bills: but this margin, which was 9 per cent. before, having itself to be calculated in depreciated currency, become apparently – but only apparently – greater.

In order that this may be properly understood, it may be necessary to state the mode in which the value of bills on England is calculated in America. The

---

[*] In a criticism on the second edition of this work, two further causes have been suggested which no doubt were also in operation: the general contraction of credit throughout the States, and the enormous war expenditure; both of which circumstances would unquestionably lead to the absorption of a considerable amount of currency.

basis of the calculation is that forty dollars are equal to £9, so that the dollar would be equal to 4s. 6d. But as this assumed par of exchange does not coincide with the actual value of the gold in the dollar and the sovereign, the £9 being worth 9 per cent. more than the forty dollars, gold for gold,* (by which the value of the dollar is reduced to about 4s. 1½d.,) the calculation has to be rectified, when bills on England are bought, by 9 dollars being added to every 100 dollars of the purchase-money. It was a fact that, as long as a gold currency existed on both sides of the Atlantic, the actual par of exchange between New York and London was about 9 per cent. nominal premium, or, as it was technically phrased, bills on London stood, when the exchanges were in a state of equilibrium, at 109. This difference (or corrective premium) of 9 per cent. *in gold currency* would be modified, either upwards or downwards, by the various other influences to which the Foreign Exchanges have been shown to be subject, by the state of indebtedness, the rate of interest, in fact, by supply and demand; but it constituted the mean specie point. After the depreciation of the currency, when prices of bills, as of other articles, were no longer expressed in dollars having a certain value in gold, but in dollars of depreciated value, it was to be expected that the same actual difference of 9 per cent. in gold would still enter into the price of foreign bills, but that it would be expressed in its equivalent of paper dollars; in other words, that these 9 per cent. would also be increased in exact proportion to the premium on gold. Thus we arrive at the following result: – if, before the issue of paper money, the purchaser of a bill on England paid 100 dollars and 9 dollars for it, he would, if the premium on gold had risen to 50 per cent., in the first place pay 150 dollars instead of the 100, and in the second 13½ dollars instead of nine dollars, or half as much again as what we may call the correcting premium. Thus, if the price of bills, when gold stood at 150, was 163½, this price would correspond to the price of 109 at the time when there was no premium on gold. The price might rise to 165 or fall to 161, according as there was supply or demand, but the mean point would be ascertained by the process which has been described.

Disturbing causes were introduced by legislative enactments which interfered with the free commerce in gold, and consequently tended to vary occasionally the relative value between bills and gold, by encumbering all operations in the latter with certain charges and inconveniences. Taxes on transactions in gold would have the same force as increased charges on specie shipments, and would thus have a tendency to widen the margin between the premium on gold and the premium on bills.

* The exact difference between the gold contained in 9 sovereigns and in 40 dollars is nearer 9½ than 9 per cent., but the quotation given in the text is accurate enough for the general argument.

And, besides the taxes imposed on operations in gold, there were other circumstances which induced those who had occasion to buy either foreign bills or gold, to give a preference to the latter, so that a somewhat artificial demand arose. For instance, fears were continually entertained that the export of gold might at any time be prohibited, either directly or indirectly; and thus, naturally, the preference was given to that species of remittance of which the export could not be forbidden. Or again, if gold or bills were to be purchased in order to be hoarded or held some little time before being used as remittances, interest would be lost upon gold but earned upon bills; for when these came to be sold, they would be worth so much more, as being nearer their maturity. Similarly, there were charges and risks, needless to specify, incident upon the holding of gold, which were not incurred in the holding of bills, and thus many considerations (but especially the constant interference of the government) would tend to widen the margin between gold and bills, and create violent perturbations at particular moments which could not be accounted for simply by the depreciation of the currency.

The extraordinary state of the Foreign Exchanges in America during the period with which we have been dealing, is peculiarly difficult to explain in a simple form, but is all the more instructive because it offers the opportunity of viewing the different elements of value in simultaneous and sometimes conflicting operation. The depreciation of the currency by the issue of 'greenbacks' exercised, it is true, so overwhelming an influence, as to have rendered difficult the discovery of the operation of other elements of value. These, however, so long as any foreign trade subsists, can never be entirely absent. According as the Americans have remitted their funds to this country, in order to secure a portion of their fortune against the contingency of progressive depreciation, so has there been a demand for bills upon England. Immense sums are said to have been remitted to English bankers by American correspondents, because this was clearly the safest course by which to secure their fortunes against loss and at the same time to earn a moderate interest. In America every species of banking investments was subject to daily depreciation, and such fortunes as consisted in securities payable in dollars, were rapidly melting away. Investments in gold were largely resorted to, but, as we have explained, they were dangerous, on account of the action of the government, and unremunerative, owing to the loss of interest. Remittances to foreign countries combined the advantage of security with that of remunerative employment for capital, and many millions sterling have been sent to Europe for this purpose. Some surprise has been caused by the fact that the gold remittances from New York have not been so great as might have been expected. But a portion of the capital which thus found its way to England flowed through an indirect channel. It was sent from the ports of California

179

instead of from the port of New York. By the adoption of this course, the great risks on the transmission of gold from California to New York were avoided, while the object of remittances to Europe was as conveniently attained. Without these bullion remittances the demand for bills must have been even greater than it was; for the Americans required funds in England, not only for the purposes which have just been indicated, but also for the payment of the large quantities of military stores purchased in this country, and for that amount of European manufactures which, however much the Americans may curtail their trade, they are obliged to purchase for immediate wants. No cotton bills being obtainable in New York, owing to the blockade, and fewer corn bills existing, owing to the reduction of that trade in consequence of plentiful harvests in Europe, no doubt the demand for bills (notwithstanding the Californian remittances) has been great, and this demand has increased the premium on sterling bills. But this increase of the premium, it will be remembered, can never exceed the expense, the risks, and the inconveniences, in their widest sense, on bullion remittances. For as soon as this margin between the premium on gold and the premium on bills on England, exceeded the 9 per cent. to which we have alluded, plus the premium on these 9 per cent. and plus the expenses on shipping the bullion, – those who desired to remit, would, as explained before, rather ship the bullion itself; and as the export of gold had not been prohibited, a remittance in gold could always be made. With many apparent discrepancies, the upward course of the American exchanges was really governed by the few simple principles which have been discussed in the earlier portion of this treatise. Amidst the complexity of the particular combination, the effect of the few leading causes which lay at the bottom of the whole, stands out clearly enough, and, it may be repeated, the rise in the price of foreign bills, owing to the unlimited issue of greenbacks, could be predicted with the most absolute certainty.

It is less easy to explain the rapid fall which followed on the battle of Gettysburg and the opening up of the Mississippi. But the difficulty lies rather in explaining the fall in the premium on gold than the fall in the prices of foreign bills, the latter being simply the consequence of the former. It is true, indeed, that in a question of the interpretation of the Foreign Exchanges, the premium on gold is only a collateral issue. But as we have followed the rise in gold, it may be interesting briefly to examine its fall. If a redundancy of currency created the premium, it would seem natural that only a diminution of the over-issue should cause a corresponding fall. The conversion of some portion of greenbacks into stock was a measure operating in this direction, but it was accompanied by fresh issues, which neutralized its effect. Besides, this conversion was in operation before the fall, even at the time when the premium was rising, and therefore cannot have contributed to the sudden fall in any great degree. The result would rather be due to the belief suddenly springing up that the quantity of paper money would really be reduced, either by a further more effectual conversion, or by a redemption in bullion at a shorter date than appeared possible during the darker period of Northern prospects. It is scarcely possible to judge whether the fall in gold was justified or not, without venturing on an opinion as to the ability or the intention of the Washington government to reduce that currency which it has for its own purposes created; but the belief on the part of the American community that this intention and ability did exist, no doubt exercised some portion of the influence which actual measures taken by the Government would have produced. This belief had the further effect of inducing persons, who had hoarded gold from a fear of a further depreciation of the currency, (and who had even before been somewhat alarmed by the measures taken against this very hoarding by the Government), to sell their stock of gold as fast as possible, giving up the idea of a further rise. And the Government, too, is said to have contributed, by somewhat artificial means, to a premature decline in the premium on gold, by throwing large sums on the market which it had been able to accumulate, as it was thought, for this very purpose. If so, a reaction is highly probable. An over-issue of paper money can only be counteracted by a subsequent contraction. It may be possible, perhaps, by artificial means, to discount this result, but not to produce it. And thus it is to be anticipated that, unless measures are taken to follow up temporary expedients by permanent improvements, the price of gold may once more advance.[*] On the other hand, the adoption of such measures is facilitated by the fact of the position of the Americans being favourable in this respect – that their currency is depreciated simply by internal and not by external causes. Probably they owe less to Europe than they have done at any other previous time in late years, and they have the further advantage that the large deposits which they have made in Europe, give them the power, at any moment they may want it, of regaining a great portion of the gold which they have lost. As to the extent to which the revival of the cotton trade may affect the exchanges, and compel Europe to send bullion to America, many circumstances will have to be considered. It will be a question of time, rather than of indebtedness. The Americans will be in need of large quantities of goods from this side, and the question will be, whether they can supply us faster with cotton than we can supply them with goods. The probability is, that we shall be more urgent for cotton than they for manufactures; but it is less certain that the quantity of cotton required will be immediately available, whereas the

---

[*] The correctness of this view was practically demonstrated even before the second edition was issued. An advance in gold again took place, which has since, with many fluctuations, made further progress. – December, 1863.

181

export of our manufactures on its former scale can, if necessary, at once be renewed. However, on the whole, as we may certainly assume that we shall immediately want the cotton, and as, from the disorganization of the cotton trade, credit will be less available, and cash payments more imperative, the probable necessity of an export of bullion on our part seems to preponderate, though not to the extent that is generally believed. A most important consideration will be, whether the Americans will be anxious to receive gold with a view to re-establish a metallic currency, or whether, owing little to foreign countries, they will be content to let their depreciated currency continue in the state in which the end of the war may find it, fancying, perhaps, that it may right itself. What, it may be asked, will be the value of gold to them, if they neither require it for internal circulation, which, they may think, can be managed as well by paper, nor for the payment of foreign liabilities, from which, under our hypothesis, they will be comparatively free?

Nevertheless, gold will be the only equivalent which, if they do not immediately take large quantities of goods from Europe, we shall be able to offer them for cotton. Consequently we may expect one of two things to happen. Either, though they may not have the immediate intention of improving their currency, the premium on gold, through the abundant supply which the circumstances indicated will place at their disposal, will fall to such a degree as to hasten their action in spite of their indifference; or, what is quite as probable, the temptation will rather be to increase their imports than to improve their currency; a great inflation of prices and of trade in general will ensue; the inducement which a redundant circulation of paper money so often creates, of importing to an unlimited extent, will have its full effect; and foreign liabilities will thus be created which will absorb that surplus of gold of which the situation described has given them the command. In the former case American finance may possibly issue from its ordeal without a catastrophe, in the latter and more probable case, a terrible collapse will, in the end, be inevitable.

The foregoing remarks upon particular instances where the Foreign Exchanges offered peculiar opportunities for analysis, are not intended to be historical or exhaustive, but only illustrative of the general question of interpretation which forms the special subject of the present chapter. In the description of the American Exchanges in 1861, it was proved that the omission of the most important element of value, namely, relative indebtedness, led in the first place to an erroneous interpretation of the perfectly natural efflux of bullion, and in the second to a mistaken estimate of its probable duration. In the course of the same exchanges during the two following years, it was the depreciation of the currency to which, while interpreting the remarkable fluctuations which have occurred, we mainly found we had to look. In both cases, indeed, it was seen, that it was indispensable not to lose sight of other elements of value, while attributing the chief influence to one; but it is, above all, important that a real and fundamental cause should always be sought, and that it should not be supposed, as it sometimes is, that the action of speculators can more than modify, hasten, or retard natural causes. For instance, when specie is being exported, it is sometimes supposed to be merely what is called an exchange operation, undertaken by a certain class of speculators, whose business it is to make a profit out of the variations in the price of foreign bills at different moments, buying them when they are cheap and selling them at a profit, and sometimes sending bullion abroad to buy up bills on their own country, if the prices should be temporarily below or touching specie point. Gold will of course not be exported so long as these speculators in exchange, or cambists, as they are technically called, can procure short bills. They wish to place funds at a certain spot. As long as they can procure short bills in the quantities they desire – as long, that is to say, as there are sufficient foreign debts owing to their own country, payable immediately, which can be transferred to them, and which they can pass on to others – they will not export gold. An efflux of gold accordingly proves, whoever the exporters may be, that the supply of short bills on other countries is being exhausted, that there is little more to claim at the moment from the country to which the bullion is despatched, and that the balance of indebtedness is temporarily against the country in question.

A further inference may be deduced from the foregoing remarks. It is often supposed that gold is never exported unless to give a profit to those who despatch it. But this is manifestly a fallacious idea. The expression which is so often made use of, that the rates of exchange in any country are at such a point that no profit is to be made on shipments of gold to it, must be carefully guarded from leading to a misconception. Such a fact is valuable to know, to a certain degree; but it does not prove that the despatch of bullion may not be natural and necessary nevertheless. It must be sent by those who are in debt to that country, if they cannot find bills. It is far more important to inquire, Is the balance of indebtedness discharged? The exchanges may remain exactly at specie point for a long time, offering no prospects of profits to any cambists, yet compelling the constant flow of bullion in order to discharge liabilities. It is indispensable to consider what debts have to be paid, before a judgment as to the drain of bullion can be formed. It is not so superfluous as many might believe, to dwell so frequently and so strongly upon this point, because, as a matter of fact, language is continually held, even among men who should be well versed in questions of this kind, which is practically at variance with the principles here put forth, though, in theory, they command immediate assent.

The question of profits on exchange operations can be reduced within very narrow limits. If carried beyond them, it only serves to obscure the plain operation of natural causes, without being essential to the real understanding of the subject. Profits can habitually be realized by those who, when they observe that there is a prospect of the demand for bills exceeding the supply, purchase in anticipation, in order to sell at a higher price when the natural buyers, who require the bills for remittances, enter the market later on. And even when the exchanges reach the specie point, profits, though on a very limited scale, are made by those who, by having establishments identical with their own in foreign cities, and having a machinery specially organized for the purpose, are able, by the avoidance of commission and the reduction of charges, to make bullion shipments at a cheaper cost than the actual merchants or manufacturers who have the remittances to make. They despatch the gold and sell the bills drawn against this gold to those who require to send funds abroad, realizing a fractional profit for the convenience which they afford. This, however, is in reality a matter of detail, and, as far as the exchanges and the principles which determine them are concerned, it is perfectly indifferent whether the debtors to foreign countries – that is to say, importers, merchants, or consumers – remit gold themselves, or pay a slight profit to cambists and bullion dealers, who, shipping it in large quantities, retail the bills drawn there against to such as require to remit.

It is only in perfectly abnormal times that large profits are to be made on specie shipments, and only when the countries to which the shipments are made, lie at a very considerable distance; so that those who have the sagacity to ship in time, or before others deem it necessary, have the advantage of being able to buy up bills below the specie point, owing to the urgent necessity of the sellers of the bills to receive the equivalent immediately; otherwise, it has been proved to be abundantly clear that the seller of such a bill, – rather than allow such as have bullion on the spot by having shipped it in anticipation, to make a profit which would be his own loss, – would send his bill to be encashed, and wait for the returns in specie himself. Where there can be immediate action and immediate communication, as between London and Paris, there can be scarcely any further profits upon shipments of gold beyond those which can be effected by an economy of charges. Only those who have a machinery for the purpose can gain a profit which, in reality, is a kind of commission paid by the rest of the community. At a distance, there is much more margin; as, where months may elapse before bills can, by their natural process, be converted into coin, those who can undertake to give this coin on the spot can often make their own terms.

The limits are, therefore, clear enough within which the natural action of the exchanges may be checked or intensified by the operations of cambists. In the case of a gradual fall in the exchanges in a distant country, where, if left to themselves, they might recede below specie point, because the unfortunate drawers of bills, being unable to wait the arrival of specie for their own account, might require their equivalent immediately, it might modify the position very much if speculators in foreign bills had foreseen the occurrence, and sent out specie to anticipate their wants, securing to themselves a moderate profit, but saving the drawers from a much heavier sacrifice. These are points which it is necessary to understand and appreciate, and which come into consideration in interpreting the exchanges of a given country at any given moment, but they can never impair the correctness of those elements of value which in principle determine the price of bills.

Of these it has repeatedly been pointed out, that the balance of indebtedness, in its widest sense, is the most fundamental, entering in a greater or less degree into almost every case in which Foreign Exchanges are concerned. But the interpreter of the fluctuations in Foreign Exchanges will bear in mind that there are limits to the variations produced by this one particular cause. He will remember the peculiar features in the rates of exchange which would point to differences in currency, as distinguished from other disturbing causes. These will be remarkable for extending far beyond the limits within which such fluctuations as are caused by excessive imports or exports, are ordinarily confined, and for being far more arbitrary and eccentric in their movements. So, too, he will not forget the influence of credit or discredit, and at any time of panic or other temporary derangement of confidence, the discount at which bills are sold will not be mistaken for the result of an adverse balance of trade or a depreciated currency. And, again, it will be borne in mind that sudden movements in the exchanges, either upwards or downwards, may reflect the position of the rate of interest in different countries, not only in the case of long dated bills, the variations in the prices of which, when they differ from the variations of bills payable on demand, are regulated exclusively by the value of money and by credit; but also in the case of those bills on demand themselves, as indicating that a high or low rate of interest is causing certain movements of capital from one country to another. The most general fact of which the exchanges are the sign, is the degree of intensity to which the demand for bills on a foreign country exists, for whatever purpose this demand may arise; and it is clear that such a demand may be caused as much by a desire to remit a certain amount of capital to that country for the sake of employing it at a high rate of interest, as for the purpose of paying a debt. A high rate of interest attracts capital from abroad, and the effect of this attraction is immediately perceptible in the exchanges. By recalling the most elementary view of the transactions with which the exchanges are concerned, and by realizing the fact that foreign bills, to the prices of which so much importance is attached, are but the instruments by which payments are effected between different countries, it becomes clear at once that in the prices paid for such bills we may discern the strength of the current in which capital is setting towards one point or another, and that the effect of every influence which may be brought to bear, to arrest or to hasten the force of this tide, will be registered with unerring certainty in the variations of the so-called 'rates of exchange.' Hence arises that intimate connection between the variations in the rate of interest, and the fluctuations in the Foreign Exchanges, which has long been recognised as one of the first principles to be kept in view in the study of monetary questions.

W. Stanley Jevons (1835–82)

Extract from *Money and the Mechanism of Exchange* (1875).

CHAPTER I.

BARTER.

SOME years since, Mademoiselle Zélie, a singer of the Théâtre Lyrique at Paris, made a professional tour round the world, and gave a concert in the Society Islands. In exchange for an air from *Norma* and a few other songs, she was to receive a third part of the receipts. When counted, her share was found to consist of three pigs, twenty-three turkeys, forty-four chickens, five thousand cocoa-nuts, besides considerable quantities of bananas, lemons, and oranges. At the Halle in Paris, as the prima donna remarks in her lively letter, printed by M. Wolowski, this amount of live stock and vegetables might have brought four thousand francs, which would have been good remuneration for five songs. In the Society Islands, however, pieces of money were very scarce; and as Mademoiselle could not consume any considerable portion of the receipts herself, it became necessary in the mean time to feed the pigs and poultry with the fruit.

When Mr. Wallace was travelling in the Malay Archipelago, he seems to have suffered rather from the scarcity than the superabundance of provisions. In his most interesting account of his travels, he tells us that in some of the islands, where there was no proper currency, he could not procure supplies for dinner without a special bargain and much chaffering upon each occasion. If the vendor of fish or other coveted eatables did not meet with the sort of exchange desired, he would pass on, and Mr. Wallace and his party had to go without their dinner. It therefore became very desirable to keep on hand a supply of articles, such as knives, pieces of cloth, arrack, or sago cakes, to multiply the chance that one or other article would suit the itinerant merchant.

In modern civilized society the inconveniences of the primitive method of exchange are wholly unknown, and might almost seem to be imaginary. Accustomed from our earliest years to the use of money, we are unconscious of the inestimable benefits which it confers upon us; and only when we recur to altogether different states of society can we realize the difficulties which arise in its absence. It is even surprising to be reminded that barter is actually the sole method of commerce among many uncivilized races. There is something absurdly incongruous in the fact that a joint-stock company, called 'The African Barter Company, Limited,' exists in London, which carries on its transactions upon the West Coast of Africa entirely by bartering European manufactures for palm oil, gold dust, ivory, cotton, coffee, gum, and other raw produce.

The earliest form of exchange must have consisted in giving what was not wanted directly for that which was wanted. This simple traffic we call *barter* or *truck*, the French *troc*, and distinguish it from sale and purchase in which one of the articles exchanged is intended to be held only for a short time, until it is parted with in a second act of exchange. The object which thus temporarily intervenes in sale and purchase is money. At first sight it might seem that the use of money only doubles the trouble, by making two exchanges necessary where one was sufficient; but a slight analysis of the difficulties inherent in simple barter shows that the balance of trouble lies quite in the opposite direction. Only by such an analysis can we become aware that money performs not merely one service to us, but several different services, each indispensable. Modern society could not exist in its present complex form without the means which money constitutes of valuing, distributing, and contracting for commodities of various kinds.

Want of Coincidence in Barter.

The first difficulty in barter is to find two persons whose disposable possessions mutually suit each other's wants. There may be many people wanting, and many possessing those things wanted; but to allow of an act of barter, there must be a double coincidence, which will rarely happen. A hunter having returned from a successful chase has plenty of game, and may want arms and ammunition to renew the chase. But those who have arms may happen to be well supplied with game, so that no direct exchange is possible. In civilized society the owner of a house may find it unsuitable, and may have his eye upon another house exactly fitted to his needs. But even if the owner of this second house wishes to part with it at all, it is exceedingly unlikely that he will exactly reciprocate the feelings of the first owner, and wish to barter houses. Sellers and purchasers can only be made to fit by the use of some commodity, some *marchandise banale*, as the French call it, which all are willing to receive for a time, so that what is obtained by sale in one case, may be used in purchase in another. This common commodity is called a *medium of exchange*, because it forms a third or intermediate term in all acts of commerce.

Within the last few years a curious attempt has been made to revive the practice of barter by the circulation of advertisements. *The Exchange and Mart* is a newspaper which devotes itself to making known all the odd property which its advertisers are willing to give for some coveted article. One person has some old coins and a bicycle, and wants to barter them for a good concertina. A young lady desires to possess 'Middlemarch,' and offers a variety of old songs, of which she has become tired. Judging from the size and circulation of the paper, and the way in which its scheme has been imitated by some other weekly papers, we must assume that the offers are sometimes accepted, and that the printing press can bring about, in some degree, the double coincidence necessary to an act of barter.

Want of a Measure of Value.

A second difficulty arises in barter. At what rate is any exchange to be made? If a certain quantity of beef be given for a certain quantity of corn, and in like manner corn be exchanged for cheese, and cheese for eggs, and eggs for flax, and so on, still the question will arise – How much beef for how much flax, or how much of any one commodity for a given quantity of another? In a state of barter the price-current list would be a most complicated document, for each commodity would have to be quoted in terms of every other commodity, or else complicated rule-of-three sums would become necessary. Between one hundred articles there must exist no less than 4950 possible ratios of exchange, and all these ratios must be carefully adjusted so as to be consistent with each other, else the acute trader will be able to profit by buying from some and selling to others.

All such trouble is avoided if any one commodity be chosen, and its ratio of exchange with each other commodity be quoted. Knowing how much corn is to be bought for a pound of silver, and also how much flax for the same quantity of silver, we learn without further trouble how much corn exchanges for so much flax. The chosen commodity becomes *a common denominator* or *common measure of value*, in terms of which we estimate the values of all other goods, so that their values become capable of the most easy comparison.

Want of Means of Subdivision.

A third but it may be a minor inconvenience of barter arises from the impossibility of dividing many kinds of goods. A store of corn, a bag of gold dust, a carcase of meat, may be portioned out, and more or less may be given in exchange for what is wanted. But the tailor, as we are reminded in several treatises on political economy, may have a coat ready to exchange, but it much exceeds in value the bread which he wishes to get from the baker, or the meat from the butcher. He cannot cut the coat up without destroying the value of his handiwork. It is obvious that he needs some medium of exchange, into which he can temporarily convert the coat, so that he may give a part of its value for bread, and other parts for meat, fuel, and daily necessaries, retaining perhaps a portion for future use. Further illustration is needless; for it is obvious that we need a means of dividing and distributing value according to our varying requirements.

In the present day barter still goes on in some cases, even in the most advanced commercial countries, but only when its inconveniences are not experienced. Domestic servants receive part of their wages in board and lodging: the farm labourer may partially receive payment in cider, or barley, or the use of a piece of land. It has always been usual for the miller to be paid by a portion of the corn which he grinds. The *truck* or barter system, by which workmen took their wages in kind, has hardly yet been extinguished in some parts of England. Pieces of land are occasionally exchanged by adjoining landowners; but all these are comparatively trifling cases. In almost all acts of exchange money now intervenes in one way or other, and even when it does not pass from hand to hand, it serves as the measure by which the amounts given and received are estimated. Commerce begins with barter, and in a certain sense it returns to barter; but the last form of barter, as we shall see, is very different from the first form. By far the greater part of commercial payments are made at the present day in England apparently without the aid of metallic money; but they are readily adjusted, because money acts as the common denominator, and what is bought in one direction is balanced off against what is sold in another direction.

CHAPTER II.

EXCHANGE.

MONEY is the measure and standard of value and the medium of exchange, yet it is not necessary that I should enter upon more than a very brief discussion concerning the nature of value, and the advantage of exchange. Every one must allow that the exchange of commodities depends upon the obvious principle that each of our wants taken separately requires a limited quantity of some article to produce satisfaction. Hence as each want becomes fully satiated, our desire, as Senior so well remarked, is for variety, that is, for the satisfaction of some other want. The man who is supplied daily with three pounds of bread, will not desire more bread; but he will have a strong inclination for beef, and tea, and alcohol. If he happen to meet with a person who has plenty of beef but no bread, each will give that which is less desired for that which is more desired. Exchange has been called *the barter of the superfluous for the necessary*, and this definition will be correct if we state it as *the barter of the comparatively superfluous for the comparatively necessary*.

It is impossible, indeed, to decide exactly how much bread, or beef, or tea, or how many coats and hats a person needs. There is no precise limit to our desires, and we can only say, that as we have a larger supply of a substance, the urgency of our need for more is in some proportion weakened. A cup of water in the desert, or upon the field of battle, may save life, and become infinitely useful. Two or three pints per day for each person are needful for drinking and cooking purposes. A gallon or two per day are highly requisite for cleanliness; but we soon reach a point at which further supplies of water are of very minor importance. A modern town population is found to be satisfied with about twenty-five gallons per head per day for all purposes, and a further supply would possess little utility. Water, indeed, may be the reverse of useful, as in the case of a flood, or a damp house, or a wet mine.

Utility and Value are not intrinsic.

It is only, then, when supplied in moderate quantities, and at the right time, that a thing can be said to be useful. Utility is not a quality *intrinsic* in a

193

substance, for, if it were, additional quantities of the same substance would always be desired, however much we previously possessed. We must not confuse the usefulness of a thing with the physical qualities upon which the usefulness depends. Utility and value are only accidents of a thing arising from the fact that some one wants it, and the degree of the utility and the amount of resulting value will depend upon the extent to which the desire for it has been previously gratified.

Regarding utility, then, as constantly varying in degree, and as variable even for each different portion of commodity, it is not difficult to see that we exchange those parts of our stock which have a low degree of utility to us, for articles which, being of low utility to others, are much desired by us. This exchange is continued up to the point at which the next portion given would be equally useful to us with that received, so that there is no gain of utility: there would be a loss in carrying the exchange further. Upon these considerations it is easy to construct a theory of the nature of exchange and value, which has been explained in my book* called 'The Theory of Political Economy.' It is there shown that the well-known laws of supply and demand follow from this view of utility, and thus yield a verification of the theory. Since the publication of the work named, M. Léon Walras, the ingenious professor of political economy at Lausanne, has independently arrived at the same theory of exchange,† a remarkable confirmation of its truth.

Value expresses Ratio of Exchange.

We must now fix our attention upon the fact that, in every act of exchange, a definite quantity of one substance is exchanged for a definite quantity of another. The things bartered may be most various in character, and may be variously measured. We may give a weight of silver for a length of rope, or a superficial extent of carpet, or a number of gallons of wine, or a certain horse-power of force, or conveyance over a certain distance. The quantities to be measured may be expressed in terms of space, time, mass, force, energy, heat, or any other physical units. Yet each exchange will consist in giving so many units of one thing for so many units of another, each measured in its appropriate way.

Every act of exchange thus presents itself to us in the form of *a ratio between two numbers*. The word *value* is commonly used, and if, at current rates, one ton of copper exchanges for ten tons of bar iron, it is usual to say that the value

* 'The Theory of Political Economy.' 8vo. 1871 (Macmillan).
† Walras, Éléments d'Économie politique pure. Lausanne, Paris (Guillaumin), 1874.

of copper is ten times that of the iron, weight for weight. For our purpose, at least, this use of the word value is only an indirect mode of expressing a ratio. When we say that gold is more valuable than silver, we mean that, as commonly exchanged, the weight of silver exceeds that of the gold given for it. If the value of gold rises compared with that of silver, then still more silver is given for the same quantity of gold. But value like utility is no intrinsic quality of a thing; it is an extrinsic accident or relation. We should never speak of the value of a thing at all without having in our minds the other thing in regard to which it is valued. The very same substance may rise and fall in value at the same time. If, in exchange for a given weight of gold, I can get more silver, but less copper, than I used to do, the value of gold has risen with respect to silver, but fallen with respect to copper. It is evident that an intrinsic property of a thing cannot both increase and decrease at the same time; therefore value must be a mere relation or accident of a thing as regards other things and the persons needing them.

CHAPTER III.

THE FUNCTIONS OF MONEY.

WE have seen that three inconveniences attach to the practice of simple barter, namely, the improbability of coincidence between persons wanting and
persons possessing; the complexity of exchanges, which are not made in terms
of one single substance; and the need of some means of dividing and distributing valuable articles. Money remedies these inconveniences, and thereby
performs two distinct functions of high importance, acting as –

(1) A medium of exchange.

(2) A common measure of value.

In its first form money is simply any commodity esteemed by all persons, any
article of food, clothing, or ornament which any person will readily receive,
and which, therefore, every person desires to have by him in greater or less
quantity, in order that he may have the means of procuring necessaries of life
at any time. Although many commodities may be capable of performing this
function of a medium more or less perfectly, some one article will usually be
selected, as money *par excellence*, by custom or the force of circumstances. This
article will then begin to be used as a measure of value. Being accustomed to
exchange things frequently for sums of money, people learn the value of other
articles in terms of money, so that all exchanges will most readily be calculated
and adjusted by comparison of the money values of the things exchanged.

A Standard of Value.

A third function of money soon develops itself. Commerce cannot advance far
before people begin to borrow and lend, and debts of various origin are contracted. It is in some cases usual, indeed, to restore the very same article which
was borrowed, and in almost every case it would be possible to pay back in the
same kind of commodity. If corn be borrowed, corn might be paid back, with
interest in corn; but the lender will often not wish to have things returned to
him at an uncertain time, when he does not much need them, or when their
value is unusually low. A borrower, too, may need several different kinds of

196

articles, which he is not likely to obtain from one person; hence arises the convenience of borrowing and lending in one generally recognized commodity, of which the value varies little. Every person making a contract by which he will receive something at a future day, will prefer to secure the receipt of a commodity likely to be as valuable then as now. This commodity will usually be the current money, and it will thus come to perform the function of a *standard of value*. We must not suppose that the substance serving as a standard of value is really invariable in value, but merely that it is chosen as that measure by which the value of future payments is to be regulated. Bearing in mind that value is only the ratio of quantities exchanged, it is certain that no substance permanently bears exactly the same value relatively to another commodity; but it will, of course, be desirable to select as the standard of value that which appears likely to continue to exchange for many other commodities in nearly unchanged ratios.

A Store of Value.

It is worthy of inquiry whether money does not also serve a fourth distinct purpose – that of embodying value in a convenient form for conveyance to distant places. Money, when acting as a medium of exchange, circulates backwards and forwards near the same spot, and may sometimes return to the same hands again and again. It subdivides and distributes property, and *lubricates* the action of exchange. But at times a person needs to condense his property into the smallest compass, so that he may hoard it away for a time, or carry it with him on a long journey, or transmit it to a friend in a distant country. Something which is very valuable, although of little bulk and weight, and which will be recognised as very valuable in every part of the world, is necessary for this purpose. The current money of a country is perhaps more likely to fulfil these conditions than anything else, although diamonds and other precious stones, and articles of exceptional beauty and rarity, might occasionally be employed.

The use of esteemed articles as a store or medium for conveying value may in some cases precede their employment as currency. Mr. Gladstone states that in the Homeric poems gold is mentioned as being hoarded and treasured up, and as being occasionally used in the payment of services, before it became the common measure of value, oxen being then used for the latter purpose. Historically speaking, such a generally esteemed substance as gold seems to have served, firstly, as a commodity valuable for ornamental purposes; secondly, as stored wealth; thirdly, as a medium of exchange; and, lastly, as a measure of value.

Separation of Functions.

It is in the highest degree important that the reader should discriminate care-fully and constantly between the four functions which money fulfils, at least in modern societies. We are so accustomed to use the one same substance in all the four different ways, that they tend to become confused together in thought. We come to regard as almost necessary that union of functions which is, at the most, a matter of convenience, and may not always be desirable. We might certainly employ one substance as a medium of exchange, a second as a measure of value, a third as a standard of value, and a fourth as a store of value. In buying and selling we might transfer portions of gold; in expressing and calculating prices we might speak in terms of silver; when we wanted to make long leases we might define the rent in terms of wheat, and when we wished to carry our riches away we might condense it into the form of precious stones. This use of different commodities for each of the functions of money has in fact been partially carried out. In Queen Elizabeth's reign silver was the common measure of value; gold was employed in large payments in quantities depending upon its current value in silver, while corn was required by the Act 18th Elizabeth, c. VI. (1576), to be the standard of value in drawing the leases of certain college lands.

There is evident convenience in selecting, if possible, one single substance which can serve all the functions of money. It will save trouble if we can pay in the same money in which the prices of things are calculated. As few people have the time or patience to investigate closely the history of prices, they will probably assume that the money in which they make all minor and temporary bargains, is also the best standard in which to register debts and contracts extending over many years. A great mass of payments too are invariably fixed by law, such as tolls, fees, and tariffs of charges: many other payments are fixed by custom. Accordingly, even if the medium of exchange varied considerably in value, people would go on making their payments in terms of it, as if there had been no variation, some gaining at the expense of others.

One of our chief tasks in this book will be to consider the various materials which have been employed as money, or have been, or may be, suggested for the purpose. It must be our endeavour, if possible, to discover some substance which will in the highest degree combine the characters requisite for all the different functions of money, but we must bear in mind that a partition of these functions amongst different substances is practicable. We will first pro-ceed to a brief review of the very various ways in which the need of currency has been supplied from the earliest ages, and we will afterwards analyse the physical qualities and circumstances which render the substances employed more or less suited to the purpose to which they were applied. We may thus arrive at some decision as to the exact nature of the commodity which is best adapted to meet our needs in the present day.

CHAPTER IV

EARLY HISTORY OF MONEY.

LIVING in civilized communities, and accustomed to the use of coined metallic money, we learn to identify money with gold and silver; hence spring hurtful and insidious fallacies. It is always useful, therefore, to be reminded of the truth, so well stated by Turgot, that every kind of merchandise has the two properties of measuring value and transferring value. It is entirely a question of degree what commodities will in any given state of society form the most convenient currency, and this truth will be best impressed upon us by a brief consideration of the very numerous things which have at one time or other been employed as money. Though there are many numismatists and many political economists, the natural history of money is almost a virgin subject, upon which I should like to dilate; but the narrow limits of my space forbid me from attempting more than a brief sketch of the many interesting facts which may be collected.

Currency in the Hunting State.

Perhaps the most rudimentary state of industry is that in which subsistence is gained by hunting wild animals. The proceeds of the chase would, in such a state, be the property of most generally recognised value. The meat of the animals captured would, indeed, be too perishable in nature to be hoarded or often exchanged; but it is otherwise with the skins, which, being preserved and valued for clothing, became one of the earliest materials of currency. Accordingly, there is abundant evidence that furs or skins were employed as money in many ancient nations. They serve this purpose to the present day in some parts of the world.

In the book of Job (ii. 4) we read, 'Skin for skin, yea, all that a man hath will he give for his life;' a statement clearly implying that skins were taken as the representative of value among the ancient Oriental nations. Etymological research shows that the same may be said of the northern nations from the earliest times. In the Esthonian language the word *râha* generally signifies

200

money, but its equivalent in the kindred Lappish tongue has not yet altogether lost the original meaning of skin or fur. Leather money is said to have circulated in Russia as late as the reign of Peter the Great, and it is worthy of notice, that classical writers have recorded traditions to the effect that the earliest currency used at Rome, Lacedæmon, and Carthage, was formed of leather.

We need not go back, however, to such early times to study the use of rude currencies. In the traffic of the Hudson's Bay Company with the North American Indians, furs, in spite of their differences of quality and size, long formed the medium of exchange. It is very instructive, and corroborative of the previous evidence to find that, even after the use of coin had become common among the Indians the skin was still commonly used as the money of account. Thus Whymper says,[*] 'a gun, nominally worth about forty shillings, brought twenty "skins." This term is the old one employed by the company. One skin (beaver) is supposed to be worth two shillings, and it represents two marten, and so on. You heard a great deal about "skins" at Fort Yukon, as the workmen were also charged for clothing, etc., in this way.'

Currency in the Pastoral State.

In the next higher stage of civilization, the pastoral state, sheep and cattle naturally form the most valuable and negotiable kind of property. They are easily transferable, convey themselves about, and can be kept for many years, so that they readily perform some of the functions of money.

We have abundance of evidence, traditional, written, and etymological, to show this. In the Homeric poems oxen are distinctly and repeatedly mentioned as the commodity in terms of which other objects are valued. The arms of Diomed are stated to be worth nine oxen, and are compared with those of Glaucos, worth one hundred. The tripod, the first prize for wrestlers in the 23rd Iliad, was valued at twelve oxen, and a woman captive, skilled in industry, at four.[†] It is peculiarly interesting to find oxen thus used as the common measure of value, because from other passages it is probable, as already mentioned, that the precious metals, though as yet uncoined, were used as a store of value, and occasionally as a medium of exchange. The several functions of money were thus clearly performed by different commodities at this early period.

In several languages the name for money is identical with that of some kind of cattle or domesticated animal. It is generally allowed that *pecunia*, the Latin word for money, is derived from *pecus*, cattle. From the Agamemnon of

---

[*] 'Travels in Alaska, etc.,' by F. Whymper, p. 225.

[†] Gladstone, 'Juventus Mundi,' p. 534.

Æschylus we learn that the figure of an ox was the sign first impressed upon coins, and the same is said to have been the case with the earliest issues of the Roman *As*. Numismatic researches fail to bear out these traditions, which were probably invented to explain the connection between the name of the coin and the animal. A corresponding connection between these notions may be detected in much more modern languages. Our common expression for the payment of a sum of money is *fee*, which is nothing but the Anglo-Saxon *feoh*, meaning alike money and cattle, a word cognate with the German *vieh*, which still bears only the original meaning of cattle. As I am informed by my friend, Professor Theodores, the same connection of ideas is manifested in the Greek word for property, κτῆμα, which means alike possession, flock, or cattle, and is referred by Grimm to an original verb κέτω or κετάω, to feed cattle. It is even supposed by Grimm that the same root reappears in the Teutonic and Scandinavian languages, in the Gothic, *skatts*, the modern High German, *schatz*, the Anglo-Saxon, *scät*, or *sceat*, the ancient Norsk *skat*, all meaning wealth, property, treasure, tax, or tribute, especially in the shape of cattle. This theory is confirmed by the fact that the Frisian equivalent, *sket*, has retained the original meaning of cattle to the present day. In the Norsk, Anglo-Saxon, and English, *scat* or *scot* has been specialized to denote tax or tribute.

In the ancient German codes of law, fines and penalties are actually defined in terms of live-stock. In the Zend Avesta, as Professor Theodores further informs me, the scale of rewards to be paid to physicians is carefully stated, and in every case the fee consists in some sort of cattle. The fifth and sixth lectures in Sir H. S. Maine's most interesting work on 'The Early History of Institutions,' which has just been published, are full of curious information showing the importance of live-stock in a primitive state of society. Being counted *by the head*, the kine was called *capitale*, whence the economical term *capital*, the law term *chattel*, and our common name *cattle*.

In countries where slaves form one of the most common and valuable possessions, it is quite natural that they should serve as the medium of exchange like cattle. Pausanias mentions their use in this way, and in Central Africa and some other places where slavery still flourishes, they are the medium of exchange along with cattle and ivory tusks. According to Earl's account of New Guinea, there is in that island a large traffic in slaves, and a slave forms the unit of value. Even in England slaves are believed to have been exchanged at one time in the manner of money.

Articles of Ornament as Currency.

A passion for personal adornment is one of the most primitive and powerful instincts of the human race, and as articles used for such purposes would be durable, universally esteemed, and easily transferable, it is natural that they should be circulated as money. The wampumpeag of the North American Indians is a case in point, as it certainly served as jewellery. It consisted of beads made of the ends of black and white shells, rubbed down and polished, and then strung into belts or necklaces, which were valued according to their length, and also according to their colour and lustre, a foot of black peag being worth two feet of white peag. It was so well established as currency among the natives that the Court of Massachusetts ordered, in 1649, that it should be received in the payment of debts among settlers to the amount of forty shillings. It is curious to learn, too, that just as European misers hoard up gold and silver coins, the richer Indian chiefs secrete piles of wampum beads, having no better means of investing their superfluous wealth.

Exactly analogous to this North American currency, is that of the cowry shells, which, under one name or another – chamgos, zimbis, bouges, porcelanes, etc. – have long been used in the East Indies as small money. In British India, Siam, the West Coast of Africa, and elsewhere on the tropical coasts, they are still used as small change, being collected on the shores of the Maldive and Laccadive Islands, and exported for the purpose. Their value varies somewhat, according to the abundance of the yield, but in India the current rate used to be about 5000 shells for one rupee, at which rate each shell is worth about the two-hundredth part of a penny. Among our interesting fellow-subjects, the Fijians, whale's teeth served in the place of cowries, and white teeth were exchanged for red teeth somewhat in the ratio of shillings to sovereigns.

Among other articles of ornament or of special value used as currency, may be mentioned yellow amber, engraved stones, such as the Egyptian scarabæi, and tusks of ivory.

Currency in the Agricultural State.

Many vegetable productions are at least as well suited for circulation as some of the articles which have been mentioned. It is not surprising to find, then, that among a people supporting themselves by agriculture, the more durable products were thus used. Corn has been the medium of exchange in remote parts of Europe from the time of the ancient Greeks to the present day. In Norway corn is even deposited in banks, and lent and borrowed. What wheat, barley, and oats are to Europe, such is maize in parts of Central America, especially Mexico, where it formerly circulated. In many of the countries surrounding the Mediterranean, olive oil is one of the commonest articles of produce and consumption; being, moreover, pretty uniform in quality, durable, and easily divisible, it has long served as currency in the Ionian Islands, Mytilene, some towns of Asia Minor, and elsewhere in the Levant.

Just as cowries circulate in the East Indies, so cacao nuts, in Central America and Yucatan, form a perfectly recognised and probably an ancient fractional money. Travellers have published many distinct statements as to their value, but it is impossible to reconcile these statements without supposing great changes of value either in the nuts or in the coins with which they are compared. In 1521, at Caracas, about thirty cacao nuts were worth one penny English, whereas recently ten beans would go to a penny, according to Squier's statements. In the European countries, where almonds are commonly grown, they have circulated to some extent like the cacao nuts, but are variable in value, according to the success of the harvest.

It is not only, however, as a minor currency that vegetable products have been used in modern times. In the American settlements and the West India Islands, in former days, specie used to become inconveniently scarce, and the legislators fell back upon the device of obliging creditors to receive payment in produce at stated rates. In 1618, the Governor of the Plantations of Virginia ordered that tobacco should be received at the rate of three shillings for the pound weight, under the penalty of three years' hard labour. We are told that, when the Virginia Company imported young women as wives for the settlers, the price per head was one hundred pounds of tobacco, subsequently raised to one hundred and fifty. As late as 1732, the legislature of Maryland made tobacco and Indian corn legal tenders; and in 1641 there were similar laws concerning corn in Massachusetts. The governments of some of the West India Islands seem to have made attempts to imitate these peculiar currency laws, and it was provided that the successful plaintiff in a lawsuit should be obliged to accept various kinds of raw produce, such as sugar, rum, molasses, ginger, indigo, or tobacco.[*] Such endeavours to establish a kind of multiple currency will be found to possess considerable interest for us in a later chapter.

The perishable nature of most kinds of animal food prevents them from being much used as money; but eggs are said to have circulated in the Alpine villages of Switzerland, and dried codfish have certainly acted as currency in the colony of Newfoundland.

Manufactured and Miscellaneous Articles as Currency.

The enumeration of articles which have served as money may already seem long enough for the purposes in view. I will, therefore, only add briefly that a

[*] See a scarce tract, entitled 'Two Letters to Mr. Wood on the Coin and Currency in the Leeward Islands,' p. 34. London, 1740.

great number of manufactured commodities have been used as a medium of exchange in various times and places. Such are the pieces of cotton cloth, called *Guinea pieces*, used for traffic upon the banks of the Senegal, or the somewhat similar pieces circulated in Abyssinia, the Soulou Archipelago, Sumatra, Mexico, Peru, Siberia, and among the Veddahs. It is less easy to understand the origin of the curious straw money which circulated until 1694 in the Portuguese possessions in Angola, and which consisted of small mats, called libongos, woven out of rice straw, and worth about 1½d. each. These mats must have had, at least originally, some purpose apart from their use as currency, and were perhaps analogous to the fine woven mats so much valued by the Samoans, and also treated by them as a medium of exchange.

Salt has been circulated not only in Abyssinia, but in Sumatra, Mexico, and elsewhere. Cubes of benzoin gum or beeswax in Sumatra, red feathers in the Islands of the Pacific Ocean, cubes of tea in Tartary, iron shovels or hoes among the Malagasy, are other peculiar forms of currency. The remarks of Adam Smith concerning the use of hand-made nails as money in some Scotch villages will be remembered by many readers, and need not be repeated. M. Chevalier has adduced an exactly corresponding case from one of the French coalfields.

Were space available it would be interesting to discuss the not improbable suggestion of Boucher de Perthes, that, perhaps, after all, the finely worked stone implements now so frequently discovered were among the earliest mediums of exchange. Some of them are certainly made of jade, nephrite, or other hard stones, only found in distant countries, so that an active traffic in such implements must have existed in times of which we have no records whatever.

There are some obscure allusions in classical authors to a wooden money circulating among the Byzantines, and to a wooden talent used at Antioch and Alexandria, but in the absence of fuller information as to their nature, it is impossible to do more than mention them.

CHAPTER V.

QUALITIES OF THE MATERIAL OF MONEY.

MANY recent writers, such as Huskisson, MacCulloch, James Mill, Garnier, Chevalier, and Walras, have satisfactorily described the qualities which should be possessed by the material of money. Earlier writers seem, however, to have understood the subject almost as well. Harris explained these qualities with remarkable clearness in his 'Essay upon Money and Coins,' published in 1757, a work which appeared before the 'Wealth of Nations,' yet gave an exposition of the principles of money which can hardly be improved at the present day. Eighty years before, however, Rice Vaughan, in his excellent little 'Treatise of Money,' had written a brief but satisfactory statement of the qualities requisite in money. We even find that William Stafford, the author of that remarkable dialogue of the Elizabethan age (1581), called 'A Brief Conceipte of English Policy,' showed perfect insight into the subject. Of all writers, M. Chevalier, however, probably gives the most accurate and full account of the properties which money should possess, and I shall in many points follow his views.

The prevailing defect in the treatment of the subject is the failure to observe that money requires different properties as regards different functions. To decide upon the best material for money is thus a problem of great complexity, because we must take into account at once the relative importance of the several functions of money, the degree in which money is employed for each function, and the importance of each of the physical qualities of the substance with respect to each function. In a simple state of industry money is chiefly required to pass about between buyers and sellers. It should, then, be conveniently portable, divisible into pieces of various size, so that any sum may readily be made up, and easily distinguishable by its appearance, or by the design impressed upon it. When money, however, comes to serve, as it will at some future time, almost exclusively as a measure and standard of value, the system of exchange, being one of perfected barter, such properties become a matter of comparative indifference, and stability of value, joined perhaps to portability, is the most important quality. Before venturing, however, to discuss such complex questions, we must proceed to a preliminary discussion of the

206

properties in question, which may thus perhaps be enumerated in the order of their importance: –

      1. Utility and value.
      2. Portability.
      3. Indestructibility.
      4. Homogeneity.
      5. Divisibility.
      6. Stability of value.
      7. Cognizability.

1. Utility and Value.

Since money has to be exchanged for valuable goods, it should itself possess value, and it must therefore have utility as the basis of value. Money, when once in full currency, is only received in order to be passed on, so that if all people could be induced to take worthless bits of material at a fixed rate of valuation, it might seem that money does not really require to have substantial value. Something like this does frequently happen in the history of currencies, and apparently valueless shells, bits of leather, or scraps of paper, are actually received in exchange for costly commodities. This strange phenomenon is, however, in most cases capable of easy explanation, and if we were acquainted with the history of every kind of money the like explanation would no doubt be possible in other cases. The essential point is that people should be induced to receive money, and pass it on freely at steady ratios of exchange for other objects; but there must always be some sufficient reason first inducing people to accept the money. The force of habit, convention, or legal enactment may do much to maintain money in circulation when once it is afloat, but it is doubtful whether the most powerful government could oblige its subjects to accept and circulate as money a worthless substance which they had no other motive for receiving.

Certainly, in the early stages of society, the use of money was not based on legal regulations, so that the utility of the substance for other purposes must have been the prior condition of its employment as money. Thus the singular *peag* currency, or *wampumpeag*, which was found in circulation among the North American Indians by the early explorers, was esteemed for the purpose of adornment, as already mentioned, (p. 24). The cowry shells, so widely used as a small currency in the East, are valued for ornamental purposes on the West Coast of Africa, and were in all probability employed as ornaments before they were employed as money. All the other articles mentioned in Chapter IV., such as oxen, corn, skins, tobacco, salt, cacao nuts, etc., which have performed the functions of money in one place or other, possessed independent utility and value. If there are any apparent exceptions at all to this rule, they would doubtless admit of explanation by fuller knowledge. We may, therefore, agree with Storch when he says: – 'It is impossible that a substance which has no direct value should be introduced as money, however suitable it may be in other respects for this use.'

When once a substance is widely employed as money, it is conceivable that its utility will come to depend mainly upon the services which it thus confers upon the community. Gold, for instance, is far more important as the material of money than in the production of plate, jewellery, watches, gold-leaf, etc. A substance originally used for many purposes may eventually serve only as money, and yet, by the demand for currency and the force of habit, may maintain its value. The cowry circulation of the Indian coasts is probably a case in point. The importance of habit, personal or hereditary, is at least as great in monetary science as it is, according to Mr. Herbert Spencer, in morals and sociological phenomena generally.

There is, however, no reason to suppose that the value of gold and silver is at present due solely to their conventional use as money. These metals are endowed with such singularly useful properties that, if we could only get them in sufficient abundance, they would supplant all the other metals in the manufacture of household utensils, ornaments, fittings of all kinds, and an infinite multitude of small articles, which are now made of brass, copper, bronze, pewter, German silver, or other inferior metals and alloys.

In order that money may perform some of its functions efficiently, especially those of a medium of exchange and a store of value, to be carried about, it is important that it should be made of a substance valued highly in all parts of the world, and, if possible, almost equally esteemed by all peoples. There is reason to think that gold and silver have been admired and valued by all tribes which have been lucky enough to procure them. The beautiful lustre of these metals must have drawn attention and excited admiration as much in the earliest as in the present times.

2. Portability.

The material of money must not only be valuable, but the value must be so related to the weight and bulk of the material, that the money shall not be inconveniently heavy on the one hand, nor inconveniently minute on the other. There was a tradition in Greece that Lycurgus obliged the Lacedæmonians to use iron money, in order that its weight might deter them from overmuch trading. However this may be, it is certain that iron money could not be used in cash payments at the present day, since a penny would weigh about a pound, and instead of a five-pound note, we should have to deliver a ton of iron. During the last century copper was actually used as the chief medium of exchange in Sweden; and merchants had to take a wheelbarrow with them when they went to receive payments in copper dalers. Many of the substances used as currency in former times must have been sadly wanting in portability. Oxen and sheep, indeed, would transport themselves on their own legs; but corn, skins, oil, nuts, almonds, etc., though in several respects form- ing fair currency, would be intolerably bulky, and troublesome to transfer.

The portability of money is an important quality, not merely because it enables the owner to carry small sums in the pocket without trouble, but because large sums can be transferred from place to place, or from continent to continent, at little cost. The result is to secure an approximate uniformity in the value of money in all parts of the world. A substance which is very heavy and bulky in proportion to value, like corn or coal, may be very scarce in one place and over abundant in another; yet the supply and demand cannot be equalized without great expense in carriage. The cost of conveying gold or sil- ver from London to Paris, including insurance, is only about four-tenths of one per cent.; and between the most distant parts of the world it does not exceed from two to three per cent.

Substances may be too valuable as well as too cheap, so that for ordinary transactions it would be necessary to call in the aid of the microscope and the chemical balance. Diamonds, apart from other objections, would be far too valuable for small transactions. The value of such stones is said to vary as the square of the weight, so that we cannot institute any exact comparison with metals of which the value is simply proportional to the weight. But taking a one-carat diamond (four grains) as worth £15, we find it is, weight for weight, 460 times as valuable as gold. There are several rare metals, such as iridium and osmium, which would likewise be far too valuable to circulate. Even gold and silver are too costly for small currency. A silver penny now weighs $7\frac{1}{4}$ grains, and a gold penny would weigh only half a grain. The pretty octagonal quarter-dollar tokens circulated in California are the smallest gold coins I have seen, weighing less than four grains each, and are so thin that they can almost be blown away.

3. Indestructibility.

If it is to be passed about in trade, and kept in reserve, money must not be sub- ject to easy deterioration or loss. It must not evaporate like alcohol, nor putrefy like animal substances, nor decay like wood, nor rust like iron. Destructible articles, such as eggs, dried codfish, cattle, or oil, have certainly been used as currency; but what is treated as money one day must soon after- wards be eaten up. Thus a large stock of such perishable commodities cannot be kept on hand, and their value must be very variable. The several kinds of corn are less subject to this objection, since, when well dried at first, they suffer no appreciable deterioration for several years.

4. Homogeneity.

All portions or specimens of the substance used as money should be *homogeneous*, that is, of the same quality, so that equal weights will have exactly the same value. In order that we may correctly count in terms of any unit, the units must be equal and similar, so that twice two will always make four. If we were to count in precious stones, it would seldom happen that four stones would be just twice as valuable as two stones. Even the precious metals, as found in the native state, are not perfectly homogeneous, being mixed together in almost all proportions; but this produces little inconvenience, because the assayer readily determines the quantity of each pure metal present in any ingot. In the processes of refining and coining, the metals are afterwards reduced to almost exactly uniform degrees of fineness, so that equal weights are then of exactly equal value.

5. Divisibility.

Closely connected with the last property is that of divisibility. Every material is, indeed, mechanically divisible, almost without limit. The hardest gems can be broken, and steel can be cut by harder steel. But the material of money should be not merely capable of division, but the aggregate value of the mass after division should be almost exactly the same as before division. If we cut up a skin or fur the pieces will, as a general rule, be far less valuable than the whole skin or fur, except for a special intended purpose; and the same is the case with timber, stone, and most other materials in which reunion is impossible. But portions of metal can be melted together again whenever it is desirable, and the cost of doing this, including the metal lost, is in the case of precious metals very inconsiderable, varying from ¼d. to ½d. per ounce. Thus, approximately speaking, the value of any piece of gold or silver is simply proportional to the weight of fine metal which it contains.

6. Stability of Value.

It is evidently desirable that the currency should not be subject to fluctuations of value. The ratios in which money exchanges for other commodities should be maintained as nearly as possible invariable on the average. This would be a matter of comparatively minor importance were money used only as a measure of values at any one moment, and as a medium of exchange. If all prices were altered in like proportion as soon as money varied in value, no one would lose or gain, except as regards the coin which he happened to have in his pocket, safe, or bank balance. But, practically speaking, as we have seen, people do employ money as a standard of value for long contracts, and they often maintain payments at the same invariable rate, by custom or law, even when the real value of the payment is much altered. Hence every change in the value of money does some injury to society.

It might be plausibly said, indeed, that the debtor gains as much as the creditor loses, or *vice versâ*, so that on the whole the community is as rich as before; but this is not really true. A mathematical analysis of the subject shows that to take any sum of money from one and give it to another will, on the average of cases, injure the loser more than it benefits the receiver. A person with an income of one hundred pounds a year would suffer more by losing ten pounds than he would gain by an addition of ten pounds, because the degree of utility of money to him is considerably higher at ninety pounds than it is at one hundred and ten. On the same principle, all gaming, betting, pure speculation, or other accidental modes of transferring property involve, on the average, a dead loss of utility. The whole incitement to industry and commerce and the accumulation of capital depends upon the expectation of enjoyment thence arising, and every variation of the currency tends in some degree to frustrate such expectation and to lessen the motives for exertion.

7. Cognizability.

By this name we may denote the capability of a substance for being easily recognized and distinguished from all other substances. As a medium of exchange, money has to be continually handed about, and it will occasion great trouble if every person receiving currency has to scrutinize, weigh, and test it. If it requires any skill to discriminate good money from bad, poor ignorant people are sure to be imposed upon. Hence the medium of exchange should have certain distinct marks which nobody can mistake. Precious stones, even if in other respects good as money, could not be so used, because only a skilled lapidary can surely distinguish between true and imitation gems.

Under cognizability we may properly include what has been aptly called *impressibility*, namely, the capability of a substance to receive such an impression, seal, or design, as shall establish its character as current money of certain value. We might more simply say, that the material of money should be *coinable*, so that a portion, being once issued according to proper regulations with the impress of the state, may be known to all as good and legal currency, equal in weight, size, and value to all similarly marked currency. We shall afterwards consider more minutely what is involved in the manufacture of a good coin.

CHAPTER VI.

THE METALS AS MONEY.

IT need not be pointed out in detail that, though the numerous commodities mentioned in Chapter IV. possess, in a greater or less degree, the qualities essential to the material of money, they cannot for a moment compare in this respect with many of the metals. Some of the metals seem to be marked out by nature as most fit of all substances for employment as money, at least when acting as a medium of exchange and a store of value. Accordingly, we find that gold, silver, copper, tin, lead, and iron have been more or less extensively in circulation in all historical ages. So closely have silver and copper become associated in people's minds with their use as money, that we find their names adopted as the names of money. In Greek ἄργυρος means equally silver, silver coin, and money generally; in Latin, *aes* is copper, bronze, or brass, and also money and wages; in French, *argent* is both silver and money. The same association of meanings could be pointed out in many other languages, including our own. Though our pence are now made of bronze, we still speak of them as *coppers*.

With the exception of iron, the principal metals are peculiarly indestructible, and undergo little or no deterioration when hoarded up or handed about. Each kind of metal is approximately homogeneous, piece differing from piece in nothing but weight, the differences of fineness being ascertained and allowed for in the case of gold and silver. The metals are also perfectly divisible, either by the chisel or the crucible, and yet a second melting will always reunite the pieces again with little cost or loss of material. Most of them possess the properties of cognizability and impressibility in the highest degree. Each metal has its characteristic colour, density, and hardness, so that it is easy for a person with very slight experience to distinguish one metal from another. Their malleability enables us to roll, cut, and hammer them into any required form, and to impress a permanent design by means of dies. With the exception of porcelain coins, which have been used in Siam, I am not aware that coins have ever been made of any substance except metal.

213

In respect to steadiness of value the metals are probably less satisfactory, regarded as a standard of value, than many other commodities, such as corn. From the earliest ages metals must have been most highly valued, as we may learn from the way in which they are esteemed by savages in the present day. But their value has suffered and is suffering an almost continuous decline, owing to the progress of industry, and the discovery of new mechanical and chemical means for their extraction. Even the order of their values becomes changed. According to Mr. Gladstone, iron was, in the Homeric age, much more valued than *chalkos*, or copper, which latter was then the most common and useful metal. Lead was little known or valued, but gold, silver, and tin held the same places at the head of the list which they hold at the present day.

Iron.

Proceeding to consider briefly each of the more important metals, the statements of Aristotle, Pollux, and other writers prove that iron was extensively employed as money in early times. Not a single specimen of such money is now known to exist, but this is easily accounted for by the rapidity with which the metal rusts. In the absence of specimens, we do not know the form and size of the money, but it is probable that it consisted of small bars, ingots, or spikes, somewhat similar to the small bars of iron which are still used in trading with the natives of Central Africa. Iron money is still, or was not long since, used in Japan for small values; but its issue from the mint has been discontinued.

The use of pure iron coins in civilized countries at the present day is out of the question, both because of the cheapness of the metal, and because the coins would soon lose the sharpness of their impressions by rusting, and become dirty and easily counterfeited. But it is quite possible that iron or steel might still be alloyed with other metals for the coining of pence.

Lead.

Lead has often been used as currency, and is occasionally so mentioned by the ancient Greek and Latin poets. In 1635 leaden bullets were used for change at the rate of a farthing a piece in Massachusetts. At the present day it is still current in Burmah, being passed by weight for small payments. The extreme softness of the metal obviously renders it quite unfit for coining in the pure state. It is one of the components of pewter, which has frequently been coined.

Tin.

Tin has also been employed as money at various times. Dionysius of Syracuse issued the earliest tin coinage of which anything is certainly known; but as tin was in early times procured from Cornwall, it can hardly be doubted that the first British currency was composed of tin. In innumerable cabinets may be found series of tin coins issued by the Roman emperors; the kings of England also often coined tin. In 1680 tin farthings were struck by Charles II., a stud of copper being inserted in the middle of the coin to render counterfeiting more difficult. Tin halfpence and farthings were also issued in considerable quantities in the reign of William and Mary (1690 to 1691). Tin coins were formerly employed among the Javanese, Mexicans, and many other peoples, and the metal is said to be still current by weight in the Straits of Malacca.

Tin would be in many respects admirably suited for making pence, possessing a fine white colour, perfect freedom from corrosion, and a much higher value than copper. Unfortunately, its softness and tendency to bend and break when pure are insuperable obstacles to its employment as money.

Copper.

This metal is in many respects well suited for coining. It does not suffer from exposure to dry air, possesses a fine distinct red colour, and takes a good impression from the dies, which impression it retains better than the majority of other metals. Accordingly, we find that it has been continually employed as currency, either alone or in subordination to gold and silver. The earliest Hebrew coins were composed chiefly of copper, and the metallic currency of Rome consisted of the impure copper, called *aes*, until B.C. 269, when silver was first coined. In later times copper has not only been generally used for coins of minor value, but, in Russia and in Sweden, a hundred years ago, it formed the principal mass of the currency. Its low value now stands in the way of its use. A penny, if made so as to contain metal equivalent to its nominal value, would weigh 870 grains, or more than an ounce and three-quarters troy. Its value is also subject to considerable fluctuations. Moreover, it is unlikely that copper in a pure state will be coined for the future, since bronze is now known to be so much more suitable for coinage.

Silver.

I need hardly say that silver is distinguished by its exquisite white lustre, which is not rivalled by that of any other pure metal. Certain alloys, indeed, such as speculum metal, or Britannia metal, have been made of almost equal lustre, but they are either brittle, or so soft as not to give the metallic ring of silver. When much exposed to the air silver tarnishes by the formation of a black film of silver sulphide; but this forms no obstacle to its use as currency, since the film is always very thin, and its peculiar black colour even assists in distinguishing the pure metal from counterfeit. When suitably alloyed, silver is sufficiently hard to stand much wear, and next after gold it is the most malleable and impressible of all the metals.

A coin or other object made of silver may be known by the following marks: – (1) a fine pure white lustre, where newly rubbed or scraped; (2) a blackish tint where the surface has long been exposed to the air; (3) a moderate specific gravity; (4) a good metallic ring when thrown down; (5) considerable hardness; (6) strong nitric acid dissolves silver, and the solution turns black if exposed to light.

Silver has been coined, it need hardly be said, in all ages since the first invention of the art, and its value relatively to gold and copper suits it for taking the middle place in a monetary system. Its value too remains very stable for periods of fifty or a hundred years, because a vast stock of the metal is kept in the form of plate, watches, jewellery, and ornaments of various kinds, in addition to money, so that a variation in the supply for a few years cannot make any appreciable change in the total stock. Productive silver mines exist in almost all parts of the world, and wherever lead is produced, a small but steady yield of silver is obtained from it by the Pattinson method of extraction.

Gold.

Silver is beautiful, yet gold is even more beautiful, and presents indeed a combination of useful and striking properties quite without parallel among known substances. To a rich and brilliant yellow colour, which can only be adequately described as golden, it joins astonishing malleability and a very high specific gravity, exceeded only by that of platinum and a few of the rarest or almost unknown metals. We can usually ascertain whether a coin consists of gold or not, by looking for three characteristic marks: (1) the brilliant yellow colour; (2) the high specific gravity; (3) the metallic ring of the coin when thrown down, which will prove the absence of lead or platinum in the interior of the coin.

If there remain any doubt about a metal being gold, we have only to appeal to its solubility. Gold is remarkable for its freedom from corrosion or solution, being quite unaffected and untarnished after exposure of any length of time to dry, or moist, or impure air, and being also insoluble in all the simple acids. Strong nitric acid will rapidly attack any coloured counterfeit metal, but will not touch standard gold, or will, at the most, feebly dissolve the copper and silver alloyed with it.

In almost all respects gold is perfectly suited for coining. When quite pure, indeed, it is almost as soft as tin, but when alloyed with one-tenth or one-twelfth part of copper, becomes sufficiently hard to resist wear and tear, and to give a good metallic ring; yet it remains perfectly malleable and takes a fine impression. Its melting point is moderately high, and yet there is no perceptible oxidization or volatilization of the metal at the highest temperature which can be produced in a furnace. Thus old coin and fragments of the metal can be melted into bullion at a very slight loss, and at a cost of not more than one halfpenny per ounce troy, or little more than one-twentieth of one per cent.

Platinum.

This is one of those comparatively rare metals which have been known only in recent times. Its extremely high melting-point, and low affinity for oxygen, render it one of the most indestructible of all substances, whilst its white colour, joined to its excessively high specific gravity, are marks which cannot be mistaken. As it seemed in these respects well suited for currency, the Russian government, which owns the principal platinum mines in the Ural mountains, commenced to coin it, in 1828, into pieces intended to have the values of twelve, six, and three roubles. Several objections to this use of the metal soon presented themselves. The appearance of platinum being inferior to that of silver or gold, it is seldom or never employed for purposes of ornament, and its only extensive use is in the construction of chemical apparatus. Hence there is no large stock of the metal kept on hand, and the localities where it is found being few, the supply is incapable of being much increased, so that any variation of demand is sure to cause a great change in its value. Moreover, the cost of making the coins was very great, owing to the extreme difficulty of melting platinum, and the worn coins could not be withdrawn and recoined without much additional cost. Platinum being thus found to be quite unfitted for currency, the scheme was abandoned in 1845, and the existing coins withdrawn from circulation.

Great improvements having been lately made in the modes of working platinum, it was proposed by M. de Jacobi, the representative of Russia at the International Monetary Conference held at Paris, in 1867, that platinum should be employed for the coinage of five-franc pieces. It is not likely that such a suggestion will be adopted.

Nickel.

This metal was formerly regarded as the bane of the metallurgist, but has recently assumed an important place in manufacturing industry, and even in monetary science. It is used only in alloy with other metals, and for the purposes of coinage it is usual to melt up one part of nickel with three of copper. The smaller coins of Belgium, and the one-cent pieces of the United States have been made of this material and seem to be very convenient. In 1869 and 1870-1, pence and halfpence, to the value of £3000, were executed in the same alloy, at the English mint, for the colony of Jamaica. These are some of the most beautiful coins which have ever been issued from Tower Hill, and are in most respects admirably suited for circulation. But they were unfortunately made much too large and heavy; not only were they thus rendered less convenient, but when in 1873, the Deputy Master of the Mint was requested to supply a further quantity of the same coins, he found that the price of nickel had risen very much, so that the materials for the coinage alone would cost more than the nominal value of the coins to be produced. This rise in price was due partly to the small number of nickel mines yet worked, and partly to the great demand for the metal occasioned by the German government, which has chosen the same alloy for the ten and five-pfennig pieces of its new monetary system. These coins, which are now being issued, are of a convenient size, rather less than a shilling and sixpence respectively, and appear to be in every way admirably suited to their purpose. The German empire will soon possess the best instead of the worst fractional currency in the world. The variableness in the price of nickel, which is at present a cause of embarrassment, may after a time become less serious, when the stock in use and the annual produce become larger.

Other Metals.

The metals yet mentioned are but a small number of those now known by chemists to exist, and it would be unwise to assume as certain that money must always be made in the future of the same materials as in the past. It is just conceivable, on the one hand, that in the course of time, some metal still more valuable than gold may be introduced. Roughly speaking, the order in which the metals have hitherto acted, as the principal medium of exchange, is (1) copper, (2) silver, (3) gold; as a general decline in the values of the metals took place, the more valuable replaced the less valuable, and the more portable gold is now rapidly taking the place of silver. Some still more valuable metal, such as the scarce and intractable iridium or osmium, or the remarkable metal palladium, might possibly take the place of gold. This, however, is barely more than a matter of scientific fancy.

On the other hand, many metals exist which might be produced more cheaply than silver, such as aluminium or manganese. It may be well worthy of inquiry whether in such metals may not be found the best solution of the fractional currency difficulty, to be afterwards more fully discussed (p. 132).

Alloys of Metals.

At one time or another an immense number of different alloys or mixtures of metals have been coined. It would be strictly correct to say, indeed, that metals have seldom been issued except in the state of alloy. Even gold and silver, as usually coined, are either alloyed with each other or with copper. The latter metal, too, has generally been employed in union with other metals. The Roman *as* consisted, not of pure copper, but of the mixed metal *aes*, an alloy of copper and tin, partially resembling the bronze which has quite recently been introduced for small money in France, England, and other countries. Brass was largely coined by some of the Roman emperors. In many cases, no doubt, the early metallurgists in smelting an ore obtained a natural alloy of all the metals contained therein, and being unable to separate them were obliged to use the mixture. Thus we may explain the curious metal containing from sixty to seventy parts of copper, twenty to twenty-five of zinc, five to eleven of silver, with small quantities of gold, lead, and tin, which was employed to make the *stycas*, or small money, of the early kings of Northumbria.

Monarchs or states in difficulty have often coined the metal which they could most easily obtain. The Irish money issued by James II. was said to have been coined from a mixture of old guns, broken bells, waste copper, brass, and pewter, old kitchen furniture, and in fact any refuse metal which his officers could lay their hands upon. He attempted to make pewter crowns circulate for the value of silver ones.

CHAPTER VII.

COINS.

IT is clear that the metals far surpass all other substances in suitability for the purpose of circulation, and it is almost equally clear that certain metals surpass all the other metals in this respect. Of gold and silver especially we may say, with Turgot, that, by the nature of things, they are constituted the universal money independently of all convention and law. Even if the art of coining had never been invented, gold and silver would probably have formed the currency of the world; but we have now to consider how, by shaping weighed pieces of these metals into coins, we can make use of their valuable properties to the greatest advantage.

The primitive mode of circulating the metals, indeed, was simply that of buying and selling them against other commodities, the weights or portions being rudely estimated. Some of the earliest specimens of money consist of the *aes rude*, or rough, shapeless lumps of native copper employed as money by the ancient Etruscans. In the Museum of the Archiginnasio at Bologna may be seen the skeleton of an Etruscan, half embedded in earth, with the piece of rough copper yet within the grasp of the bony hand, placed there to meet the demands of Charon. Pliny, moreover, tells us that, before the time of Servius Tullius, copper was circulated in the rude state. Afterwards copper, brass, or iron were, it is probable, employed in the form of small bars or spikes, and the name of the Greek unit of value, *drachma*, is supposed to have been derived from the fact that six of these metal spikes could be grasped in the hand, each piece being called an *obolus*. Such is supposed to have been the first system of money which was passed purely by *tale*, or number of pieces.

Gold is most readily obtained from alluvial deposits, and then has the form of grains or dust. Hence this is the primitive form of gold money. The ancient Peruvians enclosed the gold dust for the sake of security in quills, and thus passed it about more conveniently. At the gold diggings of California, Australia, or New Zealand, gold dust is to the present day sold directly against other goods by the aid of scales. The art of melting gold and silver, and fashioning them by the hammer into various shapes was early invented. Even in the present day the poor Hindoo, who has saved up a few rupees, employs a silver-smith to melt them up and beat them into a simple bracelet, which he wears in the double character of an ornament and a hoard of wealth.

Similarly, the ancient Goths and Celts were accustomed to fashion gold into thick wires, which they rolled up into spiral rings and probably wore upon their fingers until the metal was wanted for trading purposes. There can be lit-tle doubt that this ring money, of which abundant specimens have been found in various parts of Europe and Asia, formed the first approximation to a coin-age. In some cases the rings may have been intentionally made of equal weight; for Cæsar speaks of the Britons as having iron rings, adjusted to a cer-tain weight, to serve as money. In other cases the rings, or amulets, were bought and sold by aid of the balance; and in certain Egyptian paintings men are represented as in the act of weighing rings. It is probable that the necessity for frequent weighings was avoided by making up sealed bags containing a cer-tain weight of rings, and such perhaps are the bags of silver given by Naaman to Gehazi in the Second Book of Kings (v. 23). Ring money is said to be still current in Nubia.

Gold and silver have been fashioned into various other forms to serve as money. Thus the Siamese money consists of very small ingots or bars bent dou-ble in a peculiar manner. In Pondicherry and elsewhere gold is circulated in the form of small grains or buttons.

The Invention of Coining.

The date of the invention of coining can be assigned with some degree of probability. Coined money was clearly unknown in the Homeric times, and it was known in the time of Lycurgus. We might therefore assume, with various authorities, that it was invented in the mean time, or about 900 B.C. There is a tradition, moreover, that Pheidon, King of Argos, first struck silver money in the island of Ægina about 895 B.C., and the tradition is supported by the exist-ence of small stamped ingots of silver, which have been found in Ægina. Later inquiries, however, lead to the conclusion that Pheidon lived in the middle of the eighth century B.C., and Grote has shown good reasons for believing that what he did accomplish was done in Argos, and not in Ægina.

The mode in which the invention happened is sufficiently evident. Seals were familiarly employed in very early times, as we learn from the Egyptian paintings or the stamped bricks of Nineveh. Being employed to signify posses-sion, or to ratify contracts, they came to indicate authority. When a ruler first undertook to certify the weights of pieces of metal, he naturally employed his seal to make the fact known, just as, at Goldsmiths' Hall, a small punch is used to certify the fineness of plate. In the earliest forms of coinage there were no attempts at so fashioning the metal that its weight could not be altered without destroying the stamp or design. The earliest coins struck, both in Lydia and in the Peloponnesus, were stamped on one side only. The Persian money, called the *larin*, consists of a round silver wire, about six centimetres long, bent in two, and stamped on one part which is flattened for the purpose. It is probably a relic of ring money. The present circulation of China is composed to a considerable extent of the so-called Sycee silver, which consists of small shoe-shaped ingots, assayed and stamped, according to some accounts, by the government.

What is a Coin?

Although, in rings, grains, or stamped ingots, we have an approximation to what we call coin, it is plain that we must do something more to make convenient money. The stamp must be so impressed as to certify, not only the fineness and the original weight, but also the absence of any subsequent alteration. To coin metal, as we now understand the art, is to form it into flat pieces of a circular, oval, square, hexagonal, octagonal, or other regular outline, and then to impress designs from engraved dies upon both sides, and sometimes upon the edges. Not only is it very costly and difficult to counterfeit coins well executed in this manner, but the integrity of the design assures us that no owner of the coin has tampered with it. Even the amount of ordinary wear and tear, which the coin has suffered, may be rudely inferred from the sharpness or partial effacement of the designs, and the roundness of the edges. 'Pieces of money,' says M. Chevalier, 'are ingots of which the weight and the fineness are certified.' There is nothing in this definition to distinguish coins from Sycee silver, or from the ordinary stamped bars and ingots of bullion. I should prefer, therefore, to say, *coins are ingots of which the weight and fineness are certified by the integrity of designs impressed upon the surfaces of the metal.*

Various Forms of Coins.

From time to time coins have been manufactured in very many forms, although circular coins vastly predominate in number. Among the innumerable issues of the German states may be found octagonal and hexagonal coins. A singular square coin, with a circular impress in the centre, was issued from Salzburg by Rudbert in 1513. Siege-pieces have been issued in England and elsewhere in the form of squares, lozenges, etc. Some of the most extraordinary specimens of money ever used are the large plates of pure copper which circulated in Sweden in the eighteenth century. These were about three-eighths of an inch in thickness, and varied in size, the half-daler being 3½ inches square, and the two-daler piece as much as 7½ inches square, and 3½ pounds in weight. As the whole surface could not be covered with a design, a circular impress was struck near to each corner, and one in the centre, so as to render alteration as difficult as possible.

Among Oriental nations the shapes of coins are still more curious. In Japan, the principal part of the circulation consists of silver *itzibus*, which are oblong, flat pieces of silver, covered on both sides with designs and legends, the characters being partly in relief and partly incised. The smaller silver coins have a similar form. Among the minor Japanese coins are found large, oval, moulded pieces of copper or mixed metal, each with a square hole in the centre. The Chinese *cash* are well known to be round discs of a kind of brass, with a square hole in the centre to allow of their being strung together. The coins of Formosa are similar, except that they are much larger and thicker. All the copper and base metal coins of China, Japan, and Formosa are distinguished by a broad flat rim, and they have characters in relief upon a sunk ground, somewhat in the manner of Boulton and Watt's copper pence. They are manufactured by moulding the metal, and then filing the protuberant parts smooth. Such coins stand wear, and preserve their design better than European coins, but they are easily counterfeited.

The most singular of all coins are the scimitar-shaped pieces formerly circulated in Persia.

The best Form for Coins.

It is a matter of considerable importance to devise the best possible form for coins, and the best mode of striking them. The use of money creates, as it were, an artificial crime of false coining, and so great is the temptation to engage in this illicit art that no penalty is sufficient to repress it, as the experience of two thousand years sufficiently proves. Thousands of persons have suffered death, and all the penalties of treason have been enforced without effect. Ruding is then unquestionably right in saying, that our efforts should be directed not so much to the punishment of the crime, as to its prevention by improvements in the art of coining. We must strike our coins so perfectly that successful imitation or alteration shall be out of the question.

There are four principal objects at which we should aim in deciding upon the exact design for a coin.

1. To prevent counterfeiting.

2. To prevent the fraudulent removal of metal from the coin.

3. To reduce the loss of metal by legitimate wear and tear.

4. To make the coin an artistic and historical monument of the state issuing it, and the people using it.

For the prevention of counterfeiting, our principal resource is to render the mechanical execution of the piece as perfect as possible, and to strike it in a way which can only be accomplished with the aid of elaborate machinery. When all coins were made by casting, the false coiner could work almost as skilfully as the moneyer. Hence, in the Roman empire, it was difficult to distinguish between true and false coin. Hammered money was a great improvement on moulded money, and milled money on hammered money. The introduction of the steam coining press by Boulton and Watt was the next great improvement; and the knee-joint press of Ulhorn and Thonnelier, now used in nearly all mints, except that on Tower Hill, forms the last advance in the mechanism for striking coin.

The utmost attention ought to be paid to the perfect execution of the milling, legend, or other design, impressed upon the edge of modern coins. This serves at once to prevent clipping or tampering with the coin, and to baffle the skill of the counterfeiter. The coins of ancient nations were issued with rough, unstamped edges, and the first coin marked with a legend on the edge was a silver coin of Charles IX. of France, issued in the year 1573. The English coinage was first grained or marked on the edge in 1658 or 1662, when the use of the mill and screw was finally established in the mint. All the larger coins now issued from the English, and, indeed, from most other mints, bear a milled or serrated edge, produced by ridges on the internal surface of the collar which holds the coin when being struck between the two dies. These collars are difficult to make, and useless when made except in the coining-press, and the counterfeiter cannot imitate the milling by hand work, it being almost impossible to use a file with sufficient regularity.

The French five-franc pieces bear a legend on the edge in raised letters, the words being 'Dieu protége la France.' Such raised letters are quite beyond the art of the counterfeiter. The English crown has a legend, 'Decus et Tutamen,' and the year of the reign in incised letters, which could obviously be imitated by the use of punches. The new German gold coins are issued with smooth edges, the ten-mark piece having only a few slight incised marks, and the twenty-mark piece bearing the legend, 'Gott mit uns,' in faint letters; this is surely a far less satisfactory protection than the milled edge adopted in most other mints. It may be worthy of inquiry, whether the milled edge might not be combined with a legend or other design in relief, so as to render imitation still more difficult. One or two centuries ago, silver coins used to have a kind of ornamental beading on the edge. Elaborate patterns, produced by machinery with perfect regularity, and altogether incapable of imitation by hand, might now be substituted.

Coins as Works of Art.

I have in the previous section considered the best form of a coin as regards the prevention of counterfeiting. The falsification of coins, the loss which they undergo by abrasion, and the best means of avoiding these evils will be treated in Chapter XIII. Of the use of coins as artistic medals it would not be appropriate to speak at any length. I must however remark that many of the coins still issued from the English mint are monuments of bad taste. It is difficult to imagine poorer designs than those upon the shilling and sixpence, descending from a time when art in many branches was at its apogee in England. As our architecture and art manufactures of many kinds are regenerated by the efforts of private persons, is it too much to hope that a government department will follow? The florin is indeed an immense advance upon the shilling, being in some respects a reversion to the style of old English money. A very beautiful pattern crown piece was produced in 1847, in a somewhat similar style, but never issued. Mr. Lowe, when Master of the Mint, gave us back the old George and Dragon sovereign, which is much superior to the shield and wreaths. I think, however, that the time has come for a general improvement in our coins.

Historical Coins.

Some states have utilized their coins as monuments of important events, such as conquests, jubilees, the accession of monarchs, etc. The German states, especially Prussia, have struck a long series of beautiful coins down to the Krönung's Thaler of 1861, and the Sieges Thaler of 1871. Some of these coins are at once treasured up in cabinets in the manner of medals. If it is possible to conceive literature destroyed, and modern cities and their monuments in ruins and decay, such medallic coins would become the most durable memorials, and the history of the kings of Prussia would be traced out by future numismatists as that of the great dynasties of Bactria has lately been recovered.

In 1842 M. Anténor Joly brought before the French legislative chambers a scheme for a system of historical money, and he renewed his proposal in 1852. M. Ernest Dumas has also suggested the issue of twenty-centime bronze pieces, which should serve either as money or as historical medals. Such schemes have not been carried out in France, and in England no coins of the sort have been struck. Except the mere expense of a new set of dies, I see no objection to the issue of historical money.

The Royal Attribute of Coining.

Every civilized community requires a supply of well-executed coins, and there arises the question, How shall this money be provided? The coins of each denomination must contain exactly equal weights of fine metal, and must bear an impress proving that they do so. Can we trust to the ordinary competition of manufacturers and traders to keep up a sufficient supply of such coins, just as they supply buttons or pins and needles? Or must we establish a government department, under strict legislative control, to secure good coinage?

As almost every opinion finds some advocate, there are not wanting a few who believe that coinage should be left to the free action of competition. Mr. Herbert Spencer especially, in his 'Social Statics,' advanced the doctrine that, as we trust the grocer to furnish us with pounds of tea, and the baker to send us loaves of bread, so we might trust Heaton and Sons, or some of the other enterprising firms of Birmingham, to supply us with sovereigns and shillings at their own risk and profit. He held that just as people go by preference to the grocer who sells good tea, and to the baker whose loaves are sound and of full weight, so the honest and successful coiner would gain possession of the market, and his money would drive out inferior productions.

Though I must always deeply respect the opinions of so profound a thinker as Mr. Spencer, I hold that in this instance he has pushed a general principle into an exceptional case, where it quite fails. He has overlooked the important law of Gresham (to be explained in the next chapter), that better money cannot drive out worse. In matters of currency self-interest acts in the opposite direction to what it does in other affairs, as will be explained, and if coining were left free, those who sold light coins at reduced prices would drive the best trade.

This conclusion is amply confirmed by experience; for at many times and places coins have been issued by private manufacturers, and always with the result of debasing the currency. For a long time the copper currency of England consisted mainly of tradesmen's tokens, which were issued very light in weight and excessive in number. In Mr. Smiles' 'Lives of Boulton and Watt' (p. 391), there is printed an interesting letter, in which Boulton complains that in his journeys he received on an average at the toll-gates two counterfeit pennies for one true one. The lower class of manufacturers, he says, purchased copper coin to the nominal value of thirty-six shillings for twenty shillings in silver, and distributed it to their work-people in wages, so as to make a considerable profit. The multitude of these depreciated pieces in circulation was so great, that the magistrates and inhabitants of Stockport held a public meeting, and resolved to take no halfpence in future but those of the Anglesey Company, which were of full weight. This shows, if proof were needed, that the separate action of self-interest was inoperative in keeping bad coin out of circulation, and it is not to be supposed that the public meeting could have had any sufficient effect. In China the current small money called *cash* or *le*, is commonly manufactured by private coiners, and the consequence is that the size, quality, and value of the coins have fallen very much.

In my opinion there is nothing less fit to be left to the action of competition than money. In constitutional law the right of coining has always been held to be one of the peculiar prerogatives of the Crown, and it is a maxim of the civil law, that *monetandi jus principum ossibus inhæret*. To the executive government and its scientific advisers, who have minutely inquired into the intricacies of the subject of currency and coinage, the matter had better be left. It should as far as possible be removed from the sphere of party struggles or public opinion, and confided to the decision of experts. No doubt, in times past, kings have been the most notorious false coiners and depreciators of the currency, but there is no danger of the like being done in modern times. The danger lies quite in the opposite direction, that popular governments will not venture upon the most obvious and necessary improvement of the monetary system without obtaining a concurrence of popular opinion in its favour, while the people, influenced by habit, and with little knowledge of the subject, will never be able to agree upon the best scheme.

CHAPTER VIII.

THE PRINCIPLES OF CIRCULATION.

BEFORE proceeding to consider the actual monetary systems adopted by modern or ancient nations, it is desirable to dwell for a short time upon the different meanings which may be attributed to the word *money*, and upon the natural principles which govern the use and circulation of coins. We must, in the first place, distinguish three things which, in the practical working of a currency system, are often separate, namely, the actual coins employed, the numbers by which they are expressed, and the relation of those numbers to the assumed unit of value. We must further distinguish coins according as their values depend upon the metal they contain, the metal for which they can be exchanged, or the other coins for which they are the legal equivalent.

The Standard Unit of Value.

It is essential, in the first place, to decide clearly what we mean by a *standard unit of value*. This must consist of a fixed quantity of some concrete substance, defined by reference to the units of weight or space. Value may seem to some people to be a purely mental phenomenon, and a pound would then have to be defined, as Lord Castlereagh asserted, by a *sense of value*. But we might as well define a yard by a sense of length, or a grain by a sense of weight. Just as every quantity in physical science is defined by reference to some concrete standard specimen, so, if we are to measure and express value at all, we must fix upon definite quantities of one or more definite and unchangeable commodities for the purpose.

The expression, *standard unit of value*, will indeed be almost inevitably misunderstood as implying the existence of something of fixed value. As we have seen, however (p. 11), value merely expresses the essentially variable ratio in which two commodities exchange, so that there is no reason to suppose that any substance does for two days together retain the same value. All that a standard of value means is, that some uniform unchangeable substance is chosen, in terms of which all ratios of exchange may be expressed and calculated,

228

without any regard whatever to the feelings or mental phenomena which the commodities produce in men. For reasons already stated, one or other of the metals, gold, silver, or copper, has usually been considered most suitable for constituting the standard substance.

The absolute weight or magnitude of the unit of money is a matter of little or no importance, provided that all people agree upon the same unit, and that it be permanently and exactly defined, and afterwards adhered to. Before the English yard was fixed, it would not have mattered whether it was a few inches longer or shorter; it does not matter, indeed, whether the inch, the foot, the furlong, or the mile is the unit, provided that one of them is definitely fixed, and the others referred to it by known ratios. So, it is really indifferent whether we regard the pound troy of standard gold, or the ounce, or the fixed number of grains in the sovereign, as our standard. It is only requisite that every contract expressed in money shall enable us to ascertain exactly how much standard gold is due from one person to another.

M. Chevalier and some other continental economists have argued elaborately in favour of a universal standard unit of value, coinciding with the metric system of weights. They wish the unit of value to be ten grams of gold exactly, and seem to think that there is some magical efficacy in the correspondence of money and weights. This correspondence might perhaps be a slight convenience to those bullion dealers who have to calculate the metallic value of coins before melting or exporting them, or to those mint officials who have to adjust and test the weights of coins; to all other persons it would be a matter of complete indifference. Those who use coins in ordinary business need never inquire how much metal they contain. Probably not one person in ten thousand in this kingdom knows, or need know, that a sovereign should contain 123·27447 grains of standard gold. Besides, if we agree to accept a precise metrical quantity of one metal as our standard, the weights of the coins composed of other metals will be complicated fractional amounts, to be determined with reference to the accidental market values of the metals.

All we can say, then, is that the standard unit of value is some entirely arbitrary weight of the standard metal, the exact amount of which, being a matter of indifference on general grounds, should be fixed as seems most convenient in reference to the habits of nations or other accidental circumstances.

Coin, Money of Account, and Unit of Value.

It is desirable to distinguish clearly between three things which, although definitely related to each other, need not be identical. The unit of value, or standard weight of the selected metal, is not necessarily made into a coin. It may be a quantity too great or too small for coining. All that is requisite is that the current coins shall be multiples or submultiples of the unit, or easily expressible in terms of the unit. Nor is it even requisite that the numbers in which we express value should be numbers of coins, or numbers of units of value. The *money of account*, as it is called, may differ both from the current money and the standard money. This is well illustrated in the Anglo-Saxon system of currency. The unit of value was the Saxon pound of standard silver, which was far too large to be coined. The only coins issued in any considerable quantity by the Anglo-Saxon kings, were silver pennies and a few halfpennies; yet the usual money of account was the shilling, which, after varying from four to five pence, was fixed by William I. at twelve pence, as it has ever since continued. No coin called a shilling was issued before the reign of Henry VII. Though the shilling has survived, other moneys of account have been forgotten, as, for instance, the *mancus*, which was equal to thirty pennies, or six shillings of five pence each. The *mark*, the *ora*, and the *thrimsa* were other moneys of account used by the Anglo-Saxons.

In our present English system the three moneys happen to coincide, which is doubtless a matter of some convenience. The sovereign is at once the principal coin, the unit of value, and the money of account in all the larger transactions, although in the expression of smaller sums the shilling is yet preferred. In France at the present time the money of account and the unit of value is the franc in gold; but as this weighs only 0·3226 gram, or about five grains, it is coined only in five, ten, and twenty-franc gold pieces, with subsidiary silver coins. In Russia, before the time of Peter the Great, the rouble was an imaginary money of account, consisting of one hundred copper copecks.

When Montesquieu affirmed that the negroes on the West Coast of Africa had a purely ideal sign of value called a *macute*, he misunderstood the nature of money of account. The macute served with the negroes as the name for a definite, though probably a variable, number of cowry shells, the number being at one time 2000. The macute has also been coined in silver pieces of eight, six, and four macutes, struck by the Portuguese for use in their colonies, the macute being worth about 2¾d.

When the currency of a country undergoes a change, the units of coinage, account and value are likely to become separated. Sometimes a new system of accounts is applied to an old coinage, as in Norway at the present time. The Stockholm government is endeavouring to introduce the Swedish decimal system of currency, and some merchants are said already to keep their accounts in kroner and öre, although the money in circulation consists almost wholly of the old skillings and the paper specie-dalers. On the other hand, the coinage is sometimes changed, and yet the old method of accounts retained, especially as regards foreign transactions. Thus the rates of foreign exchange between the United States and England were, until last year, quoted in terms of a dollar valued at 4*s.* 6*d.*, in accordance with a law of 1789. This rate seems to have been the traditional par of exchange of the Mexican dollar, and it was still retained even when the American dollar had been coined so as to be worth only 49·316 English pence.

There are two causes which have often led to a difference between coinage and money of account. The coins may, by legitimate abrasion, or by fraudulent clipping and sweating, become much reduced below their proper weights, yet an *agio*, or allowance, being made for the average depreciation, the old standard of value and money of account may be retained, as was the case in Amsterdam, Hamburg, and other towns. When a depreciated currency is issued in a country, the money of account may either change with it or remain as before; and it is an exceedingly difficult, if not insoluble problem, to decide whether, in particular periods of English history, prices were expressed in the new depreciated or the old good money. Professor J. E. T. Rogers has pointed out, in his admirable 'History of Agriculture and Prices in England,' printed by the Clarendon Press (vol. i. p. 175), that, in the fourteenth century, the coinage, though apparently passed by tale, was often weighed. In the ancient college accounts which he has investigated, he finds charges entered both for the cost of scales to make the weighings, and for the deficiency of weight of the coins.

In many countries, even at the present day, the circulating medium consists not of any one simple and well-connected series of coins, but of a miscellaneous collection of coins of various sizes and values, imported from foreign states. In such cases the money of account must necessarily differ from the mass of the coins, of which the value is usually estimated by a tariff expressed in terms of the money of account. In the German states, a few years ago, French and English gold was freely accepted in this manner. In Canada there is an intricate confusion of monetary systems. There being no national mint, the circulation consists of many species of foreign coins, chiefly varieties of the dollar. The monetary unit is a dollar, taken as equal to fifty English pence; but this is represented by bank notes, and not by any coin. At the same time there are two different moneys of account: the Halifax Currency Pound, divided into twenty shillings of twenty pence each, and defined by the fact that sixty such pence are equal to a dollar; and, secondly, the Halifax Sterling Currency, which perpetuates, for the purpose of expressing the rates of foreign exchange, the old valuation which makes a dollar equal to 4*s.* 6*d.*

Standard and Token Money.

We must distinguish between coins according as they serve for *standard money* or for *token money*. A standard coin is one of which the value in exchange depends solely upon the value of the material contained in it. The stamp serves as a mere indication and guarantee of the quantity of fine metal. We may treat such coins as bullion, and melt them up or export them to countries where they are not legally current; yet the value of the metal being independent of legislation will everywhere be recognised.

Token coins, on the contrary, are defined in value by the fact that they can, by force of law or custom, be exchanged in a certain fixed ratio for standard coins. The metal contained in a token coin has of course a certain value; but it may be less than the legal value in almost any degree. In our English silver coinage the difference is from 9 to 12 per cent., according to the market price of silver; in our bronze coinage the difference is 75 per cent. The metal contained in the French bronze coins is in like manner equal in value to little more than one quarter of the current value. In many cases the difference has been far greater, as for instance in some of the old kreutzer pieces lately current in the German states. Woods's halfpence, which at one time created so much discontent in Ireland, or the small money previously issued by Charles II. in Ireland, are extreme instances of depreciated token money.

Metallic and Nominal Values of Coins.

It has been usual to call the value of the metal contained in a coin the *intrinsic value* of the coin; but this use of the word *intrinsic* is likely to give rise to fallacious notions concerning the nature of value, which is never an intrinsic property, or existence, but merely a circumstance, or external relation (see p. 9). To avoid any chance of ambiguity, I shall substitute the expression, *metallic value*, and I shall distinguish this from the *nominal, customary,* or *legal value*, at which a coin actually does, or is by law required, to exchange for other coins.

There are two ways in which the metallic value of a coin may be reduced below its nominal value, namely, by reducing either the weight or the fineness of the metal. English silver coin is still maintained at the 'ancient right standard' of 11 oz. 2 dwts. in the troy pound, which has existed from time immemorial. By the Act of 1816 the silver coins which had previously been, in theory at least, standard money, were reduced in weight by 6 per cent., and thus rendered token money, which they still continue to be. In France and other countries belonging to the Monetary Convention, the smaller silver coins of two francs, one franc, and fifty centimes, have been converted into tokens by reducing the fineness of the silver from 900 to 835 parts in 1000. It does not seem to be a matter of any importance which mode is adopted; but the English mode, so long as it does not render the coins inconveniently small, is perhaps slightly the better, because some persons can satisfy themselves as to the weight of a coin, but none are able to test its fineness, unless they are professional assayers.

It need hardly be stated that coins which circulate by law in one country as tokens may be accepted in other countries at their metallic value.

Legal Tender.

Money must further be distinguished, according as it is or is not *legal tender*, or has or has not what the French call *cours forcé*. By legal tender is denoted such money as a creditor is obliged to receive in requital of a debt expressed in terms of money of the realm. One great object of legislation is to prevent uncertainty in the interpretation of contracts, and accordingly the Coinage Act defines precisely what will constitute a legal offer of payment on the part of a debtor, as regards a money debt. If a debtor tender to his creditor the amount of a debt due in legal tender money, and it be refused, the creditor may indeed apply for it, or sue for it afterwards, but the costs of the action will be thrown upon him.

But there seems to be no legal necessity that exchanges or contracts shall be made in money of the realm. At common law, contracts for the direct barter of two commodities, or for purchase and sale in terms of any kind of money, will be valid, provided it is clear what the terms of the contract mean. Accordingly, the sixth section of the Coinage Act (33 Vict. c. 10), while enacting that every contract, sale, payment, bill, note, transaction, or matter relating to money, shall be made or done according to the coins which are current and legal tender in pursuance of this Act, yet adds, 'unless the same be made, executed, entered into, done or had, according to the currency of some British possession or some foreign state.'

If I understand the matter aright, then, every person is at liberty to buy, sell, or exchange in terms of any money or commodity whatsoever which he prefers; and the fact that certain coins, up to certain limits, are legal tender, only means that the state provides a definite medium of exchange and defines precisely what that is. The Act requires that *English money* shall be the money issued by the mint, in accordance with the terms of the Act. Of course it remains quite open to a creditor to receive payment in coins which are not legal tender, if he like to do so, and I presume there would be nothing to prevent him entering into a contract to that effect. If a man contracted to sell goods to the extent of £100, and to receive payment in bronze pence and halfpence, it would no doubt be a valid contract, although no single quantity of pence exceeding twelve pence is a legal tender.

The exact meaning of the term, legal tender, may of course vary from country to country, and the above remarks apply only to countries under the English law.

The Force of Habit in the Circulation of Money.

No one can possibly understand many social phenomena unless he constantly bears in mind the force of habit and social convention. This is strikingly true in our subject of money. Over and over again in the course of history, powerful rulers have endeavoured to put new coins into circulation or to withdraw old ones; but the instincts of self-interest or habit in the people have been too strong for laws and penalties. Though in particular instances it may be difficult to explain occurrences which happen in the circulation of coins, yet a close analysis of the character of those who handle money, and their motives for holding or paying it away, will throw much light upon the subject.

We must notice, in the first place, that the great mass of the population who hold coins have no theories, or general information whatever, upon the subject of money. They are guided entirely by popular report and tradition. The sole question with them on receiving a coin is whether similar coins have been readily accepted by other people. Thus in the remote parts of Norway at the present time, the old paper daler notes are preferred to the beautiful new twenty-kroner gold pieces. By far the greater number of the people possess no means of learning the metallic, or even the legal, value of an unfamiliar coin. Few people have scales and weights suitable for weighing a coin, and no one but an assayer or analytical chemist can decide upon its fineness. Many a traveller who has carried good new coin into a country where it happened to be strange, has had to suffer a loss in paying it away. When our bronze pence were quite a novelty, I happened to take some with me into a remote part of North Wales, and they were rejected.

People in general accept coin simply on the ground of its familiar appearance. So entirely is this the case among very ignorant populations, that it has often been found desirable to maintain unchanged the impress on successive issues of coins. In many cases coins have been struck for this purpose with the date of a long past year, or even the effigy of a dead sovereign. The Maria Theresa dollar is still coined by the Austrian mint, with exactly the same design and date as when first issued in 1780, because it is the favourite coin in some of the states of North Africa, and various parts of the Levant. The British Government, when undertaking the Abyssinian expedition, procured a large stock of these coins for paying the natives. In the same way Mexican dollars are usually worth rather more than silver bullion, because of their easy currency in the East.

To the supremacy of habit, and the absence of means of estimating the real value of coin, is obviously due the depreciation which currencies have undergone. False coiners and kings alike find that, if they can only make new coins look and feel exactly like old coins, the people will accept depreciated money without question.

The annals of coinage, in this and all other countries, are little more than a monotonous repetition of depreciated issues both public and private, varied by occasional meritorious, but often unsuccessful, efforts to restore the standard of the currency. A curious instance of successive attempts to beguile a people are found in certain Roman denarii of the Consular times. False coiners having issued plated denarii among the subject Germans, the people appeared to have notched them with files to test their genuineness. The Germans having thus become accustomed to see genuine *notched* coins, the Roman government found it desirable to issue new coins notched in a similar manner. But the forgers were not to be beaten. They issued plated denarii with the notches all complete, apparently displaying good metal within; and notched false coins of this kind exist to the present day in numismatic cabinets.

Gresham's Law.

Though the public generally do not discriminate between coins and coins, provided there is an apparent similarity, a small class of money-changers, bullion-dealers, bankers, or goldsmiths make it their business to be acquainted with such differences, and know how to derive a profit from them. These are the people who frequently *uncoin* money, either by melting it, or by exporting it to countries where it is sooner or later melted. Some coins are sunk in the sea or lost, and some are carried abroad by emigrants and travellers who do not look closely to the metallic value of the money. But by far the greatest part of the standard coinage is removed from circulation by people who know that they shall gain by choosing for this purpose the new heavy coins most recently issued from the mint. Hence arises the practice, extensively carried on in the present day in England, of *picking and culling*, or, as another technical expression is, *garbling* the coinage, devoting the good new coins to the melting-pot, and passing the old worn coins into circulation again on every suitable opportunity.

From these considerations we readily learn the truth and importance of a general law or principle concerning the circulation of money, which Mr. Macleod has very appropriately named the Law or Theorem of Gresham, after Sir Thomas Gresham, who clearly perceived its truth three centuries ago. This law, briefly expressed, is that *bad money drives out good money*, but that *good money cannot drive out bad money*. At first sight there may seem to be something paradoxical in the fact, that when beautiful new coins of full weight are issued from the mint, the people still continue to circulate, in preference, the old depreciated ones. Many well-intentioned efforts to reform a currency have thus been frustrated, to the great cost of states, and the perplexity of statesmen who had not studied the principles of monetary science.

In all other matters everybody is led by self-interest to choose the better and reject the worse; but in the case of money, it would seem as if they paradoxically retain the worse and get rid of the better. The explanation is very simple. The people, as a general rule, do not reject the better, but pass from hand to hand indifferently the heavy and the light coins, because their only use for the coin is as a medium of exchange. It is those who are going to melt, export, hoard, or dissolve the coins of the realm, or convert them into jewellery and gold leaf, who carefully select for their purposes the new heavy coins.

Gresham's law alone furnishes a sufficient refutation of Mr. Herbert Spencer's doctrine, already noticed (p. 64) that money ought to be provided by private manufacturers. People who want furniture, or books, or clothes, may be trusted to select the best which they can afford, because they are going to keep and use these articles; but with money it is just the opposite. Money is made to go. They want coin, not to keep it in their own pockets, but to pass it off into their neighbours' pockets; and the worse the money which they can get their neighbours to accept, the greater the profit to themselves. Thus there is a natural tendency to the depreciation of the metallic currency, which can only be prevented by the constant supervision of the state.

From Gresham's law we may infer the necessity of two precautions in the regulation of the currency. In the first place, the standard coins, as issued from the mint, should be as nearly as possible of the standard weight, otherwise the difference will form a profit for the bullion-broker and exporter. In the second place, adequate measures must be taken for withdrawing from circulation all coins which are worn below the least legal weight, otherwise they will continue to circulate as token coins for an indefinite length of time. All commerce consists in the exchange of commodities of equal value, and the principal money should consist of pieces of metal so nearly equal in metallic contents, that all persons, including bullion dealers, bankers, and other professed dealers in money, will indifferently substitute one coin for another. But it is obvious that these remarks do not apply to coins intended to serve as tokens, since the current value of tokens exceeds their metallic value, and every one who uses them otherwise than in ordinary circulation will lose the difference. Hence the weight of a token coin is comparatively a matter of indifference, so long as people will receive them, and the deficiency of weight is not too great a temptation to the false coiner.

In England at the present day the force of habit, and the absence of means of discrimination, lead to the depreciation of our gold standard coinage by abrasion. Only while a sovereign exceeds 122·5 grains in weight is it legally a sovereign; but people go on paying and receiving indifferently, in ordinary trade, sovereigns of which the metallic values differ 2d. or 4d., and sometimes even 6d. or 8d. Every standard coin thus tends to degenerate into a token coin, and such a coin can only be withdrawn from circulation by the state.

Extension of Gresham's Law.

Gresham's remarks concerning the inability of good money to drive out bad money, only referred to moneys of one kind of metal, but the same principle applies to the relations of all kinds of money, in the same circulation. Gold compared with silver, or silver with copper, or paper compared with gold, are subject to the same law that the relatively cheaper medium of exchange will be retained in circulation and the relatively dearer will disappear. The most extreme instance which has ever occurred was in the case of the Japanese currency. At the time of the treaty of 1858, between Great Britain, the United States, and Japan, which partially opened up the last country to European traders, a very curious system of currency existed in Japan. The most valuable Japanese coin was the kobang, consisting of a thin oval disc of gold about 2 inches long, and 1¼ inch wide, weighing 200 grains, and ornamented in a very primitive manner. It was passing current in the towns of Japan for four silver itzebus, but was worth in English money about 18s. 5d., whereas the silver itzebu was equal only to about 1s. 4d. Thus the Japanese were estimating their gold money at only about one-third of its value, as estimated according to the relative values of the metals in other parts of the world. The earliest European traders enjoyed a rare opportunity for making profit. By buying up the kobangs at the native rating they trebled their money, until the natives, perceiving what was being done, withdrew from circulation the remainder of the gold. A complete reform of the Japanese currency is now being carried out, the English mint at Hong Kong having been purchased by the Japanese government.

What happened in an extreme degree in Japan has often happened in England and other European countries, in a less degree. If the ratio of gold and silver in the coinage, as legally current, differs only one or two per cent. from the commercial ratio, it may become profitable to export the one metal rather than the other, and in this way, as we shall see, the main part of the currency of France was changed from silver into gold between 1849 and 1869. In fact the character of the coinage of most nations has been determined in a similar manner, and England and the United States were thus led to adopt a principal gold currency. There is every reason to believe that in ancient Rome, both in the time of the Republic and of the Empire, great difficulties were encountered in regulating the currency of silver alongside of copper, and the perplexity became worse when gold coin was introduced.

CHAPTER IX.

SYSTEMS OF METALLIC MONEY.

WE are now in a position to analyse the construction of the various systems of metallic money which have existed, or do exist, or which might be conceived to exist. The systems actually brought into operation are more numerous than is commonly supposed, and I have nowhere met with an adequate classification of them. M. Courcelle-Seneuil, indeed, has satisfactorily described some of the principal systems, and MM. Chevalier, Garnier, and other writers, both continental and English, have given other brief classifications. But we must now take a comprehensive view of the possible ways in which two, three, or more metals may be employed in the construction of a more or less useful monetary system.

There seem to be five distinct modes in which a government may deal with metallic money.

1. It may confine itself to providing a system of weights and measures, and may then allow the precious metals to be passed about from hand to hand, like other commodities, in terms of the national weights and measures, and in the form which individuals find to be most convenient. This we may call the system of *currency by weight*.

2. To save the trouble of frequent weighing, and the uncertainty of fineness of the metal, it may coin one or more metals into pieces of certain specified weights and fineness, and may afterwards allow the public to make their contracts and sales in one or other kind of coin, as they deem expedient. This may be described as the system of *unrestricted currency by tale*.

3. To prevent misunderstandings, the government, while emitting various coins in various metals, may ordain that all contracts expressed in money of the realm shall, in the absence of express provision to the contrary, be taken to mean money of one kind of metal, specially named, while other coin shall be left to circulate at varying market rates compared with this principal kind of coinage. This is *the single legal tender system*.

4. The government may emit coins of two or more kinds of metal, and enact that money contracts may be discharged in one or other kind, at certain rates fixed by law. This is the *multiple legal tender system*.

5. While maintaining one kind of coin as the principal legal tender, in which all large money contracts must be fulfilled, coins of other kinds of metal may be ordered to be received in limited quantities, as equivalent to the principal coin. For this the name *composite legal tender system* may be proposed.

Currency by Weight.

The order in which I have enumerated the principal systems of metallic money, is not only the logical order, but it is the historical order in which the systems have, for the most part, been introduced. There is overwhelming evidence to prove that simple currency by weight is the primitive system. Before the invention of the balance, lumps and grains were no doubt exchanged according to a rude estimation of their bulk or weight; but afterwards the balance became a necessary instrument in all important transactions. In the Old Testament we find several statements clearly implying that the ancient Hebrews used to pass money by weight. In Genesis (xxiii. 16) Abraham is represented as weighing out to Ephron 'four hundred shekels of silver, current money with the merchant,' but the silver in question is believed to have consisted of rough lumps or rings not to be considered coin. In the Book of Job (xxviii. 15) we are told that 'wisdom cannot be gotten for gold, neither shall silver be weighed for the price thereof.'

Aristotle, in his Politics (Book I., chap. ix), gives an interesting account of his view of the origin of money, and distinctly tells us that the metals were first passed simply by weight or size, and Pliny makes a similar assertion. That it was so, we may infer from the remarkable fact that, even when no use was made of it, the custom of bringing a pair of scales survived as a legal formality in the sale of slaves at Rome.

There can be little doubt that every system of coinage was originally identical with a system of weights, the unit of value being the unit of weight of some selected metal. The English pound sterling was certainly the Saxon pound of standard silver, which was too large to be made into a single coin, but was divided into two hundred and forty silver pennies, each equal to a *pennyweight*. In the English and Scotch *pounds*, and the French *livre*, we have the vestiges of a uniform international system of money and weights, the establishment of which is attributed to Charlemagne, but which unfortunately became differentiated and destroyed by the various depreciations of the coinage in one country or another. Most of the other principal units of value were originally units of weight, such as the shekel, the talent, the as, the stater, the libra, the mark, the franc, the lira.

In the Old Testament the notion of money is expressed three times by the Hebrew word kesitah, which is translated in certain old versions into words meaning *lamb*. This might seem to be an additional proof of the former use of cattle as a medium of exchange; but I am informed by my learned friend, Professor Theodores, that this translation probably arises from an accidental blunder, and that the original meaning of the word kesitah, was that of 'a certain weight,' or 'an exact quantity.' The corresponding word in the Arabic, kist, is said to denote a pair of scales.

Currency by weight still exists among considerable portions of the human race. In the Burman empire, for instance, three kinds of metal are current, namely, lead, silver, and gold, and all payments are made by the balance, the unit of weight for silver being the tical. In the Chinese empire and Cochin China, there is indeed a legal tender currency of *cash* or *sapeks* but gold and silver are usually dealt in by weight, the unit being the tael. A very interesting account of Chinese money, by M. le Comte Rochechouart, will be found in the *Journal des Economistes* for 1869 (vol. xv. p. 103). According to this writer, both gold and silver are treated simply as merchandise, and there is not even a recognized stamp, or government guarantee of the fineness of the metal. The traveller must carry these metals with him, as a sufficient quantity of strings of *cash* would require a waggon for their conveyance. Yet in exchanging silver or gold he is sure to suffer great losses, both from the falsity of balances and weights, and the uncertain fineness of the metal. In buying a tael of gold the traveller may have to give eighteen taels of silver; but in selling it he will often not obtain more than fourteen taels.

Whatever be the inconveniences of the method, currency by weight is yet the natural and necessary system to which people revert whenever the abrasion of coins, the intermixture of currencies, the fall of a state, or other causes destroy the public confidence in a more highly organized system. Though the silver penny among the Anglo-Saxons was supposed to correspond with a *pennyweight*, there was a practice of giving *compensatio ad pensum*, which really amounted to taking the coins by weight, to allow for abrasion and inaccurate or false coinage. The *as* was at first equal in weight to a Roman pound, but it was rapidly lessened, so that at the epoch of the First Punic War, it did not exceed two ounces, and by the time of the Second Punic War it had sunk to one ounce. The Roman people had naturally reverted to weighing the metal, and the *aes grave* was money reckoned by weight instead of by *tale*.

In the present day currency by weight is far more extensively practised then might be supposed, because, in many parts of the world, the currency consists of a miscellaneous assortment of old gold, silver, and even copper coins, which have been brought thither from other countries, and have been variously worn, clipped, or depreciated. In such countries the only means of avoiding loss and fraud is to weigh each coin, and the impress passes for little more than an indication of the fineness of the metals. In all large international transactions, again, currency by weight is the sole method. The regulations of a state concerning its legal tender have no validity beyond its own frontiers; and as all coins are subject to more or less wear and uncertainty of weight, they are received only for the actual weight of metal they are estimated to contain. The coin of well-conducted foreign mints is bought and sold by weight without melting; but the coin of minor states, which have occasionally depreciated their money, is melted up and treated simply as bullion.

Unrestricted Currency by Tale.

The simplest way for a state to manage its money might seem to be to revert to the primitive notion of a coin, and issue pieces of gold, silver, and copper, certified to be equal to units of weight, leaving all persons free to make contracts or sales in terms of any of these metals. These pieces of certified metal would then be so many commodities thrown into the markets and allowed to take their natural relative values.

Such appears to have been the system intended to be established by the French Revolutionary Government in terms of the abortive law of Thermidor, an III. Discs of ten grams each were to be struck in gold, silver, and copper, and then put in circulation, without any attempt to regulate their currency. If I understand his meaning correctly, M. Garnier has recently brought forward a somewhat similar scheme, proposing to make the gram of gold at nine-tenths the unit of value, and to coin pieces of one, two, five, eight, or ten grams concurrently with standard silver pieces, which are in France already multiples of the gram. M. Chevalier's proposed system of international money, partially at least, involves the same notion; for he considers that the principal currency should consist of decagrams of gold. But, as Mr. Bagehot has well remarked, there is no object whatever, as regards the greater mass of the population, in having coins simply related to the system of weights, because most people never need take any account of the weight at all. They need only know how many copper coins are equal to one silver coin, and how many silver to one gold coin. Now, if we carry out M. Chevalier's scheme consistently and fully, and make all the coins multiples of the gram, we shall oblige all people to be constantly working complex arithmetical sums. No one could give exactly correct change without calculating how many silver ten-gram pieces are, at the market price of silver, equal to one gold ten-gram piece. The necessity for calculation occasions needless loss of time and trouble, and a factitious gain is

242

sure to accrue to the expert and unscrupulous at the expense of the poor and ignorant.

Owing to these obvious objections no government has ever, I believe, carried into practice a system of money of the kind described. Nevertheless, currencies approximating to it in nature have come to exist in many parts of the world by the intermixture of coinages of different states. There are many half-civilized nations which have no national coinage, but employ the coins which happen to reach them in the course of trade. On the West Coast of Africa the Spanish dollar is the best known coin, but Danish, French or Dutch coins also circulate. In several of the South American states the currency is in a state of complete confusion, consisting of a mixture of American eagles, gold doubloons, silver dollars, English sovereigns, piastres, etc., together sometimes with several different issues of coinage of the South American states variously depreciated. Even in British possessions we find the same state of things. In the British West Indian Islands, American, Mexican, Spanish, and other dollars, circulate concurrently with English money; but it should be added that in most cases the Spanish dollar is treated as the standard of value, and other coins are quoted in terms of it.

In Eastern countries there is a similar intermixture of coinage. In Singapore the Indian rupee mingles with Spanish and Mexican dollars. Persia has a rude coinage of its own, so uncertain in weight that it has to be dealt in by the balance, but Russian, Turkish, and Austrian gold coins circulate by tale. Some of the best-regulated nations have allowed, or even promoted, the currency of various foreign coins. In Germany, French and English gold coins used to be accepted, according to a well-recognised tariff. The circulation of English, French, Spanish, Mexican, and other gold coins in the United States was legalized by an Act of June 28th, 1834, repealed by an Act of February 21st, 1857, which however allows certain foreign coins to be received at government offices.

In England we have for many generations enjoyed a very pure currency, so that we are unconscious of the inconveniences arising from a confusion of coins of different values. But in the early part of this century Spanish dollars were put into circulation for a time in England.

In former centuries the mixture of coinages was far more common than at present. No country had a currency free from strange coins. It is impossible to open an old book on commerce without finding long tables of coins which the merchant might expect to meet with; and the business of money-changing was a lucrative and common one.

It will be understood, that only so long as coins are known by the fresh sharp appearance of the impression to be of full weight, and are accepted according to tariff, does the system of currency by tale or number exist. The

243

silver dollar, being a large coin, is subject to comparatively little abrasion, so that people learn to receive dollars of various species at certain well-established rates. Thus the dollar has practically been for several centuries the international money of the tropical countries. But so soon as coins bear evidence of wear or ill-treatment, they must be circulated by weight, and we revert to a more primitive system.

M. Feer-Herzog has described, as the system of *parallel standards*, that in which a state issues coins in two or more metals, and then allows them to circulate by tale at ratios varying according to the market values of the metals. He cites, as recent examples, the rixdaler in silver, employed as the internal money of Sweden in combination with the ducat in gold, serving as international money. The government of India, again, has on several occasions tried to introduce a parallel standard of gold alongside of the single silver legal tender now existing there. Gold mohurs have long been more or less in circulation in India, and are supposed to form at present about one-tenth part of the coinage. They are of exactly the same weight and fineness as the silver rupee, and are usually valued at from 15 to $15^2/_3$ rupees. It seems probable, however, that what M. Feer-Herzog calls the system of parallel standards will coincide according to circumstances, either with that which I have described as the system of unrestricted currency by tale, or that of a single legal tender, with an additional commercial money of varying value. The Indian currency must certainly be classed under the latter head. There cannot in fact be two different parallel standards used both at the same time; and though it is not uncommon for a state to coin moneys in two metals, and leave its subjects to pay in one or other at will, yet one of the two is generally recognized as the standard of value.

Single Legal Tender System.

The system of currency naturally adopted by the first coiners of money was that of a single legal tender. Coins of one kind of metal, or even a single series of coins of uniform weight, were at first thought sufficient. Iron in small bars was the single legal tender in Lacedæmon, and possibly in some other early states. *Aes* was undoubtedly the legal tender among the Romans for a length of time. In China the sole measure of value and legal tender to the present day consists of brass *cash* or *sapeks*, strung together in lots of a thousand each. In England silver was the only metal coined from the time of Egbert to that of Edward III., with the doubtful exception of a very few small pieces of gold. Silver was the sole legal tender and measure of value, and few coins except silver pennies were issued. In Russia and Sweden, during part of last century, copper was the sole legal tender.

A single metal currency has the great advantages of simplicity and certainty. Every one knows exactly what he is to pay or receive, and when the coins are of one size or of a few sizes, simply related to each other, like the early English coins, no one is subject to loss by errors of calculation. But there is the obvious disadvantage that, according as the metal chosen is cheap or dear, large or small transactions will be troublesome to effect. To pay a few hundred pounds in Swedish copper plates, or Chinese strings of *cash*, a cart would be required for conveyance, and the counting of *cash* is almost impracticable. A silver coinage again does not admit of coins sufficiently small for minor transactions. It is difficult to understand how retail trade was carried on when the silver penny weighed 22½ grains, and the precious metals were far more precious than at present. The penny was, indeed, cut up into halfpence and farthings, *i.e. four-things*; but even the farthing must have been equal in purchasing power to our three-penny or fourpenny piece. The mass of the currency appears to have consisted of silver pennies.

Accordingly it is found that, if a government issue coins only of a single metal, the people will introduce and circulate coins of other metals for their own convenience. In Anglo-Saxon times gold byzants from Byzantium were used in England, and the gold coins of Florence, thence called florins, were much esteemed both here and in other parts of Europe. In later centuries, too, in the absence of a legitimate copper coinage, tradesmen's tokens came into general circulation.

Multiple Legal Tender System.

Out of a single legal tender naturally grew up systems of a double or even a multiple legal tender. The Plantagenet kings of England, for instance, finding that though they coined only silver the people made use of gold, eventually began to issue gold coins, and fixed the rates at which they should be exchanged for silver coins. In the absence of any special regulations to the contrary this constituted a double tender system. As, after a time, the ratio of values of the metals would fail to coincide with that involved in the relative weights of the coins, it became requisite to fix by royal proclamation a new value for one metal in terms of the other. From 1257 to 1664 the gold and silver currency of England was thus regulated, no coins of copper or any inferior metal being then issued. From 1664 to 1717 no proclamations were made upon the subject, and the value of the guinea was allowed to vary in terms of the shilling. At one time it rose nearly to 30s., owing partly to the decreased value of silver, but chiefly to the clipped and worn state of the silver money. During this interval, then, the country had a single silver standard.

245

In the early part of the last century a great deal of discussion took place upon the unsatisfactory state of the silver currency, and Sir Isaac Newton, the Master of the Mint, was requested to report upon the best measures to be adopted. In 1717 he made a celebrated report, recommending that the government should revert to the practice of fixing the price of the guinea, and he suggested 21s. as the best rate. His advice being accepted, the guinea has ever since been valued at 21s. Then there was again a double standard in England, any one being at liberty to pay in either kind of coin. In practice, however, it is almost impossible that the commercial value of the metals should coincide with the legal ratio. At the rate adopted by Sir Isaac Newton, gold was overvalued by rather more than 1½ per cent.; to that extent it was more valuable as currency than as metal. Therefore, in accordance with the Law of Gresham, and the principles laid down in Chapter VIII., the full weight silver coin was withdrawn or exported, and gold became the practical measure of value, which it has ever since continued to be.

In every other part of the world, where attempts have been made to combine two metals as concurrent standards of value, similar results have followed. In Massachusetts, in 1762, gold was made a legal tender, as well as silver, at the rate of 2½d. per grain; but, being overvalued as much as 5 per cent, the silver coinage rapidly disappeared from circulation. Various laws were passed to remedy this inconvenient state of things, but without success so long as this valuation of gold was maintained.

In these and many other cases which might be quoted, a government had attempted to combine a circulation of gold with that of silver, without being aware of all the principles involved in the experiment. It was hardly, perhaps, till the time of the French Revolution that the double standard system was consciously selected as the best method. Since the celebrated law, known as 'La loi du 7 Germinal, an XI.,' was adopted by the Revolutionary Government, the system has become identified with the policy of the French economists. The history of the origin of this law was almost unknown, until M. Wolowski described it in a series of valuable articles published in the *Journal des Economistes* for 1869.

As early as 1790 Mirabeau presented to the National Assembly a celebrated memoir on monetary doctrines, in which, amid a curious mixture of true and false views, he decided in favour of silver as the principal money, on the ground of the greater abundance of silver compared with gold. He proposed to make silver the *constitutional money*, that is, the legal tender, and to employ gold and copper as *additional signs* of value. These ideas were only so far carried out that the franc was defined first as ten grams of silver by the decree of the 1st August, 1793, and was afterwards definitively fixed at five grams by the law of the 28th Thermidor, an III. The old gold pieces of twenty-four and forty-eight livres continued to circulate, while the ten-gram gold pieces ordered by the decree to be struck were not really issued.

In the year IX. Gaudin proposed that the ratio of 15½ to 1 should be adopted in fixing the weight of the gold coins relatively to the silver ones. Thus, while the franc was defined as consisting of five grams of silver nine-tenths fine, the twenty-franc gold piece was to contain 6·451 grams of gold of equal fineness. He seems to have thought that this ratio was sufficiently near to that of the markets to allow the coins to circulate side by side for a long time, and in case of a change; he thought that the gold pieces could be melted and reissued at a different weight. After a great amount of discussion, in which Berenger, Lebreton, Daru, and Bosc took the most prominent parts, the proposals of Gaudin were carried out, but not precisely on the ground indicated by him. It appears to have been thought unwise either to demonetize gold altogether, which would have seriously diminished the circulating medium, or to leave the value of the gold coins uncertain, which would give rise to disputes.

The ratio adopted by the legislators of the Revolution happened to overvalue silver in some degree, and hence the currency of France came to consist principally of the heavy five-francs pieces, or écus. Not until the Californian and Australian discoveries caused gold to be the cheaper money in which to make payments, did this heavy silver money gradually disappear. The action of the double standard system will be further considered in Chapter XII.

Composite Legal Tender.

We have seen that with a single metal currency there is inconvenience in making small or large payments, according as the metal chosen is dear or cheap. If two or more series of full-weight coins be issued in different metals, and allowed to vary in relation to each other, the difficulty of calculation intervenes. If they both be made legal tenders at a fixed ratio, the currency will tend to become composed alternately of one or the other metal, and money-changers will make a profit out of the conversion.

There yet remains another possible system, in which coins of one metal are adopted as the standard of value and principal legal tender, and subordinate token coins of other metals are furnished for the purpose of sub-division, being recognized as legal tender only for small amounts. The values of these token coins now depend upon that of the standard coins for which they are legally exchangeable, and care is taken to make their weights such that the metallic value will always be less than the legal value. No profit can ever be made by melting such coins, or removing them from the country, and their ratio of exchange with the principal coins is always a simple ratio fixed by law.

The composite legal tender rises naturally out of the double standard system; for, as we have seen, if, under the latter system, gold be overvalued at the legal rate, all full-weight silver coins will be withdrawn and exported by degrees, so that there will remain practically a token currency of light silver. Lord Liverpool, having in his thorough investigation of the subject of metallic money observed the superior convenience of the composite legal tender to the double legal tender, advocated its adoption in England in the most conclusive manner. His arguments will be found in his admirable 'Treatise on the Coins of the Realm in a Letters to the King' (Oxford, 1805), and his recommendations, as carried into effect in 1816, are the foundation of our present monetary system.

A composite system of currency has frequently existed in one country or another without being specially designed or recognized. It comes into existence whenever coins of gold and silver are current at rates fixed by law or custom, but the silver coins are reduced by abrasion or clipping below the corresponding weight. From the year 1717, when the guinea was fixed at 21s., until the present system was instituted in 1816, the English currency was based theoretically upon the double standard system. Practically, however, the silver coins were so scarce and worn that they served but as tokens. The tradesmen's copper tokens, too, being always of light weight, and exchangeable by custom for a certain proportion of silver coins, formed the third term in the series. But Lord Liverpool appears to have been the first to apprehend and explain the principles on which such a composite system worked, and there can be no doubt that the system, as he expounded it, is the best adapted for supplying a convenient and economical currency.

Most of the leading nations have now adopted the composite legal tender in a more or less complete form. France, Belgium, Switzerland, and Italy still adhere to the double standard in theory, but have reduced all coins of less value than five francs to the footing of token money, by reducing the fineness of the silver from 900 parts to 835 parts in 1000, or by 7¼ per cent., and by limiting the amount for which they are legal tender. The copper money of France had previously been restricted as a legal tender to sums below five francs in any one payment. In the United States, when metallic currency was generally employed, the double standard system existed in theory, but was reduced to a composite standard by the excessive overvaluing of the gold money. Moreover, by a law of 21st February, 1853, the smaller silver coins were reduced in weight and made legal tender only for sums not exceeding five dollars. The silver three-cent pieces, and the several copper, bronze, or nickel coins, issued from the United States' mints, were also token money with various limits as regards legal tender.

The new German monetary system is perfectly organized as a composite legal tender.

CHAPTER X.

THE ENGLISH SYSTEM OF METALLIC CURRENCY.

I NOW come to describe in more detail the system of metallic currency which has existed in England for more than half a century, and which seems to be the best of all as regards the principles on which coins of three different metals are combined into a composite legal tender. The legal regulations under which the English coinage is issued and circulated, can be ascertained with ease and certainty, thanks to the Act of Parliament (33 Victoria, ch. 10), which Mr. Lowe caused to be passed to simplify and consolidate the statutes on the subject.

English Gold Coin.

The English sovereign is the principal legal tender and the standard of value. It is defined as consisting of 123·27447 grains (7·98805 grams) of English standard gold, composed of eleven parts of fine gold, and one part of alloy, chiefly copper. The sovereign ought, therefore, in theory, to contain 113·00160 grains, or 7·32238 grams, of pure gold. But as it is evidently impossible to make coins of any precise weight, or to maintain them of that weight when in circulation, the weight stated is only that standard weight to which the mint workmen should aim to attain as closely as possible, both in each individual piece, and in the average.

From the weight of the sovereign we deduce the mint price of gold. For if we divide the number of grains in the sovereign into the number of grains—namely, 480—in the troy ounce, we ascertain exactly how many sovereigns and portions of a sovereign the mint ought to return for each ounce delivered in. This we find to be 3·89375, which is equivalent to £3 17s. 10½d. It comes to exactly the same thing to say in terms of the old mint indentures, that twenty-pounds' weight troy of gold are to be coined into 934 sovereigns, and one half-sovereign. I have heard of people who protested against the government fixing the price at which gold should be bought and sold by the mint, and who yet allowed that the sovereign must have some fixed weight. But the fixed price is convertible with the fixed weight, and *vice versâ*. Either follows from the other.

In practice the weight of a coin is always a matter of limits, and there must be limits both for the weight as sent out and that at which it can legally remain in circulation. The *remedy* is the technical name for the allowance made to the mint-master for imperfection of workmanship, and is defined by the Act as two-tenths of a grain (0·01296 gram). Thus the mint cannot legally issue a sovereign weighing less than 123·074 grains, or more than 123·474 grains. Since the fineness of the gold, again, can never be adjusted exactly to the standard of eleven parts in twelve, or 916·66 in a 1000, a remedy of two parts in 1000 is allowed in this respect. It is understood that the English mint succeeds in working well within the remedy both of weight and fineness.

Every sovereign issued from the mint in accordance with these regulations, and bearing the impress authorized by the Queen, is legal tender, and must be accepted by a creditor in discharge of a debt to that amount, provided that it has not been reduced by wear or ill-treatment below the weight of 122·50 grains (7·93787 grams). If a sovereign of less than this *least current weight* be tendered to any person, he is presumed by the law to detect the deficiency, and is bound to cut or deface the coin, and return it to the tenderer, who must bear the loss. If the coin so defaced should prove not to be below the limit, then the defacer has to receive it and bear the loss arising from his mistake. Any justice of the peace may decide disputes arising concerning light sovereigns in a summary manner.

The only other gold coin actually issued is the half-sovereign, of which the standard weight and remedy are exactly half those of the sovereign, the remedy in fineness the same as in the sovereign, and the least current weight 61·1250 grains (3·96083 grams). The Coinage Act also legalizes the issue of two-and five-pound gold pieces, the weights and remedies in weight being corresponding multiples of those of the sovereign. Coins of the value of five and two guineas were struck by most of the English monarchs from the time of Charles II. to that of George III. Patterns of five- and two-pound pieces have been prepared under Queen Victoria; but gold coins of this size have not been issued in the present reign, nor is it desirable, for reasons stated in Chapter XIII., that they should be issued.

English Silver Coin.

The further subdivision of the pound is effected by token coins of silver and bronze, which are made of such weights that there is no danger of their metallic values rising above the metallic value of the gold coins for which they are legally equivalent. Previous to the year 1816, the troy pound of standard silver, containing 925 parts of fine silver and 75 parts of alloy in 1000, was coined into 62 shillings, so that each shilling would contain 92·90 grains of standard metal. Under these regulations gold was rated as 15·21 times as valuable as silver. As silver, however, may sometimes become more valuable relatively to gold, Lord Liverpool very wisely recommended in his letter to the king, that the weight of the shilling should be reduced. By the Act 56 Geo. III. ch. 68, it was ordered that the troy pound of silver should be coined into 66 shillings, a reduction of weight of about 6 per cent. The new Coinage Act maintains the chief provisions of that of 1816, so that the English shilling now has the weight of 87·27272 grains of standard silver (5·65518 grams), and the weights of all the other silver coins are exactly corresponding multiples or submultiples of this. The mint remedy in weight for the shilling is a little more than the third part of a grain, and in simple proportion for the other coins. The remedy in fineness is in all cases four parts in one thousand. The denominations of coins authorized are nine in number, namely, the crown, halfcrown, florin, shilling, sixpence, groat, or fourpenny piece, threepence, twopence, and penny. All, except the crown, are coined in greater or less quantity, but the fourpence, twopence, and penny, are now only struck in very small quantities as Maundy money, which, after being distributed by the Queen annually in alms, appears to find its way into numismatic cabinets or to be melted down.

All such coins are legally current, irrespective of their weights, so long as they are not called in by proclamation, or so worn and defaced that the impress of the mint cannot be recognized. The coin in circulation is actually reduced in weight by abrasion to a considerable amount, often one-fourth or one-third of its original weight. Moreover, the fall in the value of silver relatively to gold reduces the metallic worth of the coins, so that no one can export them to foreign countries, or melt them for sale as bullion, without losing from 10 to 30 per cent. of their nominal value.

It would obviously be a cause of grievance if a person could be obliged to receive unlimited amounts of this token money in discharge of a debt. Merchants might often have thousands of pounds worth of such coins thrown upon their hands, the full value of which could only be realized by gradually putting it into circulation again. It was therefore provided by the Acts of 1816 and 1870, that silver coin shall be a legal tender only to the amount of forty shillings in any one payment. This limit was chosen apparently because the two-pound piece was in 1816 regarded as the largest coin then in circulation, or likely to be issued.

English Bronze Coinage.

The final subdivision of the pound is effected by bronze pence, halfpence, and farthings, of which the weights when issued should be respectively 145·833, 87·500 and 43·750 grains. They are composed of an alloy of 95 parts by weight

251

of copper, four parts of tin, and one part of zinc, being exactly the same kind of bronze as was previously employed by the French mints. The remedy in weight is one-fifth of one per cent., and as the coins are token money there is no least current weight. As the reasons against allowing them to be a legal tender for large sums are stronger than in the case of silver coin, it is enacted that bronze coins shall be a legal tender only to an aggregate amount of one shilling.

If a copper penny were now made to contain metal equivalent in value to the 240th part of a sovereign, its weight would be 871 grains, at the present market price of copper (£75 per ton). Thus the fractional coinage has been reduced in weight nearly to one-sixth part of what it would be as standard copper coin. The bronze of which the pence are made is worth, according to Mr. Seyd, 10*d.* per troy pound, so that the metallic values of the coins are almost exactly one-fourth part of their nominal values. A considerable profit therefore accrues upon the coinage of bronze, amounting up to the end of 1871 to about £270,000; but the reduction of weight is altogether an advantage, and is probably not carried as far as it might properly be done.

Deficiency of Weight of the English Gold Coin.

It is the theory of the present English monetary law, as we have seen (p. 107) that every person weighs a sovereign tendered to him, and assures himself, before accepting it, that it does not weigh less than 122·5 grains. In former days it was not uncommon for people to carry pocket-scales for weighing guineas, and such scales may still be occasionally seen in old curiosity shops. But we know that the practice is entirely given up, and that even the largest receivers of coin, such as the banks and railway companies, and even tax-offices, post-offices, etc., do not pay the least regard to the law. Only the Bank of England, its branches, and a few government offices, weigh gold coin in England. The result is that a large part of the gold coinage is worn below the least current weight, and all persons of experience avoid paying old sovereigns to the Bank of England. Only ignorant and unlucky persons, or else large banks and companies which cannot otherwise get rid of light coin, suffer loss. The quantity of light gold coin withdrawn by the bank did not for many years exceed half a million a year; during the last few years it has varied from £700,000 to £950,000. As the average amount of gold coined annually is four or five millions, and the coins melted or exported are for the most part new and of full weight, it follows necessarily, that the currency is becoming more and more deficient in weight.

In 1869 I ascertained, by a careful and extensive inquiry, that 31½ per cent. of the sovereigns and nearly one-half of the ten-shilling pieces were then below the legal limit. The reader who has attended to the remarks on Gresham's Law (p. 80), will see that no amount of coinage of new gold will drive out of circulation these depreciated old coins, because those who export, or melt, or otherwise treat the coins as bullion, will take care to operate upon good new ones.

Great injustice arises in some cases from this defective state of the gold currency. I have heard of one case in which an inexperienced person, after receiving several hundred pounds in gold from a bullion dealer in the city of London, took them straight to the Bank of England for deposit. Most of the sovereigns were there found to be light, and a prodigious charge was made upon the unfortunate depositor. The dealer in bullion had evidently paid him the residuum of a mass of coins, from which he had picked the heavy ones. In a still worse case, lately reported to me, a man presented a post-office order at St. Martin's-le-Grand, and carried the sovereigns received, to the stamp-office at Somerset House, where the coins were weighed, and some of them found to be deficient. Here a man was, so to say, defrauded between two government offices.

It should be stated that the government made, in July, 1870, a slight effort to promote the withdrawal of light gold, by engaging to receive it through the Bank of England at the full price of £3 17s. 9d. per ounce by weight, the price previously paid by the bank having been only £3 17s. 6½d., owing to the old sovereigns being a little below the standard in fineness. A certain increase in the amounts withdrawn has no doubt followed this measure; but the loss by deficiency in weight is still thrown upon the public, and as long as this is the case the withdrawal of light gold will continue inadequate to maintain the coinage at its standard weight.

Withdrawal of Light Gold Coin.

Some steps must soon be taken to remedy the increasing deficiency of weight of the gold coinage described above. The withdrawal may no doubt be effected in several ways. One method would be for the Queen to issue a proclamation calling in and prohibiting the circulation of all gold coins more than twenty or twenty-five years old, as it is mostly the older coins which are deficient in weight. Another method would be to oblige all revenue officers, post-masters, and others, under the control of government, to weigh all sovereigns presented to them. If necessary, the bankers of the kingdom generally might be obliged to weigh coin. But it is obvious that great trouble and inconvenience would arise from such measures. The progress of the post-office savings banks could be imperilled if every depositor of a pound were liable to be charged 2 per cent. for lightness. Considerable excitement and trouble followed the issue of the last proclamation of June, 1842, calling in light gold. To make the last holder of a coin pay for the whole cost of its circulation during thirty or forty years past, leads in many cases to gross injustice. The present law tends to throw the loss upon the poor, who have usually only one or two sovereigns at a time to pay, whereas rich people, having many, can avoid paying light gold at offices where it will be weighed.

I hold that the only thorough remedy is for the government to bear the loss occasioned by the wear of the gold, as it already bears that of the silver currency. The Bank of England should be authorized to receive all sovereigns *showing no marks of intentional damage or unfair treatment* at their full nominal value, on behalf of the mint, which should recoin the light ones at the public expense. No one would then have any reason for keeping the light gold away from the bank; the currency would soon be purged of the illegally light coins, and would thenceforth be kept up strictly to the standard weight; all loss of time and trouble would be saved to individuals, a consideration which we should not lose sight of; and, lastly, no injustice would be done, as at present, to the last holder of a light sovereign.

In opposition to such a proposal it is usually urged, that encouragement would be given to the criminal practice of sweating or otherwise diminishing the weight of the currency. I answer that, on the contrary, it is the present state of things which gives the best opportunity for illegal practices, because it renders the population perfectly accustomed to handling old and worn coins. No one now actually refuses any gold money in retail business, so that the sweater, if he exists at all, has all the opportunities he can desire. I have met with sovereigns deficient to the extent of four to five grains, or 8*d.* to 10*d.*, but they nevertheless circulate. If under a better system the gold currency consisted entirely of full-weight, fresh coins, with sharp, new, perfect impressions, attention would quickly be drawn to any coin which appeared to be worn or ill-treated in any degree. As the currency, too, would be constantly passing through the automaton weighing-machines of the Bank of England, without previously undergoing the operation of garbling by bullion brokers, sweated coins, if they existed at all, would soon be detected; whereas, according to the present system, the bank authorities have no opportunity of examining the whole coinage. It is the present state of things, then, which gives the best opportunity for tampering with the currency, though there is no evidence to show that fraudulent practices are carried on to any appreciable extent. Under the proposed new system such practices would be rendered almost impossible.

Supply of Gold Coin.

It is the theory of the English monetary law that every individual is entitled to take gold to the mint and have it coined gratuitously, all the expenses being borne by the public revenues. It is intended that the coin shall be rendered identical in value with an equal quantity of gold bullion, so that it shall, in short, be so much *certified bullion*, and shall be reconvertible into ingots without loss. Though this theory is simple and sound in some respects, it is not perfectly carried into practice. The mint never engages to deliver coin in immediate exchange for gold sent for coining, so that there is a loss of interest during the uncertain interval of coinage. If, instead of sending gold directly to the mint, the owner pursues the customary mode of selling it to the Bank of England, he receives, according to the Bank Charter Act of 1844, only £3 17s. 9d. per ounce, instead of the full mint price of £3 17s. 10½d. Moreover, it has been pointed out by Mr. E. Seyd, that, as the bank used to conduct their bullion business, there was a series of small charges or profits made for weighing, melting; assaying, the turn of the scale, the difference of the assay reports, etc., which amounted on the whole, including the above charge of 1½d. per ounce for demurrage, to 0·2828 per cent. on the value of the gold. The bank has since made some small improvements in the mode of conducting the business, but it may still be considered that the cost of converting gold bullion into sovereigns is about ¼ per cent.

Though every person whatever has the right, under the Coinage Act, of taking gold to the mint and having it coined free of charge and in order of priority without undue preference, no one ever does use the privilege, except the Bank of England. During an inquiry into the Bank Act in 1857, Mr. Twells stated that he had once sent £10,000 to the mint, and was afterwards surprised to find his firm of Spooner and Co., mentioned in a parliamentary paper as the only private firm that had ever done such a thing. The directors of the Bank of England have naturally acquired the monopoly of transactions with the mint, because they have to keep large stocks both of coin and bullion to meet the demands of the Issue Department and of their customers, including, directly or indirectly, the whole of the bankers of the United Kingdom. They can convert portions of their bullion into coin without any loss of interest or cost, whenever they find the stock of coin running down. They feel the monetary pulse of the whole community, and they have all the requisite appliances for the custody, assay, or exact weighing of bullion. Even those persons who need to possess large sums of gold often employ the bank to weigh, pack, and warehouse it, and the bank is always willing to do the work for fixed low charges. Hence it is most natural and convenient that the bank should act as the agent of the mint. Though the bank makes a certain profit out of the business, it is hardly earned at the cost of the public, but rather comes out of the economy with which the work is managed. It could in no way improve the currency of the country if every one who owned a few ounces of gold were to run with it to the mint, throwing upon the country the cost of melting and assaying insignificant ingots, and complicating the accounts and transactions of the mint.

Supply of Silver Coin.

On account of the absurd misapprehensions recently existing as to the scarcity of silver money, and the supposed right of private individuals to demand the coinage of silver, it may be well to describe exactly how the supply of silver coin is legally regulated and practically carried out. There is no law, statute, or common, which gives any private person, company, or institution, the right to take silver to the mint, and demand coin in exchange. Thus it is left in the hands of the Treasury and the mint to issue so much and such denominations of silver coins as they may think needful for the public service. This state of the law is perfectly right; because, as the silver coins are tokens, they cannot be got rid of by melting or exportation at their nominal values. If individuals were free to demand as much silver coin as they liked, a surplus might be thrown into circulation in years of brisk trade, which in a subsequent year of depressed trade would lie upon people's hands.

Practically speaking, the mint is guided in the supply of silver coin by the Bank of England, not because this bank has by law any special powers, privileges, or duties in the matter, but because, in acting as the bank of banks, and the bank of government departments, it has the best opportunities of judging when more coin is wanted. Not only do all the London bankers draw silver coin from the Bank of England when they need it, but the same is done directly or indirectly by all the other bankers in the kingdom. A deficiency of silver coin in any county is shown by the stock of the local bankers running down. They replenish their stocks either from the nearest branch of the Bank of England or from their London agents, who again draw from the Bank of England. At other times or places the bankers tend to accumulate a surplus of silver coin. Some banks in a large town may happen to have accounts with many shopkeepers, butchers, brewers, cattle-dealers, or dealers of one kind or another, who deposit silver coin in large quantities. Other banks may be largely drawn upon by manufacturers for the payment of wages, and may suffer from a deficiency of silver coin. It is a common practice, therefore, for bankers in any locality to assist each other by buying or selling superfluous silver coin as the case may require. If a superfluity of coin, however, cannot be got rid of in this way, it may be returned to the Bank of England or one of its branches.

This bank indeed is in no way bound to provide or receive large sums in silver, and it therefore usually makes a small charge of about five shillings per hundred pounds to cover the trouble and risk. In consideration of this charge the bank bears the cost of transmission by railway, examines the coin for the detection of base pieces and the withdrawal of worn coin—which latter it sends to the mint for recoinage, and acts in general as the agent of the mint.

Having the business so much in its hands, it is obvious that the department of the bank which manages the receipt and issue of silver coin can judge accurately when a fresh supply of coin is wanted. Before the stock runs too low notice is given to the mint, and money is usually advanced to the Master that he may purchase silver bullion for coinage. Under this system it is almost impossible for a deficiency of currency to arise without becoming known to the mint, and if, two or three years ago, the supply could not be made equal to the sudden demand, it was because the mint was not supplied by government with machinery adequate to the growing wants of the country. The existing system, in short, seems to be as nearly perfect as can be desired, provided that the mint be rebuilt and organized in such a manner as to enable it to meet any demand which the fluctuations of trade may occasion.

The Royal Mint.

While treating of the English system of metallic money, it is impossible to avoid expressing the wish that the House of Commons and the government will no longer delay a complete reconstruction of the Royal Mint. The mint factories, as they now stand, were very creditable to the generation which erected them; but it is needless to say that in the last fifty or seventy years we have immensely advanced, both in the art of constructing machinery and in our ideas of the arrangement and economy of manufactories. What should we think of a Cotton Spinning Company, which should propose to use a mill and machinery originally constructed by Arkwright, or to drive a mill by engines turned out of the Soho works in the time of Boulton and Watt? Yet the nation still depends for its coinage upon the presses actually erected by Boulton and Watt, although much more convenient coining presses have since been invented and employed in foreign and colonial mints.

The present mint workshops are quite inadequate for meeting the demands which may be thrown upon them by the increasing industry and wealth of the United Kingdom, not to speak of the British Empire. A few years ago it was impossible to turn out silver coin as quickly as it was required when trade was brisk, and, while one metal is being coined, there are no means of meeting the demand for other kinds of coin. As to the bronze coinage, it has generally to be obtained from Birmingham presses, and some that is issued is of very inferior execution. Even silver blanks have been obtained from Birmingham. The British mint ought to represent the skill and wealth of the British nation, and no petty considerations should be allowed to postpone so necessary a reform.

Nothing short of a complete reconstruction of the mint workshops will meet the requirements of the case. If this is to be done, much convenience and economy will arise from abandoning the large and valuable site upon Tower Hill, and erecting an entirely new mint in a more accessible position. The opinions of Mr. E. Seyd upon this subject are worthy of much attention.